# Praise for *Peaceful Parent, Happy Kids Workbook*

"Dr. Laura Markham's book is an extremely useful guide for parents in connecting with their children's emotions. It is highly gratifying to finally see a research-based guide for parents. Every parent will want a copy of this book."

**-John Gottman**, PhD
Author of *Raising an Emotionally Intelligent Child*

"*The Peaceful Parent, Happy Kids Workbook* teaches parents to manage their own emotions, connect more deeply with their children, and guide kids with respectful, attuned limit-setting. As always, Laura Markham's encouraging tone, realistic scenarios, and step-by-step instructions make her research-based advice immediately accessible to busy parents, brilliantly coaching them to create the strong, healthy child-parent relationship that every mother and father seeks."

**-Tina Payne Bryson**, Co-author of
*The Whole-Brain Child, No-Drama Discipline*, and *The Yes Brain*

"*The Peaceful Parent, Happy Kids Workbook* is more than an excellent resource; it offers a well-researched, clearly written, step-by-step process that will completely transform your parenting. In a carefully guided format, richly packed from first page to last, Dr. Laura Markham teaches the practical and powerful tools that help you skillfully regulate the emotional climate in your family. This is the must-read road map you've been looking for."

**-Linda Graham**, Author of
*Bouncing Back: Rewiring Your Brain for Maximum Resilience and Well-Being*

"Dr. Laura Markham teaches parents how to use the daily challenges of living with children as an opportunity for their own growth. The result is more mindful, peaceful parents, who can help their children grow into happy, responsible people. Clear, compelling and essential for every parent."

**-Dr. Shefali Tsabary**, *NYT's* bestselling author of
*The Conscious Parent* and *The Awakened Family*

"Dr. Laura Markham's *Peaceful Parent, Happy Kids Workbook* is full of enlightening exercises and worksheets for parents to practice how to regulate their own emotions, and build a lifelong foundation to connect and engage with their children. Mindfulness exercises bring evidence-based and user-friendly ways to integrate mindful awareness into parenting, increasing resiliency for both parent and child."

**-Mona Delahooke**, PhD
Author of *Social and Emotional Development in Early Intervention*

"I will return to Dr. Laura Markham's *Peaceful Parent, Happy Kids Workbook* again and again. I will return to it for inspiration, guidance, and practical how-to personal reflection. Most importantly, I will revisit her words out of love for my son. For I want him to benefit from the most honest, warm hearted, and peaceful energy I can bring to mothering. When friends, family, or colleagues ask me about my parenting philosophy, I always direct them to the work of Dr. Laura Markham."

**-Amy Wright Glenn**, Author of
*Birth, Breath, and Death and Holding Space*

"Dr. Laura Markham taps into fascinating brain science, meditation and mindfulness practices to help parents heal themselves and be more peaceful. With the exercises, practices and reflections in this book, *Peaceful Parent, Happy Kids Workbook* provides wonderful support to parents. Dr. Markham inspires parents to believe that they can grow into the best version of themselves."

-**Melissa Hood**, Author of *Real Parenting for Real Kids*

"I am so grateful Dr. Laura Markham has written this workbook. I believe most parents find it difficult to remember helpful guidelines and put them into practice in everyday life when we are angry or impatient with our children. This workbook walks parents through a progression of worksheets and exercises that help incorporate Dr. Markham's ideas about connection into everyday life in practical, hands-on ways. This workbook will change your relationship with your child for the better; will help you engage with your child from a place of love and mindfulness every day."

-**Jesmyn Ward**, Author of
*Sing Unburied Sing,* winner National Book Award 2017

"Laura Markham integrates mindfulness practices and spiritual wisdom with the latest research findings to give parents a toolbox for transformation. Her love for parents and children shines through this book."

-**Susan Stiffelman**, Author of
*Parenting Without Power Struggles* and *Parenting With Presence*

"*The Peaceful Parent, Happy Kids Workbook* is like a Swiss Army Knife for parents, with scripts, activities, worksheets and practical tips that parents will find effective, inspiring and fun. Dr. Laura Markham's tone is empowering, and her positive parenting approach works. Every parent will benefit from this book, and the real winners will be their children."

-**Amy McCready**, Author of *The "Me, Me, Me" Epidemic*

"Laura Markham's approach is down-to-earth, filled with respect and compassion for children and parents, and most of all, it's effective. Many parents who have benefited from Laura's writings have told me that they wish they could have her move in with them for a while and provide on-the-spot advice. This workbook is the next best thing! You will rekindle that spark of connection and joy with your children."

-**Dr. Lawrence Cohen**, Author of
*Playful Parenting* and *The Opposite of Worry*

"Dr. Markham's book is like a friend, ready to offer support and encouragement when you need it the most. She clearly demonstrates how to replace power struggles with cooperation and a sense of calm. Based on the latest brain and mindfulness research, The *Peaceful Parent, Happy Kids Workbook* is filled with hope and detailed exercises for understanding and managing your own emotions as well as those of your children. You will discover the secrets to staying emotionally connected and working together, even during the most difficult times."

-**Mary Sheedy Kurcinka**, EdD, Author of
*Raising Your Spirited Child, Kids, Parents and Power Struggles* and *Sleepless in America*

DR. LAURA MARKHAM

# Peaceful Parent,
# HAPPY KIDS

Using mindfulness and connection
to raise resilient, joyful children and
rediscover your love of parenting

Library of Congress Cataloging-in-Publication Data

Names: Markham, Laura, author.
Title: Peaceful parent, happy kids workbook : Using mindfulness and
connection to raise resilient, joyful children and rediscover your love of
parenting / by Dr. Laura Markham.
Description: Eau Claire : PESI Publishing & Media, [2018]
Identifiers: LCCN 2018000064 | ISBN 9781683731153
Subjects: LCSH: Parenting. | Parent and child.
Classification: LCC HQ769 .M286 2018 | DDC 306.874--dc23 LC record available at https://lccn.loc.
gov/2018000064

PESI
Publishing
& Media
www.pesi.com

There is no single effort more radical in its potential for saving the world than a transformation of the way we raise our children.

— Marianne Williamson,
bestselling author

# About The Author

**Dr. Laura Markham** is the author of of
*Peaceful Parent, Happy Kids: How To Stop Yelling and Start Connecting* and
*Peaceful Parent, Happy Siblings: How To Stop the Fighting and Raise Friends
for Life*. She earned her PhD in clinical psychology at Columbia University and has
worked as a parenting coach with countless families across the world. Her books have
been translated into 12 languages.

A leading advocate for parents and children, Dr. Laura is frequently interviewed by the press, from *Parents Magazine*
to *The Wall Street Journal*. She is in constant demand as a conference keynoter and workshop leader because of her
warmth in connecting with audiences and her practical, research-based interventions.

Over 130,000 moms and dads enjoy Dr. Laura's free weekly coaching posts via email. You can sign up on any page of
her website, AhaParenting.com, which serves up Aha! Moments for parents of babies through teens. She also offers a
popular online course (AhaParenting.com/peaceful-parenting-course) which deepens and further personalizes the work
in this book.

Dr. Laura's aspiration is to change the world, one child at a time, by supporting parents. The proud mother of two
thriving young adults who were raised with her peaceful parenting approach, she lives with her husband in
Brooklyn, NY.

# Contents

· · · · · · · · · · · · · · · · · · · ·

# Acknowledgements

I'd like to take this opportunity to say thank you to the tens of thousands of parents who have shared their family lives with me in so many different ways over the years. You have taught me so much, and I have loved watching your children grow. I'm honored to support you.

A special shout-out to all the parents who read an early draft of this book and took their precious time to give me such helpful feedback. You made this book so much better – Thank you!

Haim Ginott's work, still the bedrock of positive parenting, deserves particular mention. But I want to express my appreciation to all the dedicated researchers, writers and clinicians working on behalf of children and parents today. Together, we're transforming parenting, and thus humanity. We all stand on the shoulders of so many brilliant thinkers in this field. Without them, my small contribution would never have come to be.

For this book, special gratitude is due to Dr. John Gottman, whose work on emotional intelligence is foundational for all of us, to Linda Graham for the research and exercises in her book *Bouncing Back*, and to Lawrence Cohen and Patty Wipfler, who inspired many of the games I've adapted over the years and which I share with parents in this book.

To my colleagues Alyson Shumays, Beth Peterson, Devon Reehl and Aisha Reehl – I couldn't imagine a better support team. Thanks for your constant attention to detail and your creativity in advancing our work. You rock!

Linda Jackson, Karsyn Morse and the rest of their team at PESI have been a pleasure to work with in every way. I so appreciate everything each of you has done to make publishing this book possible.

I want to thank Marian Lizzi, my editor at Perigee, for helping me launch *Peaceful Parent, Happy Kids* and for Perigee's cooperation in publishing this workbook.

My gratitude, as always, to my agent Rebecca Friedman, who believes fiercely in the power of positive parenting.

To my children Eli and Alice, who continue to teach me and make me proud every day: I am eternally grateful that I was given the gift of being your mother. Thank you for the light you bring to my life.

And to my husband Daniel Cantor: A public acknowledgment could never begin to express my gratitude for our life together and my love for who you are. Thank you for always believing in me, supporting me, and loving me.

Introduction

# What Is Peaceful Parenting?

Raising children is one of the most rewarding things you will ever do. It is also stressful, exasperating, and exhausting. Given how demanding parenting is and how childish children are, how can it possibly be "peaceful"?

Peaceful parenting doesn't mean that you're perpetually blissed-out or disconnected from the messy reality of life with children. Peaceful parenting simply means regulating your own emotions so that you don't take them out on your child. Just as a medical doctor commits to the Hippocratic Oath, pledging "first, do no harm," peaceful parents commit to taking responsibility for their own emotions, so they aren't doing harm to their children.

Of course, most patients don't throw howling tantrums or otherwise provoke their doctors. Parents can count on their children pushing every button they have. But when we manage our own emotions—regardless of the child's behavior—it frees us up to respond to our child's needs, offering the loving guidance that helps any child, every time. Children who are guided with love learn in turn to love and manage themselves. They develop an inner compass that protects them and helps them make choices with integrity. They learn the skills to communicate and work things out with others, and develop the tools needed to thrive throughout their lives.

Each child is different, but research studies generally agree on what children need to become healthy, happy, responsible kids who grow into healthy, happy, responsible adults. And it is *not* perfect parents. It's a relationship with a parent who loves them and delights in them. A parent who models how to repair the relationship when things are hard. A parent who really appreciates this individual child, who guides the child with emotional generosity, and who coaches the child to be his or her best self.

I'm going to support you, step by step, to become that parent, so you can raise that child. Our guiding framework is **Three Big Ideas**. Big ideas, but simple and doable—for every parent.

## Idea 1: Regulating Ourselves Is Our First Responsibility as Parents

No one is peaceful all the time. Conflict is part of every human relationship, and all parents sometimes get angry at their children. But when we allow our anger and fear to hijack our reasoning brain, we end up in "fight, flight, or freeze" mode and our child begins to look like the enemy. We don't see our child's perspective at those moments. In fact, our agenda shifts from teaching our children and nurturing their healthy development to winning the battle. We lash out with threats or punishment.

By contrast, when we parent peacefully:

- We take responsibility for monitoring and regulating our own emotions. That means we notice, accept, and allow ourselves to feel our anger, and all our other emotions—but we resist acting on that anger. In other words, we don't visit our upset on our child.

- We take responsibility to teach our child in a healthy way. That means we set limits as necessary to guide our child's behavior, but at the same time we stay connected—we offer the child understanding and help with the emotions and needs driving the behavior.

- We accept our child's "big" emotions with compassion, just as we accept our own. This allows children to accept their emotions, which is the first step in regulating them.

XIV * DR. LAURA MARKHAM

- We take responsibility for our own self-care, so we can give our child the emotional generosity and unconditional love every child needs.

When you parent peacefully, you act as a role model for your child, showing how to regulate emotions and work through conflicts in ways that are respectful to both people. You're able to address whatever needs are driving your child's behavior—and as a result your child's behavior changes.

## Idea 2: Connection Is What Children Most Need from Parents

Parenting isn't a set of strategies. It's a relationship. When you adore and delight in your child, your child feels valued, just for being himself. That connection allows you to see your child's perspective so that you can parent responsively, which is one of the most important factors in a young child's emotional health.[1]

Children thrive when they feel connected. They trust that they will be understood, loved, and protected. When children feel disconnected from us, they don't feel safe. That means they don't think well and they can't regulate their emotions.[2]

When children don't feel safe, they do something they think will make them feel better. Sometimes that's a positive thing, like coming to us for a hug. But often they do something that's not as healthy. They tease their sibling or lash out in anger, which makes them feel more powerful. Or they whine for treats or screen time, which they hope will numb their pain. Or they look right at us and break a rule, which at least guarantees that we'll pay attention to them. Of course, the negative attention we give in those tough moments usually ends up making our child feel even more disconnected from us.

By contrast, when children feel connected to us, they're open to our influence. They are much more likely to cooperate. But, no matter how hard we work to connect as parents, life intervenes and children can start to feel disconnected. Maybe the child is highly sensitive, so she's easily overwhelmed by strong emotions, which makes her disconnect from us. Or he goes to school or daycare and orients away from us for much of the day. Or she stays home with us but life is awfully complicated: we're busy with the baby, on the phone with the doctor, caught up in our screens, or struggling with our own health, exhaustion, or finances. Or maybe we're able to be mostly patient, but, being human, we sometimes raise our voices. Disconnection is a normal part of life, no matter how aware we are. So parenting effectively requires us to constantly reconnect.[3]

When you begin prioritizing connection, you'll probably think of it as meeting your child's needs so she's happier and more cooperative. And of course you'll be right—that's why connection is your most powerful parenting tool, after managing yourself. But soon you'll notice that the sweeter, stronger relationship you're creating with your child isn't just for her. It's for you, too. In fact, those lovely moments that make your heart melt are what make all the sacrifices of parenting worth it.

## Idea 3: Emotion Coaching Is the Most Effective Discipline Strategy

What kind of discipline works to raise great kids? When we hear the word "discipline," we usually think of punishment, but the original meaning of the word "discipline" was "to learn" or "to be guided." So let's rephrase that question. What kind of guidance works to raise great kids?

Research[4] shows that the most effective guidance helps children develop emotional intelligence so they can master their emotions and therefore their behavior.[5] Effective guidance sets clear limits on behavior, but also offers understanding, right alongside those limits. The result is children who don't feel bad about themselves and are more open to the guidance. It's a virtuous circle. Over time, the child internalizes the limit and thus develops self-discipline. (In Part 3, we'll talk more about how children develop self-discipline.) This kind of guidance is most effective when the person doing the guiding is someone the child loves and trusts, someone the child knows is acting in her best interests, someone the child wants to "follow." It should be obvious that this kind of guidance can't include punishment, or the child would feel betrayed and the trust would diminish. Instead, the most effective guidance helps heal the reasons the child is misbehaving and coaches the child to develop new communication and self-management skills, so he can be his best self.

Would you rather have a boss who guided you with punishment, or with empathy? Given the obvious answer, and the research that supports this parenting approach,[6] you're probably wondering why most parenting advice suggests that parents should control children with rewards or punishments to get them to do what the parents want. These familiar ideas have shaped our view of children for generations, and most of us automatically parent the way we were raised. We aren't as punitive as we once were, but we still haven't yet caught up with the research. Thousands of studies on parenting can be boiled down to this: coaching children so they develop emotional intelligence and self-discipline is the single best way to create happier, more responsible adults. Punishment merely creates more misbehavior.[7] (If this idea is new to you, I urge you to read Alfie Kohn's book *Unconditional Parenting*, which is a terrific introduction to the research on the effects of punishment.)

## What If You've Made Mistakes As A Parent?

You will probably become more patient and empathic with your child as soon as you begin reading this book, which will encourage better behavior from your child, giving you more confidence as a parent. But you may also become more self-critical. You might even feel some shame and worry about how you've parented in the past, or even in the past five minutes. Just acknowledge those feelings, thank them for letting you know that you want to do a better job, and let them go. You've received the message. Knowing more inspires you to do the hard work to change. But berating yourself won't help at all.

Because no matter what you have done as a parent, you did the best you could. I mean that. You used the information you had, you were influenced by your past experiences, and you were reacting to the environment you were in. In fact, if an objective observer could see how hard you have tried, with all the challenges you've faced, that person might well decide that you've been heroic.

This is true even if you've done something that you now think was a terrible thing to do. If you're clear that you will work hard not to repeat that behavior, that's good enough. It's easy for all of us to feel superior to someone else who has made different choices than we have. But I truly believe that if I had been born in your body, with your genetics and family legacy, and had your childhood and experiences, then I would have done the exact same things you did. Really. You did the best you could. It's time to let yourself off the hook.

When I say that we all fall short, I'm not excusing parents who have harmed their children. I'm pointing out that you can't simultaneously feel bad about what you've done and feel good enough to do better. (Just like feeling worse doesn't help a child do better.) We all make mistakes. But if you use your past mistakes to guide you toward a better way in the future, that's a learning opportunity, not a mistake.

That doesn't mean you excuse yourself from making repairs to relationships where you've hurt someone. And it doesn't mean you excuse yourself from changing now. Use the past as a motivation to be the best parent you can be today.

Luckily, children are wonderfully resilient creatures! Your child may need to do some crying about those times when she felt so alone in the face of your anger. But whatever has happened in your relationship with your child, whatever mistakes you've made, however ugly your child is acting, however ugly you've acted—it's never too late. You can always transform your relationship with your child into a happier, closer connection.

You deserve total compassion from yourself. No matter what. Make amends for the past by accepting your child's feelings to help him heal them. That's payment enough; you don't get extra points for beating yourself up. As you learn more, you'll do better. That's why you're reading this book.

# HOW TO GET THE MOST OUT OF THIS BOOK

I'm excited to make this promise to you: if you give these ideas and practices a fair chance, by the time you finish working your way through this book, you can expect to experience a happier family life, with a lot less drama and a lot more love.

Have you read *Peaceful Parent, Happy Kids: How to Stop Yelling and Start Connecting* yet?[8] This workbook is designed to complement that book, but it can also stand alone. This workbook offers a review of the basic ideas presented in *Peaceful Parent, Happy Kids*, but it also gives you additional hands-on tools to bring those principles alive in your family life. In addition, there's much more information in this book on how emotion works and why mindfulness is so important, since I've found in the five years since writing *Peaceful Parent, Happy Kids* that those are the tools that are most useful to parents trying to transform their families. For a deeper understanding of the ideas surrounding peaceful parenting, including a breakdown of how they apply to children of different ages, you'll want to read *Peaceful Parent, Happy Kids*. If you've already read it, you'll find some recap in this book, but you'll also find that doing the exercises and applying the examples will make the principles of self-regulation, connection, and coaching come alive in your family.

This workbook will help you set a new course for your family, but only you can actually take the steps to change things with your child. The more you "work it," the more it will work for you. I suggest that you schedule some time every day to use this workbook. Even if you just read one page, it will keep the ideas present as you engage with your child. This is hard work and it takes time. It does not happen magically, but, if you do the work, I guarantee that you will see changes in your child and in yourself.

You'll notice that some of the pages suggest that you post them on your refrigerator that week to guide your practice. When you're done with those pages, you can put them in a folder or notebook that you keep with this book. There are also many journal prompts that may inspire you to write more than will fit in the space given in this workbook, so again a notebook, possibly with a pocket for loose pages, will be a valuable accompaniment to this workbook. *If you have more than one child*, you will often want to give different answers for each child. In that case, plan to photocopy the pages before you begin filling them out, and give yourself extra paper.

It's fine to turn directly to the parts of this book that most call to you, but it's important for you to know that all of these ideas work together. For instance, many people skip right to **Part 3: Coaching Instead of Controlling**, hoping they'll find a discipline secret that will make their child want to behave. But the only thing that makes a child *want* to cooperate is connection. So, if you skip **Part 2: Connection Is the Secret to Happy Parenting**, you'll end up missing the most useful "discipline" tool there is. Similarly, if you skip to "Helping Your Child with Emotions" (in Part 3) to find out how to help your child manage his emotions, you'll find some valuable tips. But your child won't learn to manage his emotions until he sees you regulate your own, which is the territory of **Part 1: Regulating Yourself**. So I encourage you to skim the whole workbook to get the basic principles, whatever your final goal.

You'll see that there are guided meditations accompanying this workbook, available as a gift to you on the Aha! Parenting website. Simply go to AhaParenting.com and look in the main menu for the "Books" tab, then click "Workbook Audios." You can also sign up on any page of AhaParenting.com for a free newsletter designed to support you to stay on track in your parenting.

Please *do* the exercises and journal prompts. I realize that's more work than simply reading. But in the advance feedback from parents like you who used early versions of this book, I heard over and over that doing the exercises is where the real transformation happens. They force us to grapple with the ideas and apply them to our own lives, so we can actually apply this philosophy in our own families and realize the benefits.

## *What To Expect From Yourself*

As you tune in to your own emotions and nurture yourself more, you may notice some old, tangled-up emotions bubbling up to be healed, now that you're becoming more self-accepting. You might notice tears nearer the surface. Don't worry, this is something you can handle. It just means you may have some days when you feel a little fragile and need some extra tenderness from yourself. As you allow yourself to feel those emotions, they'll begin to heal, and you'll find yourself feeling happier more often. In fact, you'll probably notice that you're feeling happy for no reason. That's a signal that your sense of well-being is shifting to a new, higher baseline. Enjoy it!

**Trigger warning.** This book will ask you to get to know yourself on a deeper level, from your childhood experiences to your current inner life. That can be hard work, but it's the only way to transform your relationship with your child. If you feel that it will be too upsetting to consider your childhood, if you have a background of trauma, or if you find yourself becoming very upset as you read through this book, please put the book down while you find a counselor you trust. An experienced counselor will give you the support you need to stay grounded and feel safe as you work through this book.

## What To Expect From Your Child

> When I first started peaceful parenting, my daughter began to get angry and then completely fall apart and cry, about nothing. Luckily, I had been warned to expect some emotional backpack-emptying. After she cried, she was affectionate and really tried to be helpful, much more than she was before. Soon, the meltdowns stopped, and she was so much more cooperative and affectionate all the time!
>
> — Erica, mother of three-year-old

When parents offer children more patience and understanding, kids blossom. But sometimes, first, they have to get some old, unhappy tears and fears off their chest. They do this because they've been stuffing those feelings until now, but as you become more accepting, they feel safe enough to show their past hurts to you. What heals those hurts is your compassion. So, when you begin using these ideas, please be aware that your child may briefly act a bit worse before settling into a much happier, more cooperative place. I know, you aren't reading this book to have your child act worse. I assure you this is temporary. He just needs a chance to show you those old hurts so he can heal and move on.

You can minimize this phase by focusing on connecting with your child and seeing things from her point of view. Keep setting limits: *"It's not okay to hit no matter how angry you are."* But at the same time acknowledge all emotions, even upset and angry ones: *"I see how angry you are, Madison. I'm sorry it's so hard… I'm right here."*

You'll find that the more your child feels genuinely heard and understood, the more quickly she moves past her anger to show you the hurts underneath it. And once she expresses those hurts, they begin to heal, and you'll see her transform before your eyes.

The good news is, it is never too late to heal things with your child. The older your child is, the harder it will be, because kids develop emotional armor and they lash out to keep you from getting too close. So a three-year-old will respond much faster to this new approach than an eight-year-old. But as long as you're willing to be present and loving, your child will show you her hurts. That's the beginning of restoring emotional health.

> Your delight in your child may be the most important
> factor in your child's level of happiness and cooperation.
> Why not focus on finding opportunities to delight
> in your child, beginning today?

## What To Expect From Your Partner

> My husband had been quick to punish or raise his voice when our little one got out of line, but we've been talking about peaceful parenting and he's been following my cues for guiding and coaching with love rather than bossing and being authoritarian—the only parenting style with which he was familiar! We are loving the connectedness it brings our family and the feeling of doing better.
>
> — Grace, mother of a three-year-old
>
> What if your partner isn't on board? I try to implement lots of these ideas, but my husband isn't really willing to consider alternative ways of parenting.
>
> — Camila, mother of six and eight-year-olds

This book will stimulate lots of thinking about parenting and will help you evolve your ideas and your approach. If you have a partner, or an ex-partner who co-parents with you, you'll want to think about how best to invite them into this process.

Most parents say that this workbook improves their relationship with their partner as well as with their child. That's because these ideas are universal. Everyone wants to feel understood and respected. But it's also very common for parents to begin using the peaceful parenting ideas, only to find that their partner disagrees with this new approach. After all, you're introducing a new way of relating into your family.

How to work with your partner on parenting together is beyond the scope of this book, but here are my top five tips for navigating your discussions:

1.  **Remember that you and your partner both want what's best for your child.** You may have different ideas about how to create that, but you're on the same side.

2.  **The more your partner is involved in this workbook, the better.** That way, even if one of you disagrees with these ideas, the two of you can discuss them together. (If your partner does not want to work on this book with you, consider getting your hands on the audio version of my book *Peaceful Parent, Happy Kids: How to Stop Yelling and Start Connecting*. I've been told by many parents, especially fathers, that they don't enjoy reading, but loved listening to my book while in their car. It covers the same three big ideas as this book.)

3.  **Extending emotional generosity to your partner is essential** to your relationship, and to having any influence with your partner.

4.  **Expect many discussions over time as you explore these ideas.** Keep these conversations safe by listening a lot, non-judgmentally, and by expressing your own opinions, needs, and fears rather than attacking each other's parenting or perspectives. Instead of lecturing your partner, empathize with what he or she expresses. Re-state what's being expressed and ask whether you've correctly understood it.

5.  **Role model the parent you want both of you to become.** It may not happen immediately, but over time your partner will see the difference in how your child responds to your different approaches.

For more support in working through conflict with your partner so it brings you closer, check out *Happily Ever After: Conscious Co-parenting* at AhaParenting.com.[9]

## *Does Peaceful Parenting Work With A Difficult Or Special Needs Child?*

> My heart knew he didn't need punishment and I am beyond grateful for the tools you gave me to help him navigate his world, which is clearly a very difficult and different world from the one you and I are in… I really wanted to reach out because maybe there are other special needs parents out there wondering, 'But my child has _____ [fill in the blank]—will this work?'
>
> The resounding answer for us has been yes! Because empathy is hard for him, because connection is hard for him, because he struggles in social situations, I feel that it is even more important that we set loving limits and teach him about emotions and about how to be connected and how to express love.
>
> — Andrea, mother of a five-year-old boy and a two-year-old girl

The peaceful parenting approach not only works with challenging and special needs kids, but is *even more* important for them. You can see why this is true when you consider the three basic elements of this approach:

1.  **Regulate your own emotions.** This can be even harder with a special needs child, but, since they're often even more sensitive and reactive than other children, it's especially important.

2.  **Connect.** With kids on the autism spectrum, and with children who are easily overwhelmed by connection, building a strong bond can be more challenging. But that doesn't mean it isn't important. Without that relationship, why else would the child follow your lead?

3.  **Coach instead of punishing.** Many "experts" give advice that centers on rewards and punishments, especially for children who have special needs. But all humans deserve the dignity of being coached to be their best selves, rather than being punished when they don't behave as we'd like.

Special needs children have a different experience of the world than we do, and it must often frighten them. There are many children who have an overactive alarm system, so that simple limits feel like threats to their survival and send them into extreme "fight or flight." When children act out of fear, they deserve love, not punishment. Of course, we need to set limits, but we can set them with love. This is also more effective in gaining cooperation, because *all* humans rebel against being controlled and only feel safe "following" those who they trust have their best interests at heart.

# Getting Started

**Ready for your family life to get sweeter and more peaceful? Let's do this!**

Please give yourself credit for every bit of progress in the right direction. Life is simply the slow accumulation of moments, and each moment gives you a new chance to change directions. Even if you change your reaction to only a few things that happen today, you'll find yourself heading in a new direction. Before you know it, you're in a whole new landscape.

## TAKING STOCK

A note about the workbook sections: don't feel like your answers need to be perfect, or even complete. This isn't a quiz—no one's going to grade you. But these answers are important, because they'll help you clarify what you want and how you feel. So, even if you're not sure what your answer is, writing down a bullet point or two for each question will help get these ideas moving in your brain.

What motivated you to begin this peaceful parenting workbook? What would you like to get out of it?

*I noticed that I yell a lot at my 2yr old even when I don't want to. Also, she is very whiney and cries & has meltdowns a lot so I'm sure I'm feeling then in some way. I wonder how?*

What questions about parenting your child do you have as we embark? Keep these in mind as you proceed through this workbook.

*How to reinforce & encourage good behavior? That actually is effective?*

What are your biggest strengths as a parent? Don't worry about humility; just be honest. What would an impartial observer admire if she could watch your best moments with your child or children? We're going to build on these strengths to help you be like this even more often.

*I'm fun. Present (as opposed to on my phone). Active.*

XXII * DR. LAURA MARKHAM

## PROUDEST PARENTING MOMENTS

This is a fun part. Think about the times when you've been most proud and happy about yourself as a parent. We're going to build on them. List some of those times below. In each case, reflect on what you did that made each moment possible. How can you do more of that, to create more terrific times with your child?

**( 1 )** There was the time when I:

*Cant think of anything.* _____

_____

_____

What I did that made this moment possible, and how I can do more of this in the future:

_____

_____

_____

**( 2 )** There was the time when I:

_____

_____

_____

What I did that made this moment possible, and how I can do more of this in the future:

_____

_____

_____

**( 3 )** There was the time when I:

_____

_____

_____

What I did that made this moment possible, and how I can do more of this in the future:

_____

_____

_____

**( 4 )** There was the time when I:

_____

_____

_____

What I did that made this moment possible, and how I can do more of this in the future:

_____

_____

_____

**( 5 )** There was the time when I:

_____

_____

_____

What I did that made this moment possible, and how I can do more of this in the future:

_____

_____

_____

## HOW DOES YOUR CHILD SEE YOU?

If your child had to choose three words to describe you and how you relate to her, what would she say? For each word, what example might your child give of why she sees you this way? (These words might be "positive" or "negative." Be honest. This is your starting place. Until we're clear about what's happening, we can't change it.)

**( 1 )** _____

**( 2 )** _____

**( 3 )** _____

For number **1**, what's an example of why your child sees you this way?

_____

_____

_____

For number **2**, what's an example of why your child sees you this way?

_____

_____

_____

For number **3**, what's an example of why your child sees you this way?

_____

_____

What do you want more of in your relationship with your child or children?

_____

_____

_____

What might you be willing to do or to change to have more of that?

_____

_____

_____

## HEALING THE PAST

As you learn more about the effect of our parenting on our children, you may find yourself wishing you could do some days over again. I do too! Unfortunately, no one can rewrite the past. But every one of us can start today and write a new future. And you can use your past as your motivation to create that new future.

First, we have to acknowledge those times that still make us wince and grieve for them, so that we can move on. Should you apologize? Of course, and we'll cover that in Part 2: Connection Is the Secret to Happy Parenting. But our children don't need our apologies nearly as much as they need us to change our behavior.

Right now, I invite you to acknowledge any sadness you're carrying about the past. Feel that grief fully. Say what you wish had been the case.

For example: *"I wish I had been less distracted…, I wish I had not hurt my child…,*
*I wish I had known then what I know now…"*

I wish:

_____

_____

_____

Cry if you need to. You might find yourself yawning, which is one of the ways your body releases and heals those old feelings. Just breathe deeply and let them go.

## A LETTER TO YOUR CHILD

Now, write a letter to your child on a separate piece of paper—not to show your child, but to show yourself. Acknowledge what your child deserved and what you wish had been the case. Promise to do better.

Be honest. Your child will never see this letter. But, on some deep level of the soul, he or she will feel it. And writing it will change you and help you to be the parent you want to be for your child. Put the letter away in a safe place so that you can revisit it when you need inspiration to keep trying.

Later, when you're with your child, you may feel a need to share your regret with her. Since you never want your child to feel she has to take care of you, I suggest that, as much as possible, you process these feelings in private before talking with your child. Then, simply begin by acknowledging that sometimes in the past, your child may have felt like you didn't understand. Apologize for that. Reassure your child that you love her, no matter what, and that you could never love anyone more. Your emotional generosity now will signal to your child that you're able to be a safe haven for her in a whole new way. Notice how your child looks at you with new hope. Notice how open your heart feels.

> Commit to giving yourself the support you
> need to keep choosing love every day.

## SETTING YOUR INTENTION

Now it's time to state your intention for this work we'll be doing together. Below, describe your highest and best vision of yourself as a parent. Include three words that describe the parent you're striving to be. (Why set an intention? Because if you don't know where you want to go, you're likely to end up somewhere else!)

_That I am able to direct my own negative emotions elsewhere, not at my kids or partner, in order to more effectively & lovingly guide others out of their difficulties. I am so far from a guide right now._

To realize that highest and best vision of yourself as a parent, you will need to change. You don't have to tackle everything at once, though. What one change can you commit to making now?

I, _____, commit to making this change:

_When anger & frustration bubble up, take 3 breaths, stretch, & visualize sending dark air into the past or in some black hole._

This commitment should feel manageable but hard. Now, write down any specific supports that will help you make this change a reality. What will help you stay on track? Do you need some time alone? More sleep? Is there information you need? You don't have to figure everything out at once, and your ideas will evolve as you learn more. Just map out the first steps of how you will support yourself.

## A LETTER TO YOURSELF

Change is hard work and always seems to involve taking two steps forward, but then one step back. You're bound to feel at times like you just can't reach your goals as a parent. Knowing that you'll feel like giving up at some point, what words will you need to hear? How would you encourage another parent who was struggling? Write the pep talk that will inspire you when you're feeling frustrated and stuck. Use a separate piece of paper that you can put away.

Part 1

# Regulating Yourself

> I have come to the frightening conclusion that I am the decisive element in the classroom. It is my personal approach that makes the climate, my daily mood that makes the weather. As a teacher, I possess tremendous power to make a child's life miserable or joyous. I can be a tool of torture or an instrument of inspiration. I can humiliate or heal. It is my response that decides whether a crisis will be escalated or de-escalated and a child is humanized or de-humanized.
>
> — Haim Ginott, former teacher and
> the grandfather of Peaceful Parenting[10]

Peaceful parenting doesn't mean you're peaceful all the time. A full human life constantly stimulates emotions, some of which are the opposite of peaceful. Peaceful parenting simply means that you commit to managing your own emotions, so you aren't taking them out on your child. You monitor your mental and emotional state, and take care of yourself, so that you can maintain a sense of well-being most of the time. When you get triggered, you notice it and take proactive steps to calm yourself so you can respond to the situation with maturity. Psychologists call this "emotional intelligence." But you could simply think of it as role modeling how to be a responsible grown-up, even when your child is acting like a child.

Children can be expected to act childish, so we need to train ourselves not to take their behavior personally. They aren't trying to create a problem for us; they're just acting from their own unmet needs and tangled emotions. In fact, their misbehavior signals that they're *having* a problem and need our help.

Aspiring to become more peaceful doesn't mean that you'll never get angry. It simply means that you take responsibility to work through your anger, rather than taking it out on your child. You'll still have to intervene to guide your child appropriately, but that guidance will be in your child's best interests, rather than a way for you to blow off steam.

Many parents say that anger just hijacks them and, before they know it, they're having their own tantrum. But every time you're able to interrupt your own tirade, to notice yourself getting upset—but resist taking action—you're building new neural pathways. Soon, your prefrontal cortex (the rational part of your brain) will automatically send a calming message to your amygdala (the alarm system of your brain) that says, *"When this child gets defiant, it seems like an emergency, but it really isn't."* Over time, you'll notice that you're calmer, less reactive.

I want to stress that I'm not suggesting that you should ignore your feelings when you start to get angry. If you say, *"I shouldn't feel angry,"* and just push your anger out of your awareness, then you're trying to repress your anger. Repressed emotions don't go away. They're forced out of our conscious awareness, but we still carry them in our bodies. We're still lugging them around with us, and they're always knocking on the door of our consciousness saying, *"Hey, pay attention to me!"* Sooner or later those angry feelings are going to pop out uncontrolled by our conscious mind, and then we explode.

But what if you're really good at keeping those angry feelings stuffed? That's even worse, because repressed anger just stays in your body and makes you depressed or physically ill.

# Regulating Emotions 101

**WHAT REGULATING YOUR EMOTIONS IS:**

- Noticing the feelings and the sensations in your body, which means you become conscious of the emotions. That allows your brain to integrate the message and decide how to respond wisely, instead of letting unconscious emotions hijack your actions.
- Taking responsibility to calm yourself so you can act like a responsible, kind grown-up in the situation, rather than indulging in your own tantrum.
- Monitoring your own mood and giving yourself whatever support you need to maintain a generally positive sense of well-being, which includes working through intense emotions as they arise, or as soon as possible thereafter.

**WHAT REGULATING YOUR EMOTIONS ISN'T:**

- Numbing yourself, or repressing your emotions. That doesn't work since repressed emotions are no longer under conscious control and will either make you sick or burst out unregulated.
- Blaming your child for your emotions.
- Pretending that you feel something you don't, or that you don't feel something you do. Children will always sense how you actually feel. The key is to acknowledge your emotions and take responsibility for them.

What I'm encouraging you to do is actually much harder than stuffing your feelings. I'm suggesting that you notice your anger and other emotions but that you resist acting on them. Noticing your experience without leaping to action is called "mindfulness."

Mindfulness helps you defuse your own tantrums before they even start. You might find yourself saying, "*When my child is defiant and says, 'I hate you, Mommy!' it makes me crazy—it makes my blood boil.*" If you can just notice that, then you already have the ability *not* to get hijacked into reactivity, because you're now in observer mode. Observer mode gives you a choice about how to react.

Anger is always a message that something is wrong, that something needs changing—either something outside us or (more often than we'd like to admit) something inside us. So we do need to listen to our anger, not just ignore it. But, when we're angry, we often interpret the anger as meaning that we should attack the messenger. If we consider the message after we've calmed down, we usually realize that the source of our rage was our exhaustion, or our fear, or feeling powerless. There *is* something we need to change in our life. But it might not be our child. And, even if it is, we can't control another human being, so we can't directly change our child. If we crack down with punishment, our child will change—but in ways that will almost certainly backfire. Instead, peaceful parents consider which needs and emotions are driving their child's behavior, and how to address those in order to change the behavior. Changing the environment—and ourselves—will always produce change in our child.

Every one of us will lose it if we're pushed to the edge, no matter how peaceful we try to be. So aspiring to parent more peacefully won't make you perfect. It will just help you remember that, as the grown-up, it's always your responsibility to stay away from the edge.

## WHAT'S YOUR REACTIVITY BASELINE?

On a scale of 1 to 10, how effectively have you been regulating your emotions lately?

**1      2      ③      4      5      6      7      8      9      10**

Be honest. You'll be evaluating your emotional regulation again after using this workbook, so the number you record here is your baseline. You have no place to go but up!

## Practice: Self-Regulation Successes

We've all had times when we've gotten angry and said things we later regretted. But I'm betting there are also times when you were able to stay calm, even though everything around you was pushing you over the edge, including your child.

Think about the times when you were able to successfully self-regulate. We're going to build on those. List some of those times below. In each case, reflect on what you did that helped you stay calm.

**①** There was the time when I:

_____

_____

_____

What I did that made this moment possible, and how I can do more of this in the future:

_____

_____

_____

**②** There was the time when I:

_____

_____

_____

What I did that made this moment possible, and how I can do more of this in the future:

_____

_____

_____

**③** There was the time when I:

_____

_____

What I did that made this moment possible, and how I can do more of this in the future:

_____

_____

_____

## Practice: **Your Pause Button: Stop, Drop, and Breathe**

> I saw major changes when I started using 'Stop, Drop, and Breathe.' The Pause Button keeps me from saying things I'll be sorry for, and lets me phrase things so my kids will be more likely to listen. I think it helps my kids take a breath and decide to behave better, too.
>
> — Daniel, father of four-year-old and eight-year-old

Sometime this week, you will feel annoyance, irritation, resentment, anger, or even rage in reaction to your child's behavior. As soon as you notice that you're angry, use your **Pause Button: Stop, Drop, and Breathe**. Below are the steps. Post them on your refrigerator so you have them handy. (Note: You will feel an urgent need to set your child straight. Unless someone is in physical danger, ignore it—that's a sign you're in "fight" mode. Your intervention will be more successful if you calm down first.)

### STEP 1: **Stop, Drop, and Breathe**

**Stop.** Just stop. Stop everything you're doing. Close your mouth.

**Drop** your agenda. Just for now, let it go. Step away from the fight.

**Breathe.** Take three deep breaths to calm yourself, breathing in through your nose and out through your mouth.[11] If you need more breaths, take 10. Becoming conscious of your breath stops your slide down the slippery slope toward losing it and lets you choose how to respond.

### STEP 2: **Choose Love**

The hardest part of calming down is choosing to calm down. When we're in the grip of anger, we want to lash out, not calm down. Make a conscious choice to let the anger go.

### STEP 3: **Change Your Mind**

Consciously choose an antidote—an image or thought (some people call this a mantra)—that will make you feel more calm and emotionally generous. (Not the mantra type? I'm not suggesting you start "ohmming" in traffic. Just find a thought to interrupt that anxiety loop by reassuring your worried mind.)

### STEP 4: **Calm Your Body**

Notice the sensations in your body. Shift your emotions by hugging yourself or moving your body—shake out your hands, splash water on your face.

**Once you're calm**, go back to your child. Set whatever limit is necessary or talk about what happened.

## Reflection After Practice: **What Did You Learn About Calming Yourself?**

When you tried Stop, Drop, and Breathe, how did it work? Were you able to calm yourself?

_____
_____
_____

What did you think and feel?

_____
_____
_____

What did you do?

_____
_____
_____

How did your child respond?

_____
_____
_____

What was the hardest part?

_____
_____
_____

How can you support yourself in the future to make it more likely that you can activate your Pause Button and self-regulate?

_____
_____
_____

## Practice: **Self-Regulation Resources**

Which self-calming strategies work best for you?

_____

_____

_____

How can you remember to try these strategies next time you get upset?

_____

_____

_____

Is there anyone who supports you in trying to be more regulated and could help you stay accountable in regulating your emotions?

_____

_____

_____

## UNDERSTANDING EMOTION

What is emotion? While experts disagree on an exact definition, most of us recognize our emotions as intense states of feeling that include physiological reactions in our body.

Emotions are designed to keep us alive. They're a message about something we need, motivating us to take action. Fear, for instance, motivates us to run away. Anger motivates us to protect ourselves. Loving feelings motivate us to connect and nurture.

Emotions also play an essential role in motivating us to grow. Every conscious decision we make uses the brain, and therefore creates neural structure. Since emotions motivate us, we are constantly making decisions in response to our emotions. That means that experiencing emotions builds our inner resources—emotional depth and strength, as well as compassion for others.

We learn lessons more readily when they have emotions attached. This means, for instance, that the automatic rush of fear most of us feel when we see a snake makes it more likely that we'll keep our distance whenever we see snakes, and thus more likely that we'll survive. But positive emotions also help us learn lessons, so when Daddy lifts his child high into the air, the child learns the exciting word "up"!

Emotions derive from our perceptions, which is why we have a very different reaction to a snake than to a stick. They're an automatic physiological response to a perception or need. Our perceptions are shaped by our thoughts, which in turn are shaped by our belief systems and the meaning we assign to our experiences, or what I call our "story lines."

Since our thoughts shape the way we perceive things, they're usually the trigger for our emotions. But emotions can also bypass conscious thought. When we see a stick on the path that resembles a snake, we may feel a flash of fear, even before our mind has consciously shaped the thought that we're in danger.

Here's the big secret about emotions that can change your life. Ready? When we allow ourselves to feel any emotion, it begins to fade away.

That's because emotions are a message, and once the message has been delivered, the emotion is "processed." We can then make a conscious choice about what to do with the information we've been given. Maybe the best response to feeling hurt is to withdraw from a situation in which we don't feel emotionally safe, or maybe the best response is to reach out to the loved one by whom we feel hurt, to ask for connection and repair. The decision about how to act on emotional information is made by the prefrontal cortex, which builds on the belief systems we've created based on our past experiences and integrates information from the right (more emotional) and left (more logical) sides of the brain.

## The Neural Basis Of Emotions

Many of our responses to perceptions are automatic. Just as we automatically respond to a red light by pushing the brake down while we're driving, we automatically respond to hurt by withdrawing. Some of these responses are universal and hardwired, so most other people would react in the same way—for example, we all react with fear to being grabbed from behind. But many of our responses are highly individual, learned from experience, often in childhood. For instance, we may respond to the smell of a cigarette with excitement, pleasure, relief, fear, or disgust, depending on past associations.

These automatic neural associations are simply habitual ways of responding that allow us to act rapidly without having to think through each step. They can be as simple as the neural pattern that helps you tie your shoe or as complicated as the neural pattern that allows you to play a sonata. Automatic associations are created by neurons in the brain that all fire together in a learned pattern. Neurologists say that "neurons that fire together wire together," which just means that the more often the experience is repeated, the stronger the neural associations (or pathways) become. The nervous system wires itself for efficiency by creating a predictable chain reaction of quick physical and emotional responses to any repeated experience.

Some of these automatic emotional associations serve us well. For instance, we might respond to feeling anxious by breathing more deeply, which calms the nervous system, giving it the message that there's no emergency. Other associations don't serve us as well. For instance, maybe we learned in childhood that eating would help us numb our anxiety. In addition to complicating our relationship with food, this response distracts us from the anxiety rather than helping us notice and address it.

In addition, some neural associations that served us well at some point in our lives may not serve us well now. For instance, as a child it probably wouldn't have served you to express hurt to an alcoholic parent on a rampage. It might have served you better to hide. But today when you feel hurt by your partner, it probably doesn't serve you to withdraw and hide, which just widens the gulf between you and makes future hurt more likely. It would probably serve you better to reconnect with your partner, express your needs, accept comfort, and strengthen your relationship.

## Recognizing Your Emotions

While I use the terms "feelings" and "emotions" almost interchangeably, there is a technical difference. Feelings are physical sensations in our bodies. Emotions are our interpretations of those feelings. In other words, emotions are the construct we build around those physical sensations when we add perceptions, thoughts, and beliefs so as to understand, contain, justify, and even defend against those sensations.

Research on emotions shows that humans across most cultures say they feel similar emotional states: anger, sadness, fear, anxiety, and depression. But people, even within a given culture, vary widely in identifying these emotions. In fact, many people can't distinguish between feeling depressed and feeling anxious—they feel both at once.[12] This is partly because many of us got into the habit of repressing our emotions in childhood, so we no longer recognize the physical cues that accompany them. But there's also wide variation in the physical reactions that individual humans have to emotions.[13] In each situation, our mind interprets the physical sensation using perceptions of the situation. So a thumping heart could mean you're terrified, shocked by bad news, furious, excited, or even that you've just finished an intense workout. Our behavior when we feel a given emotion also varies. Depending on your past experiences and your temperament, you might respond to anger by lashing out, crying, running away, or going numb.

If you find it challenging to identify your emotions, you're not alone. And all of us can probably become more precise in identifying what we feel. There is no one way to "map" emotions and how they relate to each other, but the **Feelings Wheel**, developed by Dr. Gloria Willcox, illustrates the wealth of emotions available to us. As you can see, the middle wheel contains more specific versions of the feelings in the central wheel. The outer wheel contains common responses to those feelings. So for instance when you're excited you might be more daring, and when you feel hurt you might become more distant. The full color version of the Feelings Wheel is worth printing out and posting. You can find it at AhaParenting.com/FeelingsWheel.

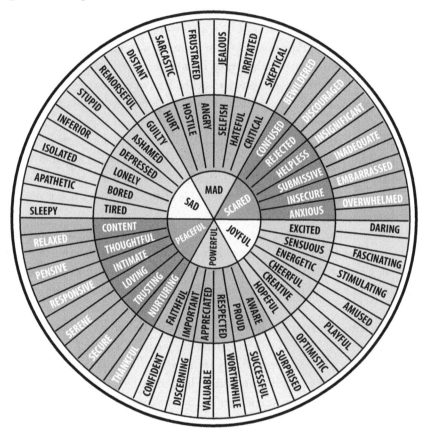

But don't worry—if you find the idea of so many emotions overwhelming, you can also think in terms of just the four basic emotions:

- **Happiness**, which includes **love, joy** and **peace**. This is our natural state, when we're in flow.
- **Fear**, which is a reaction to threat and includes **terror, anxiety** (fear of an unspecified threat), **worry** (fear of a specific threat) and the feeling of being powerless or defenseless. Note that when mammals feel fear, they often shift into **anger** as a defense.
- **Sadness**, which is a reaction to loss and disappointment, and includes **grief, depression and loneliness**. Note that many people defend against disappointment and sadness by becoming **angry**.
- **Anger**, which is a reaction to threat from within or without and includes **irritation, frustration** and **rage**. Note that when anger is not heard, the person may turn it inward so that it becomes **depression** or **numbness**.

We may respond to fear by running away (flight) or by trying to fight. If we don't feel adequately resourced for either of those responses, we may freeze, go numb, or even go into a physical or emotional collapse.

Anger may arise from the perception of an immediate threat that sends us into "fight" mode, or from a more subtle threat such as the loss of self-esteem, power, or the ability to meet our needs. But anger is always a message that something isn't working for us and that we need to make a change. Most of us assume that the person or circumstance making us angry is the problem and should change. But we can never control someone else, and we often can't control our circumstances. We can only control ourselves. So the most effective response to anger will always be to first calm our physiological response and then to consider what we can change. (Note that being peaceful does not mean denying your anger, but instead noticing it and using it to make your life better.)

In the chart below, you can see typical physical reactions to help you identify the most common emotions as well as the message that the emotion is trying to give you.

| Emotion | Common Physical Signs | Common Reactions | Message |
|---|---|---|---|
| Love and happiness | Ease, lightness, well-being, benevolence toward others | Connection, delight | Share the happiness with others. Feel gratitude so as to open the door to even more well-being. |
| Fear and anxiety | Cold hands, increase in heart rate, shallow breathing, butterflies in the stomach or stomach pain | Flight, freezing (numbness), collapse, self-medicating, defensive anger | Find safety, help, and reassurance. |
| Grief and sadness | Fatigue, pain in the chest, aching, weakness | Giving up, numbing, self-medicating | Connect with someone who can comfort you. |
| Anger and frustration | Sweating palms, tension throughout the body, trembling | Lashing out at others, resentment | Make a change in yourself or your situation. |
| Guilt | Sleep disturbance, muscle tension, stomachaches | Self-medicating, self-sabotaging, overreacting to criticism | Take action to bring yourself back into integrity. |
| Shame | Downcast eyes, lurching stomach, heaviness | Self-medicating, self-blame, defensively lashing out at others | You're judging yourself as unworthy of love based on the views of others; you need to give yourself love and acceptance. |
| Jealousy | Increased heart rate and blood pressure, upset stomach | Clinging, obsession, rage, distrust | You're feeling a loss of self-esteem from comparing yourself with others; you need to give yourself love and acceptance, and build what you're missing into your life. |

Notice that guilt, shame, and jealousy are defensive reactions, sometimes called secondary emotions. We feel them in reaction to a loss of esteem. Shame and jealousy feel terrible, but better than acknowledging that we may not be lovable because we simply aren't good enough. Guilt feels terrible, but better than seeing ourselves as a bad person.

When we're able to accept our feelings as they arise, we'll notice that minor anxiety and sadness arise continually as we go through life. We can listen to those sensations and decide how to respond productively. The emotion, having delivered its message, begins to dissipate, and we feel energized to tackle the problem, which builds our inner resources and makes our life better. But when we're frightened of our feelings, we numb them (using food, alcohol, or "little addictions" such as shopping), or repress them in our emotional backpack, which makes us sick and tired. Instead of being able to solve the problem, we find ourselves stuck in a cycle of secondary emotions—anger, shame, guilt or jealousy—blaming others or ourselves.

## Practice: Identifying Your Emotions

The first step in regulating emotions is befriending them. And any friendship begins by being able to recognize your friend! Since everyone's emotions are a bit different, each of us needs to learn to recognize our own cues. Reflect on each of your emotions: the bodily sensations that help you recognize them, the thoughts that help you interpret them, and (maybe most importantly) what you usually feel like doing to express the emotion or get rid of it. These are your cues to what you're feeling. I've given you space here for the most common emotions, but please use this practice for any emotions that you feel often.

# Fear

When I feel afraid, I notice these sensations in my body:

_____

_____

_____

I notice thoughts like this:

_____

_____

_____

I want to:

_____

_____

_____

It would be helpful if when I feel fear I could:

_____

_____

_____

# Sadness

When I feel sad, I notice these sensations in my body:

_____

_____

_____

I notice thoughts like this:

_____

_____

_____

I want to:

_____

_____

_____

It would be helpful if when I feel sadness I could:

_____

_____

_____

# Anger

When I feel angry, I notice these sensations in my body:

_____

_____

_____

I notice thoughts like this:

_____

_____

_____

I want to:

_____

_____

_____

It would be helpful if when I feel anger I could:

_____

_____

_____

## Practice: You Are Not Your Emotions: Shifting from "I Am" to "I Feel"

We usually express emotions by saying "*I am…*," as in "*I am sad*," "*I am angry*," or "*I am disappointed*." That habit communicates how overwhelmed we often feel by our emotions, but it also sets up an identification with the emotion, so we see ourselves as *being* that emotion. It's hard to imagine at that moment being something else. But feelings come and go. We aren't actually anger. We just feel angry at this moment.

Something liberating happens when we develop the habit of expressing emotions by saying "*I feel…*" For example, "*I feel sad.*" "*I feel angry.*" "*I feel disappointed.*" We break the hold the emotion has on us. Instead of being swept away by the emotion, we become more conscious of it, and we see it as a temporary state. Adopting this habit actually challenges your belief system about emotions, so you regulate more easily in those tough moments.

Let's try this right now.

- Say "*I am sad*" aloud. Notice how that feels.

- Now say "*I feel sad.*" Notice how that feels. Is it different?

Now try the same experiment with "angry." What did you notice? How can you make this new way of expressing your emotional states a habit?

_____

_____

_____

## The Emotional Backpack

Remember the discussion of emotions in the previous section? When we allow ourselves to feel our emotions, they begin to lose strength. We can move on. By contrast, when we push emotions out of our awareness, they gain power, because we lose the ability to consciously control them. So you might imagine each of us humans carrying around an "emotional backpack" crammed with feelings that we didn't feel safe enough to process when we first felt them.

Some of our emotions may have been stuffed today, or this week. But most of us also have old tangled-up fears or pain from months and even years ago. In fact, feelings from any traumatic incident that you couldn't process adequately at the time will stay in your emotional backpack until you process them. The more "reactive" you are, or the more easily you get "triggered," the more old emotions you have in your backpack, signaling you that they're waiting to be processed.

When the backpack gets too full, that feels like a threat, so we feel tense and anxious. And when something happens that upsets us, often the current situation triggers the old feelings to burst out. It's common to confuse those old feelings with whatever is going on in the present moment.

That's why a driver who gets cut off in traffic might find himself out of his car yelling at a complete stranger. Sure, he has a reason to be angry. But most of us wouldn't react that way. His overreaction is almost certainly coming from old feelings from the past, when he felt disrespected so severely that it felt like a threat to his integrity—his wholeness as a person—or even his existence. This is old baggage, not a current threat. But, in that moment, this driver is certain that the stranger driving the other car is the cause of all of his upset feelings and presents a current danger.

We call this "getting triggered" because the current situation triggers the old emotions to burst out of the emotional backpack. If we're not aware of what's happening, we react as if there's a real and present danger. Our body gears up for self-protection, as we ready ourselves for an emergency. We leap to actions that we would never take if we were thinking clearly. You can see how your child's misbehavior could have a similar effect, causing you to overreact because of your old triggers.

Mammals have limited defenses when there's a threat: fight, flight, or freeze. So, sometimes we run away ("flight") or, if that's not an option, we may "freeze" and go numb. We may even collapse, which prevents us from protecting ourselves. Or we'll leap to anger, mobilizing the body for "fight." So anger is the body's "fight" response, our defense against threat. Anger doesn't know if the threat is a current danger or old emotions that feel dangerous. Anger only knows that it's been summoned to your defense, and it's ready to vanquish the enemy. That's why you can feel enraged at your one-year-old when she won't stop throwing her food off the high chair. It's not reasonable, but old emotions from the past are fueling your current rage.

While the emotional backpack is a useful metaphor, there's obviously not really a backpack. We actually carry those old unprocessed emotions in our bodies, which as any massage therapist can tell you, is where many subconscious memories are stored. Unfortunately, even when those old feelings aren't being triggered, they don't just stay put. That's because the body experiences them as tension or contraction, which isn't healthy. Luckily, the body has mechanisms to heal itself. Just like an infection bubbles up to the surface to get healed, stuffed emotions will bubble up to get healed.

Sometimes, yawning is enough to release the held tension that started out as fear, anxiety, or worry. Or maybe we'll find ourselves laughing hard about something, which is another way the body releases stress. Sometimes we'll find ourselves crying about something unrelated. This releases stress even if we don't know the original source of the sadness. Or maybe we regularly pick fights with our partner to help us work through the upsets we're carrying, because we learned early in life that when we fight with a loved one, it eventually builds towards the tears that help us feel better. (Wouldn't it be great for our relationships if we could learn to bypass the fight and go straight to the tears?)

> Let's look at how this works with your child. He can be perfectly behaved all day at school but then come home and wreak havoc. That's because he's been stuffing feelings in his emotional backpack all day, when another child shoved him or he barely made it to the bathroom on time or the teacher scolded him. When he gets home and feels safe, the healing process will often take over, and all those feelings from his day will bubble up to get healed.
>
> But, as the feelings start to swamp the child, they don't feel good. After all, the feelings in the emotional backpack were stuffed because they were too upsetting to process at the time. They're scary. Now, when they start to surface, the child reaches for a defense against them. The best defense is a good offense. So he picks a fight with you to distract himself from those painful emotions that are coming up. He looks right at you and breaks a household rule or yells in your face. Naturally, you respond by yelling back, since you're being attacked. In response, his body mobilizes for a fight. Since it's no longer a good time to process stored feelings, those scary emotions subside into the emotional backpack, to be healed another day. Crisis averted—your child doesn't have to feel those awful emotions from his backpack. Except, of course, that now you're in a completely unnecessary altercation with your child, which can ruin the day for both of you. Not to mention that his backpack is now even more full, and will get triggered at some later point.

Any emotion that felt too vulnerable to process when we first felt it might be stuffed in our emotional backpack. Fear in its many forms, including feeling trapped, disconnected, or powerless, is so threatening to us that it often gets pushed into the backpack. So do grief and loneliness.

**Anger, however, is *not* in the backpack.** It's the body's fight response, so it's a response to threat, mobilizing you to protect yourself. That's why, although anger feels visceral, immediate, and instantaneous, it's usually a secondary emotion, a response to the threat of more vulnerable emotions getting triggered from the emotional backpack. Certainly we can get angry in response to real threats in the current moment, such as a mugger. But those intense events are fairly rare in our lives. The more we "clear" our emotional backpacks, the more we realize that most of the "threats" of daily life don't warrant more than annoyance. It's the emotional backpack getting triggered that most often spurs us to shift into "fight" mode, ready to do battle for survival.

Notice that fighting with you doesn't empty your child's emotional backpack, just as yelling at him won't empty yours. The fight response is designed to protect you from danger, so it helps you gear up for attack. It doesn't help you feel those vulnerable, scary emotions underneath the anger, which is what you need to do to empty the emotional backpack.

It would be so much easier if our child could just come home and ask for a hug and have a good cry, instead of picking a fight with us that eventually ends in tears. This book will show you how to make that more likely. But even adults often exhibit a version of this more difficult behavior. When the fear or pain in our emotional backpacks get triggered, we often erupt in anger, just as our child lashes out at us rather than crying or telling us he's afraid of something. Unfortunately, many of us (and our children) have learned that anger is an effective defense against feeling all those powerful emotions we're avoiding, so we leap to anger whenever we start to feel fear or grief. That's one reason parents get addicted to yelling.

## But What If...?

We've been focusing on you and your ability to self-regulate, without addressing your child's behavior. If—like so many parents—you're in the habit of using your anger to manage your child's behavior, you may have a lot of questions that begin with *"But what if…?"* Let's answer those questions.

**"But what if my child 'deserves' my anger?"** Remember that no matter what your child did, no human ever *deserves* to be yelled at. You're always entitled to your anger, but it's always *your* anger, not the other person's responsibility. No one else can "make" us angry.

**"But what if my child's behavior requires discipline?"** The child may well need limits (and we'll discuss how to guide children effectively in Part 3: Coaching Instead of Controlling). But any decision we make while angry will come from our fear, not our love. You'll be much more effective in intervening to guide your child once you calm down. In fact, I guarantee that your child's offense won't seem nearly so terrible, regardless of what it is.

It's our job as parents to be our child's role model in handling emotions constructively. That means never acting on our anger from that "fight, flight, or freeze" place where our child looks like the enemy and where it feels like we have to "win" while our child has to "lose." Forget about teaching your child lessons unless you feel emotionally generous and can teach lovingly. Teachable moments only happen when both people are receptive and positive. Anger and punishment are never based on love, because your child never believes your love when you're angry. He can't help but shift into fight, flight, or freeze, which means the learning parts of the brain shut down.

**"But isn't it healthy to express my anger?"** Dumping your anger on another person is never healthy; it just reinforces your rage.[14] What's healthy is to acknowledge *to yourself* how you feel, and then be brave enough to pause and notice what's under your anger—hurt, fear, sadness, disappointment. If you allow yourself to feel those sensations in your body, *without acting on them*, they begin to melt away. Once you've calmed down, you'll be better able to take care of your own hurt places, and also to intervene with your child so she learns how to manage her behavior better.

**"But doesn't my child need to learn a lesson?"** Of course, but rage, or even criticism, are not the lessons you want to teach. If you make your teachable moments into learnable moments by waiting until your child is receptive, your teaching will stick. Your child will get something even better than the lesson about behavior: a lesson about self-regulation. And, just as important, he will develop the unshakable conviction that he is wholly and unconditionally loved exactly as he is, including all those messy, passionate emotions that drive our behavior and make us human.

**"But I want my child to learn that all people get angry, that it's just part of life, it's normal and not scary."** What creates the belief that anger is scary is what the parent does with the anger. If you blow up, your child learns that anger is terrifying. Instead, if your child sees you get angry—and there is no way to avoid that in daily life—and then sees you stop and take a few deep breaths, and then state your needs without an attack or a tantrum, you've just taught your child that anger is normal and not scary. And, you've taught your child how to manage anger responsibly and use it to make things better.

**"But I don't want my child to think emotions aren't allowed."** Good point! Hopefully, we feel comfortable enough with our feelings to honor them as they come up. This means that we find ourselves shifting through different emotions all day long. Happiness, sadness, disappointment, frustration, delight—emotions are always arising and passing away. Tears are always coming to the eyes and smiles are always coming to the lips. If we accept all of these emotions and let them move through us, they dissipate, rather than triggering us. If we talk with our kids as we feel those emotions about how to respond constructively, we'll be teaching them about emotional wholeness and self-discipline. So hopefully all day long you're saying things like:

- *"My body loves feeling that beautiful sunshine!"*
- *"Oh, no! There's paint on the floor! Let's all stop and fix this."*
- *"I'm missing my sister. It makes me sad that she lives so far away."*
- *"We need to leave the house in five minutes and I'm worried about how we'll be ready. What does each person need to do now to be ready?"*
- *"I'm so frustrated trying to get this open!"*
- *"I'm upset to see toys all over the floor! We need to work together to get this room cleaned up."*

If allowing our own emotions means that we sit down on the floor and cry sometimes, I think that's a good thing for children to see. We can just explain that we're sad, so we're crying, but things will be okay. What if it upsets our child? We hold them, and reassure them that we're feeling sad about whatever it is and so we're crying, and that we will stop crying soon. We always reassure the child that our tears are not her fault, that everyone needs to cry sometimes, and that we can handle it. That's a great learning experience for a child, especially when we're able to smile at them and talk about it shortly thereafter. This kind of modeling makes it safe for kids to feel their full range of emotions. (Of course, if you're weeping on a daily basis, it's time to get some support so you can heal without involving your children in your deep emotional work.)

**"But what about being authentic with my child?"** Being authentic about the truth of your experience never requires you to "dump" it on someone else, unfiltered. As the Dalai Lama says, *"Be kind whenever possible. It is always possible."*[15]

Besides, anger by itself is not the whole truth. It's the body's defensive reaction to fear or powerlessness or grief or another deep, upsetting emotion. So if we really wanted to be authentic with our children, we would not scream at them when they resist doing their homework. We would admit the deeper truth: *"I'm terrified that you're acting like this because maybe you have a learning disability... I feel powerless to get you to do this work and I am afraid you will fail at school and ruin your life."*

But of course expressing our most primal fears to a child in the name of authenticity would also be damaging. Those fears are not the truth. Fear is rarely the truth, and never the whole truth.

The solution is to express our needs, set limits, and partner with our child to problem-solve. After all, needs are giving rise to those emotions. In this example, your need is for your child to do their homework. So you would do what we are always asking our children to do—express the need without attacking the other person: *"I need you to do your homework because the school requires it. I find it frustrating when you don't seem willing to do the homework, and I can see that you really don't enjoy it. You do have to do it, so let's find a way to make this work for you."*

**"But what if my child runs into the street? Surely that requires me to let him know I'm furious?!"** Actually, I think that requires you to let him know you were terrified. Every child takes their cues on safety from their parents; that's how the human race is still here. She's much more likely to take your terror seriously than she is to take your anger seriously. In fact, children often feel the need to respond to our anger by testing us. Occasionally telling your child how angry you are about a major infraction is probably unavoidable and won't damage her psyche, but it isn't the best way to teach lessons or get cooperation.

## Practice: **Surfacing Your Reservations**

Whenever we decide to change, part of us is motivated toward our new path. But part of us is still loyally dedicated to our previous mission. Until we acknowledge those places inside us and answer their concerns, we aren't unified in working toward our new goal. We hold ourselves back from change.

Consider the ideas you've been learning about self-regulation. Do you have any fears or reservations about trying this approach? List them on the space provided below. Then, beside each one, use what you've learned to answer that concern as well as you can. If you don't have an answer yet, put a sticky note on this page to come back and respond to these concerns later, as you find the answers throughout this book.

**(1)** _____

_____

_____

**(2)** _____

_____

_____

**(3)** _____

_____

_____

**(4)** _____

_____

_____

**(5)** _____

_____

_____

### *Your Emotional Triggers*

> "
> When asked by a student, 'Master, how do you stay centered all the time?' he responded,
> 'I'm not centered all the time. I simply recover faster.'
>
> — Morihei Ueshiba, founder of the martial art Aikido[16]

The definition of getting triggered is that old feelings in our emotional backpack are stimulated by our current experience, setting off the alarm system in our brain and sending us into a "fight, flight, or freeze" state. In other words, our emotions seize control from the prefrontal cortex and we lose access to the reasoning brain. In the moment, we often think our reaction is appropriate, because we're overestimating the threat. Only later can we see that we overreacted.

Our child often triggers us, but our child did not install that trigger. It's been there inside us for a long time. In fact, our child is giving us an opportunity to notice and heal that trigger. If we don't, we will probably take that old baggage and dump it on our child.

Virtually all of us have triggers, unless we've done a lot of work on ourselves. No matter how loving and responsive your parents were, there were almost certainly times when you experienced something that was overwhelming for you. Because it was so overwhelming, your brain wasn't able to process that experience in the way that we usually process experiences—by incorporating the memory into a neural network that stores related memories. Usually when we process memories, which happens during sleep, the emotions associated with the memory are stripped away. That's why once we've slept on something for a few nights, it usually isn't so upsetting.

But any time the memory was so upsetting that your brain wasn't able to process it as usual, the memory was stored unprocessed, with all the sensations you felt at the time. That's why when you experience something similar to that event—maybe not in actual content, but in the way it makes you feel—you're suddenly swamped with bodily sensations that are an overreaction. Those feelings aren't actually from the present experience. They are stored with that earlier unprocessed memory, which is getting triggered by the current experience.

Your psyche does this for a reason. If you almost drowned in childhood, you're more likely to stay alive later in life if you remember that experience with all the fear you felt initially. So there may have been times when a mild form of PTSD (post-traumatic stress disorder) was beneficial to human survival.

But this doesn't work so well if the experience was being humiliated by a teacher, which might make you quake when you have to speak up at a staff meeting. And it really gets in your way if the original experience was being frightened of, yelled at, or hit by a parent. If those memories were stored unprocessed, then when your child yells at you or hits you, it triggers all those feelings of fear and feeling victimized that you felt as a child. You can't think clearly. You freeze, or you lash out, either verbally or physically.

So most of us have some unprocessed emotions from childhood, which is another way of saying we're lugging these old feelings and memories around in our emotional backpacks. This unconscious "baggage" will inevitably get triggered as we go through life. It sends us right into our unconscious, which means we do and say things that we would never do if we were fully conscious and aware. See if you recognize the common responses to being triggered in the chart below.

| Fight | Flight | Freeze |
|---|---|---|
| Impatience | Fantasizing | Numbness |
| Annoyance | Spacing out | Distancing |
| Blaming | Screen usage | Falling asleep |
| Feeling victimized | Repetitive thoughts | Eating |
| Emotional and physical outbursts | Upset stomach, headache, body tension | Alcohol, drugs |
| Self-justifying | Shopping | Smoking |

Luckily, research shows[17] that you can heal your emotional triggers, simply by letting your body feel them, but not taking action based on them. Let me say that again. The key to healing your triggers is to *notice the sensations in your body,* but *resist taking action.*

Of course, first you have to notice that you've been triggered, which isn't always easy. But once you can say, "*Oh, I'm triggered, that's what's happening here!*" you can stop running or numbing or lashing out. You can heal that trigger.

Please note that noticing the feelings in your body that are associated with an old trigger does *not* mean getting all tangled up in the story line. Thinking about the story of what happened will just mire you in the muck. Remember, we feel emotions in the body. So noticing the feeling simply means noticing the sensations in your body.

## Practice: **Healing an Emotional Trigger**

Here's a simple three-step process for healing an emotional trigger. Simple, but not necessarily easy. In fact, sitting with the sensations stored in the body can feel pretty scary. Take it slow, and keep returning to Steps 1 and 2 to center yourself. You can handle this! If you feel overwhelmed, make an appointment with a counselor for support as you begin to explore your triggers.

1. **Center yourself as much as possible.** Sit comfortably, breathe deeply. Notice how the chair or floor is supporting you.

2. **Increase your sense of well-being and safety.** You can do this by remembering things you're grateful for, or surrounding yourself with love and light, or using an comforting mantra or image.

3. **Now, think of a recent event that triggered you.** You don't need to know what the old trigger was, just think of the recent event. Notice how remembering this feels in your body. Keep your attention on your body, rather then following any thoughts about the event. Keep breathing. Notice that you may want to run (flight) or eat something (freeze) or call someone to tell them off (fight). Resist all of that. When you want to jump up and check your phone, don't. When you feel an urgent need to clean the kitchen, don't. Just breathe and give yourself a hug and notice the way that sensation feels in your body. Breathe into it. You can handle this. If you feel overwhelmed, just go back to your place of well-being (Steps 1 and 2).

That's it. Those body sensations are the stored feelings from the emotional backpack that are triggering your current overreactions. When we observe them from the calm, safe perspective of our conscious adult self—what some psychologists call the "observing ego"—they begin to change and evaporate. If you can stay in your observer self, it keeps you from getting hijacked by the emotions and allows your brain to begin to rewire that neural circuit.

The next time this same old trigger is activated by some new event, you'll notice that it has less power. Every time you do this process, you diminish its emotional charge. Eventually, you'll be able to stay calm in the face of an event that would once have triggered you.

Scientists think that you're actually rewiring the neural pathways of the triggering memory by holding yourself in a feeling of safety and well-being as you revisit it.[18] This seems to deactivate the emotional charge, which allows your brain to fully process the old memory. So you may still remember the teacher humiliating you, but your takeaway will be that the teacher was having a hard day or maybe should not have been teaching. You'll feel compassion for yourself as a child, instead of shame. As a result, you won't cringe when you think of the memory, and you will feel more comfortable when you speak up in front of others.

Or you'll remember that interaction with your parent, but with compassion for you the child and even an understanding of your parent. You won't get upset at the memory. Your body won't tense up into fight, flight, or freeze mode. Your takeaway will be an ability to stay unruffled when your child is upset.

I think of this as shining the light of consciousness on the memories that we've pushed into the dark basements of our psyches. Simply bringing our own loving awareness to the shadows melts them away. One by one, we process the memories, remove the charge from the triggers, and thereby resolve them. They no longer pop up to derail us as we go through life. We feel so much freer, happier, less anxious, and able to stay calm.

Are all triggers from childhood? No, of course not. Traumas can happen to us throughout life. But the childhood traumas are usually the ones with the most power, because that is the time when we are most easily overwhelmed by our emotions. And many of the traumas we experience in later life are re-enactments of our earlier traumas.

You may be thinking that it will take your entire life to heal your triggers. And you're right. This is the work of a lifetime. But don't worry. The good news is that every step you take makes you feel better. Every time you feel those big emotions but resist acting on them by lashing out, you do some healing of that trigger and reduce its power. Over time, those triggers get deactivated.

Let's consider the situations that are most likely to trigger you into anger or upset. Not only will this help you bring more awareness to those situations; but reflecting on this question will also help develop your prefrontal cortex,[19] giving you more ability to choose a better response the next time you're triggered.

## Practice: Identifying Your Triggers

Consider the past week, month, or year. When did you get angry or very upset, so that you acted in ways you later wished you hadn't? List five situations below. Then, go back to each situation and reflect. Write some ideas for what you could have done in each situation to prevent your downhill slide.

**1** _____

_____

_____

**2** _____

_____

_____

**3** _____

_____

_____

**4** _____

_____

_____

**5** _____

_____

_____

## Practice: Interrupting Your Automatic Reaction

When we let ourselves feel an emotion and act on it according to our "pre-programmed" habitual response, the neural signals have completed their usual chain reaction. But what if we want to break that chain reaction? For instance, maybe your habitual response to your children fighting with each other is to begin screaming at them. But now you've decided that you'd like to stay emotionally regulated instead, so you can calm the storm instead of escalating it.

The next time your children fight, what can you do? It's actually pretty simple. That doesn't mean it's easy—it's one of the hardest things you can learn to do—but each time you attempt this, you're changing your brain so it gets easier the next time.

1. **Notice the message your body is trying to send you**, by noticing the emotions. You'll usually find a complex mixture, probably of:
   - anger ("*They know better than this!*")

- fear ("*Will they hate each other for life?*")
- shame ("*It's all my fault for not managing my own emotions better and being a terrible role model!*")
- powerlessness, which is a form of fear ("*I just don't know what to do to stop this fighting!*")
- or sometimes numbness, or lack of any feeling, which is a sign that you're in "freeze" mode (which will push you to withdraw instead of yelling)

2. **Notice that the emotions are pushing you toward an automatic reaction**—in this case, yelling at your children.

3. **Resist your automatic reaction.** Activate your Pause Button by taking a deep breath. Notice, but don't react. Slow yourself down. This breaks the habitual neural connections. (In this case, you might even put your hand over your mouth to help you avoid your habitual response of yelling.)

4. **Redirect your impulse toward a healthier response.** For instance, train yourself to take a deep breath and blow it out slowly, instead of yelling. Conscious breathing has been proven to be calming to the anger response. Substituting a different response begins to rewire your neural pathways.

**What if you can't resist the "pre-programmed" action, which in this case is yelling?** After all, your body thinks this is an emergency and your unconscious (that neural wiring) thinks it knows just how to handle the situation. You're primed for action.

That's why we have Step 4. It's easier to resist your habitual reaction if you give yourself something to do instead that redirects your physical energy. Instead of yelling at your child, turn away and blow out a forceful breath while you shake out your hands.

Many parents tell me that they can stop themselves from yelling mean things at their children but they can't stop themselves from yelling something, anything, even if it's just "*Stop!*" or a loud noise like "*Arrrgh!*" That's certainly better than yelling something demeaning, so it's a good step in the right direction. But it still escalates the drama. So use loud noise as a stepping stone away from demeaning words, but don't stop there. Your next step is to change the loud noise into a less threatening response.

Eventually, you'll disconnect the neural connections so that your reaction to your children fighting becomes to breathe out your upset while you move toward your children to calm the situation. We'll look at a detailed example of how to do this, in "When Your Kids are Fighting in the Car."

But first, let's take a peek at what was happening in your brain as you did this exercise.

### How The Brain Rewires

Decades of research have led scientists to the conclusion that the human brain is highly adaptable.[20] When a task is practiced repeatedly, the brain wires itself to better accomplish that task. So all habits rewire our brains. Habits such as meditation, exercise, and feeling gratitude actually change our brains and bodies so that over time we can regulate ourselves better emotionally.[21] (They help our immune, digestive, and other systems work better, too!)

This means that every time we stop ourselves from sliding into a "parent tantrum," we're building the neural pathways that help us calm down, so we can stay centered even when life throws us curve balls.[22] The only catch? These habits have to be "practiced" long enough for them to rewire the brain, and then they have to be reinforced with regular usage to maintain the wiring.

That's a big commitment. But you'll find it's so worth it. As you become more mindful, even in those moments when your blood starts to boil you'll be able to keep your emotions from hijacking you. Daily practice is what helps us choose love in those tough moments.

So here's a quick look at what actually happens in your brain when you get upset. Then we'll look at how you can rewire those automatic responses.

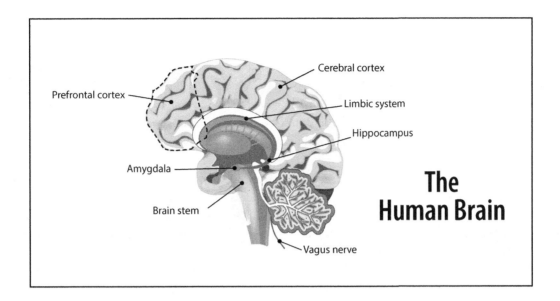

The **brain stem** is the part of your brain that keeps your breathing, digestion, and other automatic bodily functions on track. You might have heard it referred to as the "reptilian brain" or "lizard brain." It works hard to keep you alive.

The **limbic system** consists of the parts of the brain that handle emotions, motivation, behavior and memory. The limbic system connects us to others, makes sure that we learn from past experience and works hard to keep us safe. All mammals have a limbic system.

The part of the limbic system that sounds the alarm when we're in danger is the **amygdala**. When the amygdala sounds the alarm—"*Threat, threat, pay attention!*"—your **sympathetic nervous system** leaps to work, mobilizing you to defend yourself by fighting, running away (flight) or hiding (freeze). Your body is immediately swamped with stress hormones and neurotransmitters, designed to save your life. The amygdala can't evaluate the threat. Its job is simply to sound the alarm at the slightest hint of a problem. So, if you hear a loud noise, you're halfway out of your chair before you consciously think about it.

Your amygdala is always doing its best to keep you safe, but sometimes it overreacts, seeing a threat where there isn't one. So, while it makes sense for your amygdala to signal your prefrontal cortex to double-check whether there's actual danger, it doesn't make sense to hit the nuclear option when your three-year-old is defiant. For that, humor—a specialty of the prefrontal cortex—is probably your best defense.

The **cerebral cortex** is the conscious, or "thinking," part of the brain. It includes the **prefrontal cortex**, which we can think of as the executive function, or command center, of the brain. The prefrontal cortex talks to the rest of the brain to synthesize all inputs, evaluate whether a threat is real, and decide on the best response. For instance, it may decide that the noise you heard was a car backfiring instead of a gunshot, so you can sit back down in your chair.

At this point, your prefrontal cortex signals your **vagus nerve** to calm your body down. The vagus nerve, which originates in the brain stem and travels throughout the body, is the main nerve of the **parasympathetic nervous system** and is responsible for calming the body's fight or flight response and restoring your heartbeat, breathing, and other physiology to optimal function. If your vagal "tone" is strong—meaning your vagus nerve responds quickly—your body will be able to calm itself more easily after being stressed. (Strong vagal tone is also associated with optimal physical health, including reduced inflammation.)

## *Your Rewiring Toolbox*

You've already learned the first tool to rewire your brain, which is activating your Pause Button with Stop, Drop, and Breathe. Along with the other tools and exercises in this book, making Stop, Drop and Breathe a habit will reduce your amygdala's tendency to overreact and strengthen your vagal tone so you can calm down more quickly.[23]

The previous exercise, "Interrupting Your Automatic Reaction," changes your usual programming (for instance, maybe you usually deal with upsets by eating or yelling) to substitute a different choice (for instance, sharing your worry and asking for help). Every time that new response is repeated, the brain rewires to make your new choice more likely in the future.

When we reflect on a past incident that upset us, but from a place of feeling loved and loving, we develop the prefrontal cortex that helps us process and integrate past experience.[24] So I'll be giving you an exercise to disconnect old learning that no longer serves you (for instance, a belief that you aren't good enough) and substitute a new conclusion (you're more than enough, exactly as you are), as well as a journaling practice to develop your prefrontal cortex, in the section called "Healing Trauma" later in Part 1.

Another practice, which you'll begin in Part 2: Connection Is the Secret to Happy Parenting, is cultivating empathy. Not only will that help you connect more deeply with your child (and probably your partner and other people in your life), but cultivating positive emotions also increases the hormones and neurotransmitters in your body that give you a sense of safety and well-being.

Finally, thousands of research studies[25] have shown that meditation, which we can think of as a form of "brain training" can rewire your brain, reducing anxiety and depression and improving the brain's ability to return to calm. Mindfulness-based attention, including body scans and focusing on the breath, also develops the prefrontal cortex.[26] Loving-Kindness meditation develops compassion, changes behavior in relationships, and increases well-being.[27] Just eight weeks of dedicated mindfulness meditation[28] can even measurably shrink the size of the amygdala. So I encourage you to begin even a short regular daily meditation or mindfulness practice. We'll talk more about this in the Mindfulness section later in Part 1.

> Three months from now, you'll notice that you don't get triggered as often in those tough moments and that you calm down faster. You'll probably notice that you're calmer in general and less stressed. Fewer stress hormones in your system means your body will spend less time mobilized by the sympathetic nervous system and more time humming along under the guidance of the parasympathetic nervous system. This means that your immune system will work better. You'll be healthier, and less prone to putting on weight.

What you won't be able to see, because we won't do any MRIs to take pictures of your brain, is that your brain will actually change. The hippocampus, which is associated with self-awareness, insight, and compassion (as well as learning and memory), will become more dense, meaning that you'll actually grow neural connections.[29] As you increase your sense of safety and decrease how often you feel worried, your amygdala will have much less to do, which will help it to shrink in size. Your vagus nerve will become able to return you to calm more quickly. Finally, your prefrontal cortex will increase in activity and size, giving you more mental clarity, insight, and flexibility in your responses.[30]

This means that gifting yourself these new experiences of self-regulation and connection as outlined in this book will change your brain's "go-to" response from perceiving a threat, sounding the alarm, and lashing out to instead noticing that you're getting upset, calming yourself, and choosing a healthier response. All of these shifts will work together to rewire your brain, make you happier, and allow you to show up as the parent you want to be, more often. (And, in Part 3 of this book, we'll use coaching to support your child so that he or she can also grow a happier, healthier brain!)

# SELF-REGULATING IN THE MOMENT

> Between stimulus and response, there is a space. In that space lies our freedom
> and power to choose our response. In our response lies our growth and freedom.
>
> — Victor Frankl [31]

Right about now, you're probably wondering, "*Okay, okay, so what's the magic formula? When I get upset, how can I calm down?*"

The magic formula is using your Pause Button—Stop, Drop and Breathe—and **choosing** to calm down. The bad news is that this is really hard work, and you have to choose to do it each time you get angry. The good news is that it does get easier every time you make that choice, because you're building a brain that can shift out of anger more easily. This enlarges the space between your child's stimulus and your reaction, so that you have the freedom to choose a constructive response.

But this may well be the hardest work you'll ever do, and the hardest part of it is actually being *willing* to switch gears, because when you get triggered, your body goes into a state of emergency. You're flushed with flight or fight hormones and you're ready to fight. Your child looks like the enemy. On some level, you feel that your very survival depends on taking action *right now*! That's why the magic formula is simply to stop—and take a deep breath. That deep breath gives you a chance to not get hijacked.

But you still have to make the conscious choice not to act while you're triggered. It's really hard to make that choice while you're still seething. In fact, the next time you get angry, you will almost certainly find yourself saying, "*But this is an exception. I have to set this kid straight. He needs discipline RIGHT NOW!*" But that moment is not an exception. You only feel that sense of urgency because you're in fight, flight, or freeze mode.

What if it really is an exception? If there's immediate danger, of course you intervene. You won't have to think about it. But most of the time, parenting is not an emergency, even when it feels like it is.

Presuming there's no immediate danger, it doesn't matter how insolent your child has been; it doesn't matter if they're ignoring you when you've asked them three times to do something. Whatever they're doing, if you're going off the deep end, your first responsibility is to calm yourself down, before you interact with your child. That's the only way you can parent responsibly.

Remember our four-step process to shift your emotional state? (For the full details, see page 4.)

1. **Use your Pause Button.** Stop, Drop, and Breathe.

2. **Choose love.** Make the conscious choice not to act while you're triggered.

3. **Change your mind.** Reframe mentally. Use a mantra to talk yourself down and reframe your perceptions, so your mind turns off its alarm system. Choose to see things from the other person's perspective. Remind yourself of all the wonderful things about your child, to put this current "offense" into perspective.

4. **Calm your body.** Use one of the soothing strategies detailed later in this chapter.

## Example: When Your Kids are Fighting in the Car

Let's take an example of how you might do this. Say you're in the car and your children are fighting. You pull the car over to the side of the road. The children are still yelling at each other. In the past, you might have started shouting. Or, like many parents, you might have stormed around to the back of the car and thrown open the doors and started pulling your kids roughly out of their car seats, yelling the whole time.

But this time, you decide you're going to try something different. You pull the car safely to the side of the road. You turn it off and put your blinkers on. Then, you use your Pause Button, before you even open your mouth to your kids. Your job is to stop yourself from getting triggered so you can intervene effectively. You will feel an urgent need to set the kids straight, but that's "fight or flight" talking. Always calm yourself first.

Start with your **Pause Button: Stop, Drop** (your agenda, which at this moment is to stop your kids from fighting so you can drive again), and **take a deep breath** in through your nose. Let it out through your mouth. (Breathing in through the nose affects the brain's electrical signals to help you calm down and think more clearly.[32]) Then take three more slow, deep breaths in a row, in through your nose, out through your mouth.

Now that you've interrupted that cascade of stress hormones, **choose love.** At this moment, in the car, you choose to calm the storm rather than let your inner alarm turn you into a crazy person.

You've made the decision to calm yourself. But how can you actually do that? Your body, remember, is primed for an emergency here. It's ready to run away or fight an attacker. You won't be able to think well until you stop all those stress hormones from being released into your blood stream. So your next steps are to **change your mind** and **calm your body**.

Let's reframe your perceptions so your mind stops triggering that flood of adrenaline. Notice the thoughts you might be having at this moment. Notice how those thoughts make it harder for you to return yourself to calm. For instance:

| Your Perception of the Situation | How It Makes You Feel |
|---|---|
| These kids always make my life harder. | Resentful |
| This child always picks on his sister. | Ready to clobber him |
| They should know better than to fight while I'm driving. | Ready to clobber both of them |
| I can't deal with this! | Powerless, helpless |

To reframe, remind yourself of something that is just as true as your original perception, and calms your anger.

| Your Perception of the Situation | Reframed View | How It Makes You Feel |
|---|---|---|
| These kids always make my life harder. | These kids are having a hard time. They need my help. | Empathic |
| This child always picks on his sister. | He must be really unhappy. | Compassionate |
| They should know better than to fight while I'm driving. | Kids don't have the brain development to postpone a fight when they're agitated. | Ready to help them solve their problem |
| I can't deal with this! | I can handle this. | Powerful, competent |

Notice how reframing shifts you from wanting to clobber your kids to wanting to help.

## Practice: **Reframing**

Consider the last time you were furious with your child. What were your perceptions of the situation? How did those perceptions make you feel?

| Your Perception of the Situation | How It Made You Feel |
| --- | --- |
|  |  |
|  |  |
|  |  |
|  |  |

How could you reframe your perceptions of that incident to remind yourself of something that is just as true and that would have calmed your anger?

| Your Perception of the Situation | Reframed View | How It Makes You Feel |
| --- | --- | --- |
|  |  |  |
|  |  |  |
|  |  |  |
|  |  |  |

How could you remind yourself to reframe the situation in this way the next time you get angry?

_____

_____

_____

## Practice: **Using a Mantra**

> I cannot emphasize how much Stop, Drop, and Breathe and the phrase 'It's not an emergency' work for me. They snap me right out of autopilot almost every time. The other day my one-year-old was throwing toys all over while I was trying to get everyone outside. I could feel myself getting red and hot. Suddenly I stopped, took a breath and said out loud, 'It's not an emergency.' My four-year-old piped up (they hear everything!), 'Yeah, Mom, it's not an emergency, we are all safe.' I realized that we didn't have to rush and distracted the baby into playing with shoes, and we got going five minutes later than normal but without the screaming, which probably would have delayed us even more anyway!
>
> — Coralee, mother of a four-year-old and a one-year-old

One fast way to reframe when you're upset is to use a mantra, which is simply an antidote to thoughts that don't serve us. Mantras help us talk ourselves off the cliff when we're upset. You can use words or mental pictures that speak directly to the subconscious.

Say your mantras aloud and your children will pick up on them and begin using them. My 22-year-old daughter will still turn to me if I'm anxious because we're going to be late and say to me, *"Mom, it's not an emergency."* I love that, because I said it to her throughout her childhood, and she uses it herself now. (She's now calmer than I am, although as a baby she was hard to calm, and as a three-year-old she inspired comments from bystanders such as *"I pity you when she's a teenager!"*)

When you're upset, what would it help you to hear? What would be calming for you? Some examples are below. Add to the list. Then pick a few to try out. Write them down on sticky notes and put them where you'll see them—on your dashboard, your mirror, or your refrigerator.

- It's not an emergency.
- Choose love!
- Don't take it personally.
- They're acting like kids because they are kids.
- I am more than enough.
- She's not giving me a hard time; she's having a hard time.
- I'm a good parent.
- This too shall pass.
- Only love today.
- Sooner or later, they all sleep through the night.
- My kids need my love, especially when they're at their worst.
- I won't even remember this by next week.
- I breathe in love. I breathe out love.
- What would Jesus (or Buddha, or Mohammed) do?

Add your own:

1 _____

2 _____

3 _____

4 _____

5 _____

## Practice: **The Antidote of Appreciation**

When you're furious at your child, you're taking one aspect of their behavior and blowing it out of proportion. At the moment, it seems like the most important part of who they are. But, in truth, your child is a complicated human being with many wonderful traits, just as you are. You wouldn't want to be judged solely on your worst behavior, would you? That's why it's a useful antidote, when you're angry at your child, to revisit all the things you love about him. As you go down that list, you start to see his current "offense" in perspective. Then, when you talk with him about it, you're able to be much more reasonable instead of going on the attack. And he's likely to be able to take in what you're saying without going on the defensive.

Take a minute now and list below 10 things you love about your child. Post this list. Next time you're angry, read it—and really take it in—before you talk to your child.

**(1)** _____

**(2)** _____

**(3)** _____

**(4)** _____

**(5)** _____

**(6)** _____

**(7)** _____

**(8)** _____

**(9)** _____

**(10)** _____

## Practice: Soothe Your Subconscious

Another way to calm yourself quickly is to show your mind a soothing image. That's because the subconscious mind thinks in pictures. If it thinks there's an emergency and you show it an image of you and your child playing at the beach, it will feel safe and happy, and settle right down.

What mental picture could you show yourself to calm down when you're upset? For instance, when you imagine yourself beaming lovingly at your child when she was an infant, does that serve as an antidote to feelings of anger? What about an image of yourself at a peak moment? Below, describe the calming mental picture in detail, so you can summon it in those tough moments.

_____

_____

_____

_____

When you practice reframing often, you'll find that it just takes moments, even when you're stressed. So within less than a minute, you've taken a few deep breaths (Step 1), decided to shift to love (Step 2), and changed your mind (Step 3). Now, if your body is still tense and ready to fight, help it release the anger by bringing yourself back into your body (Step 4), using one of the following practices. (For a reminder of the four steps, see page 23.)

## Practice: **Help Your Body Release the Anger**

When your body is in fight, flight, or freeze mode, you're being ruled by your sympathetic nervous system, which is mobilized for action. To calm yourself, you want to shift back to your parasympathetic nervous system. Here are four easy techniques to help you make this shift physically. See which one works best for you. You'll find that the more you practice these techniques, the faster your body will calm.

- Shake your hands out while you take deep breaths and blow your breath out of your mouth, imagining that you're letting go of all fear and anger from your body.
- Hug yourself firmly by wrapping your arms around yourself, so one hand is reaching toward the opposite side of your rib cage and the other is reaching toward the opposite shoulder.
- Put one hand on your belly and one on your heart and breathe slowly, as if the air is going in and out through your hands.
- Release the feelings and shift your emotional state by tapping on the acupuncture point on the edge of your hand (the karate chop point) while you breathe deeply. Say to yourself while tapping, "*Even though I feel upset, I'm safe. I can calm myself and handle this situation.*" If you find yourself yawning, that's your body releasing stress and shifting gears.

There are many more techniques to shift your body out of anger, such as putting on music and dancing, or running your hands under cool or warm water, and we'll get to those ideas soon. But, now that you know some quick strategies to calm your mind and body, let's go back to our example of when your children are fighting in the car. You're saying your mantra, so you've reframed the way you're looking at the situation, and you've done something physical to release the stress. You may not be exactly peaceful, but you're a whole lot calmer than you were as you pulled your car off the road.

**Now you can finally turn around to talk to your children.** If you're worried that it will take you a long time to calm down and you'll be sitting on the side of the road for 15 minutes before you're able to speak to your children calmly, I understand. But the more you practice calming yourself using these strategies in any situation, the faster you'll be able to do it in a tough moment, such as in your car. So start practicing in less stressful moments and you'll be a pro before you know it.

And, remember that the exercises in this book are designed to strengthen your vagal tone and prefrontal cortex,[33] so as you work your way through this book you'll find that you're able to calm down more easily when you're upset.

But right at this moment, in the car, your children have probably stopped yelling at each other. Now they're looking at you apprehensively because they think you're about to yell at them. But you're calm enough now that you can assert your needs without attacking your children, which actually reinforces your authority as the leader. You can even partner with your children to problem-solve.

So you say, "*I need to drive safely so that we can all get where we're going safely. That's my job. What's everybody else's job?*" They'll probably look at you blankly. You point out that they have a job, too. "*Everybody's job is to make sure that it's a safe and fun trip for the family.*" Then you ask each child what they're going to do to contribute to the safety and the fun factor of the trip.

Your kids have probably forgotten what they were fighting about by now, but, if they haven't, now is when you coach them to solve their problem with each other. We'll talk more about how to do that in Part 3. As always, if you don't help them solve their problem, they won't be able to move past that to cooperate with you. But notice that you're able to coach effectively now because you're calm, and that helps your children calm down too. Your emotional regulation makes your children feel safer, so they start to respond more reasonably to you and to each other.

> You can't transform a situation of upset by acting your own upset out onto your children. First you have to transform your inner state.

**Look at what you've been able to do, just by taking a moment to calm yourself.** You turned the entire situation around, and now your kids are partnering with you to take a role in having a safe and fun trip.

This even sets a precedent for the future, so when you get into the car next time, you'll be able to say to your children, "*Okay, what are our jobs? How are we all going to work together to have a safe and fun family trip?*" This is true whether you're going on a real trip—a road trip for three days—or whether you're going to be in the car for five minutes running an errand.

By contrast, think about what would've happened if you had turned around and started screaming at your children. Yes, they might have been quiet for a minute, but then they would have been in an even worse mood. As soon as you drove one block, they would've been at each other again, taking all those bad feelings out on each other.

## How Your Thoughts Create Your Anger

Consider the last time you got angry at your child. What led up to it? Too little sleep? Too much pressure? Rushing? Worrying? The repetition of a situation that had been annoying you, over and over?

Most likely, your upset built from a series of smaller annoyances that sent you into a downward spiral. Somewhere in there were some negative thoughts: "*We'll never get there on time... I knew this wouldn't work out... Oh, no, don't start being difficult right now!... He always does this—I'm so fed up!... I wish they would do what I say without fighting about it, just this once... What part of "no" don't they understand?... I didn't sign on for this...!*"

What if you monitored your thoughts and noticed the start of the downhill slide? Could you catch that first negative thought and reframe it?

# Practice: **Your "Thoughts to Emotions" Chain Reaction**

On the next page, list the situations or behavior that make you most angry with your child.

1. For each situation, write down the anxiety-producing thoughts that spark your anger.

2. Notice that your thoughts aren't even necessarily true and don't merit a state of emergency.

3. For each situation, write what you could say to yourself instead that helps you see your child's perspective and empowers you.

## Example

| I get angry at my child when: | Because my mind tells me these catastrophic thoughts: | I could reframe to think these more constructive thoughts instead: |
|---|---|---|
| He refuses to try to use the toilet before we leave the house and then has an accident. | Everyone is staring. He's just being willful. He'll never be toilet-trained! I'm a failure as a parent. | He's still very little. He wants to be in charge of his own body. Every child learns sooner or later to use the toilet. I'm doing the best I can. No one else cares, and anyway my responsibility is to my son, not anyone who's staring. |

## *Your Turn*

**1** I get angry at my child when:

_____

_____

_____

Because my mind tells me these catastrophic thoughts:

_____

_____

_____

I could reframe to think these more constructive thoughts instead:

_____

_____

_____

**2** I get angry at my child when:

_____

_____

_____

Because my mind tells me these catastrophic thoughts:

_____

_____

_____

I could reframe to think these more constructive thoughts instead:

_____

_____

_____

**3** I get angry at my child when:

_____

_____

_____

Because my mind tells me these catastrophic thoughts:

_____

_____

_____

I could reframe to think these more constructive thoughts instead:

_____

_____

_____

## Example: Self-Regulating When One Child Hurts the Other

> The only thing that really makes me lose it is when my four-year-old repeatedly is physically violent to his two-year-old sister. I try to do what you say, and say, 'Quick, Sammy, can you get her an ice pack?' and turn him into a helper. He's good at it. But it makes me mad if they're fighting and I say 'I'm coming to help' and then he throws her to the ground and busts her head.
>
> — Wendy, mother of four-year-old and two-year-old

Infuriating, right? Most parents say that when one child hurts another, it's the hardest time for them to self-regulate. In this case, it's even worse, because Mom tried so hard to intervene, and her son still hurt his sister. Even though he knew Mom was coming, he couldn't trust that she'd be there soon enough, and he couldn't control his impulses. He is, after all, only four. It's hard for a four-year-old to resist power, especially when he's sure he's right and his sister is wrong. (Part of being four is being sure you're right. He's not likely to see his sister's side of things yet.) Of course, the two-year-old deserves protection, and we'll talk more about limit setting in Part 3 of this book. (And, if you turned right to this example because you *need* the answer, I think you'll find my book *Peaceful Parent, Happy Siblings* very helpful in doing the prevention work that avoids your child acting this way toward a sibling.[34])

But the question this mom is asking is, how do you self-regulate when your child is hurt?

The answer is, you don't. When your child is hurt, you become a raging lunatic and you will do anything to protect them and destroy anyone who threatens them.

But, of course, that's not a practical answer when the perp is also your child. It's not even a practical answer when the perp is the next-door neighbor's kid and you want to smash him to bits, but he's a child too. And that is actually the clue to how to handle this in the moment, when you're so dysregulated you can't see straight. If the neighbor's child threw your daughter to the ground so she hit her head, you wouldn't waste time screaming at him. You would fly to your child and help her. You would ignore the aggressor. Once you were calm, you would figure out how to protect your child from another incident.

This highlights our problem. With siblings, it's pretty hard to protect your child from another incident. You can't build a fence to keep your own child out of your yard. This increases your frustration that you can't keep such incidents from happening, when you've tried so hard. So the truth is, the reason you "lose it" is that you feel powerless and the rage makes you feel better. I hasten to add that you aren't wrong. Any parent would feel this way. But what are your choices? You could spank your child, but research shows that would make him more aggressive, which is just what you're trying to stop.[35] You could shame and punish him, but research (and common sense) tells us that would increase the sibling rivalry and worsen the relationship.[36] The *only* thing that will stop such incidents from happening is prevention, which includes helping your son with his jealousy and with his panic when you're on the way to help but he isn't sure you'll get there in time.

So we're back to that moment when you're furious that this scenario keeps happening and you simply *have* to express your authentic upset to your child. But what's really authentic here? It isn't your rage at your son. That's a defense against something even more primal—your anguish that you haven't been able to protect one of your children, which is your most foundational responsibility as a parent. You *need* to keep your children safe. Your need is driving your rage.

For your child to *want* to help, he has to hear your words as an expression of your need, rather than an attack on him: "*I need all of my children to be safe. I get so upset and angry when one of my children is hurt. I get even more upset and angry when one of my children hurts the other!*"

**Notice that you're clearly expressing anger.** Your child has no doubt that you're angry. But, even though your voice was passionate, you didn't blame your child. If you tell him you're furious at him for hurting his sister, he's confirmed in his fear that you don't love him—because of her! He'll be on the defensive and won't be able to change. If instead you can convey your fierce need to keep all your children from hurting each other—which is in fact what this is about—your child will be much more likely to respond by wanting to meet your need.

Does this sound too simple? He'll obviously need to feel connected to you to *want* to work with you on this, so the practice sections in Part 2: Connection Is the Secret to Happy Parenting will be essential. And he'll need to feel understood, so the emotion coaching practices in Part 3: Coaching Instead of Controlling will also be essential. Finally, he may well need to cry, to work through all of those painful feelings that are driving him to hurt his sister. And, if he only seems to hurt her when she touches his things, you may need to come up with a temporary solution to keep her away from them. You wouldn't expect a four-year-old to cross the street by himself, because he doesn't yet have the impulse control to keep himself safe. Similarly, he doesn't yet have the impulse control to manage himself when a competitor destroys something he has worked really hard to create (which is how he experiences it when his sister wrecks his castle).

## Example: When You Can't Stay Calm, Take Preventive Action

> How do I stop my rising frustration when my kids are screaming at each other or throwing things and I'm cooking dinner at the stove? How can I coach and guide them while also having to do something? I feel my anger building up when I can't do anything but referee all day and I can't get them to separate or listen.
>
> — Jen, mother of two boys

This is a great example of a time when you can't really expect to self-regulate. You've been refereeing all day, so you're worn out. Let's say you're still in the early stages of this kind of parenting, so you still have to be there to intervene, coach, model, and prevent the breakdowns and fights on the days that are rough. (As you do this kind of parenting over time, it gets easier, because your children learn how to navigate conflict constructively without your help. But let's assume you aren't there yet.) So, if you know a tough situation is coming that will make it very hard for you to stay calm (for example, you need to make dinner) so you can't be present with your children to help them work things out, it's your job to head it off at the pass. Sometimes preventive maintenance works, but in this case, you need to separate your children—calmly, kindly, but definitively, while you're still in a good mood.

Most parents don't do that, because they think they shouldn't have to, that their kids should be able to get along. I wish! That's a lot to expect of immature humans who have every reason to be unhappy with each other on a regular basis. So, if you're having the kind of day when your anger has been building because you have to constantly referee, take responsibility as the grown-up to move everyone away from the edge before you lose it. Give your kids choices, but be sure they're in separate places. Then, spend a little time connecting with each one before you start cooking. Finally, make sure that your dinner prep is very short. Your children need you in a good mood a lot more than they need a hot dinner.

> How do I Stop, Drop, and Breathe when I'm out in public with my kids and I can't reign them in? My anxiety builds and I find myself taking a breath, but not able to resolve the situation without threats.
>
> — Nick, father of two

## Example: Parenting in Public

Responding to off-track behavior in public is one of the most challenging situations for parents, because we assume that other people are watching and judging. Our own shame kicks in and our anxiety builds so we can't think clearly. Before we know it, we're hissing threats.

There are usually warning signs before our children fall apart in public. Most of us respond to those warning signs by trying to move faster. We say, *"We're almost done shopping—be patient for a few more minutes."* But a young child who's on the edge of falling apart isn't developmentally able to get back in balance without substantial parental help.

So, instead of speeding up, start by slowing down and taking a deep breath. Then, take a minute to reconnect with her—hug, make eye contact, sing to her softly, or gently twirl her around. Find ways to honor or redirect your child's impulses. *"You want to run! Let's go back outside the store for a few minutes to run, since you've been sitting in the car. Then, when we come back in the store, let's walk THIS way!"* Exaggerate your silly, slow walk, to get your child laughing. Laughter dissolves tension and creates more positivity. This approach of calming yourself and connecting might be enough to shift your child's mood and give you time to complete your errand—with both of you in a good mood.

But what if it isn't? When your child misbehaves in public, you're already in the breakdown lane, so your options are limited. Promise yourself to do more preventive maintenance starting tomorrow. And remember that, no matter how wonderful a parent you are, you will end up in the breakdown lane sometimes. That's just life with kids.

Anyone who sees you follow these steps will admire you—they'll think you're heroic and that your child is the luckiest kid in the world. Unless, of course, they think children should be controlled and their feelings punished, and in that case why would you even care what they think of your parenting?

Here's your roadmap:

1. **Use your Pause Button: Stop, Drop and Breathe.**
   - Stop. Literally stop walking or talking.
   - Drop your agenda. That includes having to get somewhere on time or even "make" your child behave.
   - Breathe in deeply and blow the breath out, at least three times.

2. **Soothe your anxiety.**
   - Remind yourself that the people around you are not your responsibility. Your only responsibility is to your child and your own integrity as a parent.
   - Use a mantra: *"They're hungry, angry, lonely, tired. I need to HALT and tend to them"* or *"They're having a problem, not trying to give me a problem."*

- Remind yourself that you can handle this. (Fear and anxiety are just the worry that we can't handle something.)
- Keep breathing and shake out your hands.

3. **Connect physically.** (We'll talk more about connecting in Part 2 of this book.)
   - Turn to your child and touch them gently.
   - Make eye contact.
   - Keep your voice warm and calm.

4. **Connect verbally** by describing the situation as non-judgmentally as possible *from your child's perspective.* In other words, connect with your child by describing what the child wants or hopes for:
   - *"Sounds like you really wanted to stop for ice cream today."*
   - *"It looks like you think that plane is really cool and you wish we could buy it."*
   - *"You're having a hard time with your brother today and you just wish he would leave you alone."*

5. **Check that your child feels understood and get agreement.**
   - *"I bet you know just what flavor you would get, right?"*
   - *"Is that right?"*
   - *"Sometimes you just need a little peace and quiet, right?"*

6. **Redirect, offer help, or set whatever limits are necessary,** now that your child feels reconnected to you and is open to your influence. (We'll talk more about setting limits in Part 3, but notice that these limits are set with an understanding of the child's perspective.)
   - *"Mint chocolate chip, huh? That sounds delicious. Next time when we get ice cream, I can't wait to watch you enjoy it. AND, no ice cream today, Zack. We've having birthday cake at the party this evening, and that's enough treats for one day. We'll have to look forward to mint chocolate chip next week."*
   - *"That plane is really cool. I know you love airplanes. I hear how much you wish you could have it, even though you know that today we're only buying a toy for your cousin's birthday. Let's put it on your wish list. If you still want it when your birthday comes, maybe you'll get lucky."*
   - *"You can get what you need without attacking your brother. You can tell your brother, 'Please give me a little time to myself. I don't feel like talking right now.' And you can ask me if I can help. Which I can! Because I was just about to ask your brother what he wants for dinner."*

7. **Regroup.** In books like this one, the child usually says something like, *"Okay Daddy, thank you Daddy!"* And sometimes that actually happens in real life, because you've stayed calm and your child feels understood. But what if, despite your best efforts, your child erupts? Sometimes, that's unavoidable with immature humans. If you erupt too, it will just make everything worse. When children get dysregulated, they need your help to re-regulate. (Promise yourself that you'll do more preventive maintenance starting tomorrow, so your child can handle disappointments with a bit more grace.) But for now, you can only control you. So remind yourself that the people watching don't matter and might even be cheering your ability to stay calm and loving. Then start over. Go back to your self-regulation toolkit, breathing deeply and consciously

calming your voice. Connect with your child to try to create safety: "*That isn't what you wanted me to say, is it? You were really hoping...*"

8. **Come up with something to say to any onlookers who comment.** Mostly, you can ignore other people as you respond to your child. But occasionally, a store clerk or some other well-meaning person will try to intervene to distract your child. So it's best to prepare yourself with a standard answer that reassures the person that, despite your child's wailing, it's not an emergency and you don't need them to fix your child or anything else. Something like, "*She'll be okay... We just need a little time alone.*"

9. **Move your child to a more private place.** If your child has a meltdown, it's impossible to attend to her and also finish your shopping. Just scoop her up and remove her from the situation. Maybe you can go to your car or to an out-of-the-way spot at the mall where you won't be disturbing other people—and where you won't be tempted to parent as onlookers think you should, so you can follow your own parenting instincts. It would be natural to be angry at your child for making a scene. But she's not trying to make a scene. She's just overwhelmed by her emotions and she needs your help to re-regulate. So continue to calm yourself and see things from her perspective, so you can empathize with how upset she is: "*You want to run around the aisles, but I need you to stay in the cart. It's hard to stay in the cart, but I need you to do it so you're safe.*" Feeling understood usually calms kids. When she's done crying, hold her and comfort her. Decide whether the two of you are up for another try and, if so, how this could work for both of you. "*Maybe for the last bit of shopping, you can walk next to me and help me find things, and then sit in the cart again at the checkout.*"

10. **Keep calming yourself.** Focusing on your "audience" will just make you more anxious and undermine your ability to help your child. Until you help her with whatever problem is causing her to scream, she will probably keep screaming, so it's better to ignore everything but staying calm and connecting with your child. Children can be expected to exhibit childish behavior. There's no shame in your child's needs clashing with the household's need to get food for the family. The only possible embarrassment here is in responding to that clash by becoming a parent you don't want to be. So, when you feel that happening, stop, take a deep breath, and shift gears. Use a mantra, such as "*This isn't an emergency... She's acting like a child because she is a child... She just needs a good cry.*" And remind yourself that you'll never see those strangers in the grocery store again. Smile ruefully in their general direction and say, "*Sometimes we all have bad days.*" Nobody can disagree with that.

Does that sound hard? It is. And of course the hardest part is staying calm yourself. That's why it's so important to practice breathing and other self-calming techniques when you aren't upset—you're developing tools for when you really need them. It's also an argument for working on any pockets of shame you notice in your own psyche. They don't help you be your best self, and they keep you from being the parent you want to be, especially when people are watching.

## Practice: Using Your Pause Button

As you begin using your Pause Button, keep a record to hone your approach. What can you learn?

( 1 ) I used my Pause Button when:

_____

_____

_____

What helped me be successful? What got in my way?

_____

_____

_____

What I learned for next time:

_____

_____

_____

( 2 ) I used my Pause Button when:

_____

_____

_____

What helped me be successful? What got in my way?

_____

_____

_____

What I learned for next time:

_____

_____

_____

( 3 ) I used my Pause Button when:

_____

_____

_____

What helped me be successful? What got in my way?

_____

_____

_____

What I learned for next time:

_____

_____

_____

**(4)** I used my Pause Button when:

_____

_____

_____

What helped me be successful? What got in my way?

_____

_____

_____

What I learned for next time:

_____

_____

_____

## Tips To Help You See The Bigger Picture When You're Angry

> My advice? Don't give up. It took at least a dozen times of me trying to stay peaceful before I saw any change in my strong-willed daughter. But now I can see a remarkable change in how she listens more often and responds more positively.
>
> — Brigitte, mother of a four-year-old

To help you motivate yourself to switch off the blood-wrath in those tough moments, here are a few reminders to help you enlarge your perspective.

**See it from your child's point of view.** Remind yourself that your child is having a hard day too. Maybe he's feeling disconnected from you, which makes kids feel unsafe so they act out. (Connection gets frayed during daily life and has to be constantly renewed.) Maybe he's actually afraid—of the mean kid at school, or the monsters in his closet, or losing your love to his sibling, or never being good enough to stop you from yelling at him. And, even if you can't understand what's driving this particular behavior, take a few minutes to remind yourself of all the wonderful things about your child, to put this issue in context.

**Ask yourself what's under your anger.** I know, you want to smack your child, and at this moment you're clear that they deserve it. But why? Did they make you feel disrespected, for instance? Then the button that just got pushed is probably from feeling disrespected in your own childhood. Guess what? This is an opportunity to heal that! Even if your child actually *did* disrespect you, you have all the respect you need inside yourself. Find that self-respect inside and give it to yourself. I'm not suggesting you let yourself get walked on. I'm suggesting you take responsibility for your own self-respect and emotional regulation.

**Take care of yourself.** Whatever deep need is triggering your anger, hug yourself and meet that need. Do you need a good cry? Do you need to give yourself permission not to get it all done? Do you need to cut back your expectations and try again tomorrow? Now that you're a grown-up, it's your responsibility to give yourself what you need. So just do it. Otherwise, you can't be the emotionally generous parent you want to be, and everyone loses.

**If you still need to, express the anger safely.** Shake out your hands, splash water on your face, or put on music and dance.

This is basic emotional self-regulation, and it's arguably the most critical emotional intelligence skill. Most of us don't come by it naturally. But, as you know from the section on Emotional Triggers, every time you resist acting when you're triggered, you're rewiring your brain. Just keep practicing, finding that moment of freedom between the stimulus (your child's behavior) and your own response. Noticing is what gives us a choice next time.

## Practice: **Self-Soothing Strategies**

A self-soothing strategy is any technique that works to help you calm down. Remember, when you're in fight, flight, or freeze mode, it means you think the situation is dangerous. You aren't really able to see the full truth of what is happening in the moment, and you aren't thinking well.

Soothing strategies reassure your subconscious that there is no danger and help you shift into more conscious awareness in the moment. Some examples of soothing strategies are deep breathing, running your wrists under cool or warm water, or playing a song that always soothes you. Sometimes the best soothing strategy is to call someone we trust to just listen to us, so we feel understood and less alone.

Make a list of soothing strategies that work for you.

(1) _____

(2) _____

(3) _____

(4) _____

(5) _____

## Practice: **Your Peaceful Place**

Everyone needs a peaceful place inside, where they can go when they're upset and need to calm down and nurture themselves. Your imagination is powerful. When you cultivate an image that inspires feelings of peace, safety, and love inside you, that place will always be waiting for you.

Close your eyes and take several deep breaths. As you breathe out, feel your body relaxing.

Now, ask your subconscious to show you a picture of a place that helps you feel serene and safe. Linger with this image, allowing the peaceful, happy feelings to fill your heart.

What do you see? What do you hear? What do you smell? What other details do you notice? Write a detailed description of your peaceful place on the next page.

_____

_____

_____

_____

_____

The more you practice imagining your peaceful place and enjoy the way it makes you feel, the more easily you'll be able pull up that image and those calming emotions, even when you're upset. Start training your subconscious today, by revisiting your peaceful place before you fall asleep tonight. To remind you, make a sticky note reminder and put it on your pillow. Keep the note and use it every night for a week, until it becomes a regular nightly habit to cultivate your peaceful place and the serenity it inspires.

## Practice: Using the RAIN Process to Work with Anger

There's a common practice taught by meditation teachers about how to sit mindfully with a difficult experience. This process, often referred to as RAIN, can be used any time you're upset, and is also useful after the fact to explore why you got so upset at the time.

The four steps of this practice are:

**R**ecognize what is happening.

**A**llow life to be just as it is.

**I**nvestigate inner experience with kindness.

**N**on-identification.

For this example, let's apply the RAIN process to the emotion of anger. Our four steps become:

**R**ecognize that you're feeling angry.

**A**ccept that you're feeling angry, and accept the circumstances that you're reacting to, instead of struggling against them.

**I**nvestigate the experience of anger with kindness.

**N**on-identifying with the anger. Just observe.

The first step is to **recognize** what you're feeling. "*Oh. I'm feeling anger. I'm livid at my kid.*" Sometimes parents are ashamed when they feel anger at their child. But there is no shame in being angry. You didn't create that anger. That anger is there like your arm or your leg. What matters is what you do with your anger, and *that* you do have control over—although it may not always feel like it—just like you have control over what you do with your arm or your leg.

We're not trying to get rid of emotions. We're trying to have a different relationship with them, so we're aware of the emotion when we start feeling it rather than after we've already reacted and done things that we regret.

The second step is **acceptance**. It's hard not to blame ourselves on some level when we're feeling enraged at our child. We know she's just a kid. We know that she wouldn't have hit her brother if we had been right there to help when they started fighting over the toy. So we often blame ourselves a bit. But then that makes us feel more angry, and, because we're defensive, we feel even more angry at our child.

It's okay to feel whatever you're feeling. You didn't ask for this feeling and you didn't create the feeling, so really, the only thing you can do is accept the feeling. When we push feelings away, when we refuse to accept them, guess where they go? Into the subconscious, otherwise known as the emotional backpack, where we lug them around until they burst out. Awareness is what lets you process feelings as they arise, so they never have to go into the backpack.

Step three is to **investigate** the feeling. That's probably a new idea, because usually we run away from angry feelings. In this case, instead of running away from the feeling, we sit with it. We recognize that we're feeling it, we accept that we're feeling it, and we even get to known it a bit.

Investigating doesn't mean analyzing, but observing. Notice that we're not asking *why* we're angry, which would focus us on justifying the anger and revisiting what our child did that upset us—that's the story line. And we're not blaming ourselves for feeling angry—we've already accepted it. This protects us from getting trapped in that vicious cycle of feeling bad about ourselves and then taking it out into the world through negative emotions.

We're simply *noticing what it feels like to feel angry*. Where do you feel it in your body? What is the sensation? Does it feel like an explosion pressing on the inside of your chest? Does it feel like your throat is tight and strangled? Maybe you can't catch your breath or your hands are balled into fists.

As you notice those physical sensations, just breathe. Just stay with the feeling in your body. Just observe. What you'll notice is that it changes. Suddenly, you may be crying, and you realize that what was under the anger was actually sadness. Or that tight feeling in your throat gets tighter and that feeling that you can't breathe gets worse. Suddenly, you notice you're feeling panicky, and you realize that what was behind the anger was fear, or helplessness.

> As you sit with any emotion, the message is received and the feelings transform, and you're able to clear your emotions at a deeper level.

All of our anger has other, more vulnerable feelings behind it, so, as you sit with the anger, you'll notice other emotions come up. As you do this, you're excavating the trigger behind the anger. As you sit, you'll notice that the anger begins to lessen. It was so strong a moment ago, and now you're not even feeling angry. You may still feel sad or scared, but the anger has melted away. It was only there to fend off the tears and fears. You don't need it anymore.

Then you'll notice that even the sadness and the fear begin to melt away, and you realize that all of these emotions are always arising and passing away. They come and they go, and you aren't in charge of them. You actually can't control them. Sometimes you can change your thoughts, and that will certainly change the feelings that come up—meaning, if you think your kid is a brat, you'll be more angry at him than if you think, "*This child is hurting; he needs my help.*" But we can't fully control our thoughts, and we don't choose our feelings. Some of them are positive and some of them don't serve us. Luckily, they arise and then they pass away. That's not who we are. They're just thoughts and emotions arising and passing away. Your yelling at your child or your being angry are not who you are. They are a small part of who you are being right now, and over time you can learn to not even act on that anger, even though the anger will probably always arise.

This leads us to the fourth step of the RAIN process, which is **not identifying** with the feelings. If these feelings are always arising and passing away, they don't have to define you. You don't have to let the fact that you got angry at your child define who you are. It was a temporary state of what I would call "forgetting," where you got hijacked by emotion. You forgot how much you love your child. You forgot your intention to show up in the world with love.

Not identifying with the emotions means we don't have to act when we get triggered. We can just observe and reframe: "*Oh, there's that anger again. I know what to do with this. Stop, drop, breathe, notice, accept, resist acting.*"

You can see how useful the RAIN process is for any emotion. We simply accept what we're feeling, without judging ourselves. We investigate it, not by analyzing but by observing. We really take in the experience of that emotion, the sensation of it in our body, and then it begins to shift, to change, to diminish, and to evaporate, because we've gotten the message. Every time you do this process, you're reducing the power of that trigger. You're peeling more layers off the onion.

## How To Stop Yelling At Your Child

> My daughter has responded so much better to my calmer parenting.
> I find she has fewer tantrums.
>
> — Andrea, mother of three-year-old

Now that you've learned the basics of self-regulation, let's explore some additional tools for those times when you're stressed and just want to scream.

Most parents yell at their children, at least occasionally. Some of us were brought up in homes where the yelling was constant, so it's just automatic for us. Some of us go through periods of yelling when we're especially stressed. And some of us have children who are particularly challenging, so that almost any adult would find themselves yelling in response to the child's daily behavior.

When parents are asked about their yelling, they usually express regret. But they also say that the child provoked the yelling with their behavior. If the child would behave, the parent wouldn't need to raise their voice. But is that really true? We all know that when we're in a good mood, we don't yell, even when our child misbehaves. Besides, all children will exhibit childish behavior. That's part of normal human development, as they learn limits and self-control. No one ever deserves to be yelled at.

Some parents are surprised when they hear me say that. But really, treating other humans with respect and kindness means we don't scream at them, no matter what. Does it help you to be screamed at, ever?

When we lose control, our children lose respect for us. They lose affection for us. Children will always love their parents—even when parents are abusive to their children, children love their parents, but that doesn't mean they respect or trust them. And children don't cooperate with a parent unless they think the parent is emotionally trustworthy.

If you're a yeller, you probably do it out of habit. You might even think, *"This is necessary; it's the only way my child listens."* But when you control with fear, your child only obeys because they're frightened for that moment. How long will that last, before your child starts yelling back or pretending they don't care?

Yelling teaches kids to yell. It does *not* teach them whatever lesson you're trying to teach at that moment, though, because when you're yelling, you're in fight, flight, or freeze mode and your child also goes into a state of emergency. When children are scared, the learning centers of the brain shut down, so they're not taking in information.

Finally, is yelling the best thing for your child's development long term? Does yelling raise children who can regulate their own emotions? Of course, we all know that it doesn't. In fact, parental yelling shapes children's brains to have overactive amygdalae (to guard them from danger) and less ability to calm themselves when they get upset. So when we make a habit of yelling, we sabotage our child's brain development.

> I love the vow of Yellibacy! I've learned that if I can control how I handle a difficult situation, it will nine times out of ten not escalate. Yelling always escalates it. Very liberating!
>
> — Teri, mother of a four-year-old daughter and an eight-year-old son

> 66
>
> Before the vow of yellibacy, I would just find myself shouting. But then after I began stopping myself in the middle of a rant, I began to see it coming—I would start to notice that I was getting more and more irritated, and often now I can just stop myself before I even start shouting.
>
> — Steve, father of two

So, if you're a yeller, I have a personal challenge for you. Take a vow of "yellibacy." Use my plan for 12 weeks to train yourself to stop yelling. Every time you find yourself yelling, just shut your mouth. Bite your tongue. Stop, Drop, and Breathe. Yes, I know that sounds too simple to work. But I've seen thousands of parents use this technique to stop yelling and you can do it, too—no matter how ingrained the habit is.

In the beginning, when you stop yelling mid-sentence, you may feel like a fool. But in fact you look like somebody who decided to control themselves—who turned away and stopped yelling, right in the middle of a yell. You're modeling anger management!

If you do that today, one time—even if you yell three other times—then tomorrow you can do it twice. The next day you can do it three times. Soon you won't be able to get out a whole tirade without stopping yourself. You'll be able to notice and stop yourself in the middle of your tantrum every time. Eventually, you'll find that you're stopping yourself before you open your mouth. Congratulations, you've stopped yelling!

Over time, you'll be able to notice when you're gathering kindling. You know what kindling is—small pieces of wood with which you start a fire. Emotional kindling is what we gather when we're stockpiling grievances, when we're saving things up instead of dealing with them. Sooner or later, you get a bonfire.

Instead of letting those irritations build up until you explode, try to take action to address what's wrong, while you can still stay calm. This may seem impossible, but you really can turn things around, and within three months you may find you can't remember the last time you yelled.

What you need is a plan, and that plan has three parts:

1. Use your Pause Button to handle those tough moments. You already know how to do this!

2. Reduce the stress you carry and increase the support you give yourself, so you have more inner resources. We'll give you these tools in the sections on self-care and mindfulness later in Part 1.

3. Monitor the circumstances when you yell so you can learn what triggers you and heal or avoid those triggers. For this, you'll need an accountability partner.

Who's the best accountability partner to know if you're yelling? Your child! Explain to your child that you want to use a respectful voice more often. You expect your child to follow your house rules and cooperate with you, but, regardless of whether or not they do, you are committed to using a respectful voice to guide your child. Tell your child that each evening, you'll ask them to give you a star if you used a respectful voice. You can download a Respectful Voice star chart at AhaParenting.com/RespectfulVoiceChart. You don't need to buy stars; your child can draw the star and color it in.

I'm not a big fan of star charts for kids because I think they focus kids on the reward, rather than the more important reasons for the desired behavior. But I don't think you're going to get the wrong lessons from a star chart, so I'm recommending that you use one. In fact, I suggest that when you get enough stars, you do something really nice for yourself. Why not give yourself all the support you can?

> Not acting on your anger creates more space for love.
> And, where there is more love, there is always more room for transformation.

Just one warning. When your child says that you don't get a star because you yelled, you'll probably find yourself excusing your yelling by saying, "*But you deserved it.*" It doesn't matter what your child does. No one ever deserves to be yelled at. You're the role model. Unless you want to teach your children that yelling is the best way to solve problems and that they can yell at you any time they're unhappy, you need to stop yelling at them.

It's also likely that you'll find yourself saying, "*I didn't really yell. I was just trying to get your attention.*" But researchers have taped parents interacting with children and they say that parents are often "not conscious of their actions, because it's habitual and they sort of lash out without really thinking about it."[37] So if your child felt like your voice was disrespectful, it probably was. Unless your child is angry while deciding whether to give you a star—which is obviously not the time to initiate your daily chat—then accept their perception about whether you yelled.

Even if you go all week and you don't get a single star, don't give up. Next week just split your star chart up into mornings and afternoons, so you have two chances to get a star each day. Sooner or later, you're going to get through a morning or an afternoon without yelling and get a star. The next week, go for two. Just keep improving over the week before.

It usually takes at least 12 weeks of tremendous effort to stop yelling. But you can do this. It's not rocket science. In the beginning it's really hard, but as you do it, you gain momentum and it gets easier, because you're building the neural pathways for self-regulation.

Start your new program of "yellibacy" today. Just start it. You'll find it's very tough. Don't be hard on yourself when you end up yelling. You may fear that you'll never get a star. That's okay. Keep plugging away. Sooner or later, you're going to get a star. Notice the circumstances. How can you give yourself that support more regularly? Then you're going to get two stars, and three, and four, and pretty soon, you'll realize that you don't yell very often and you can reliably regulate yourself!

## Practice: **Your Vow of Yellibacy**

If you don't yell or shout much, please don't skip this exercise. Use it as an opportunity to work on cultivating a respectful voice.

**1.** Print out your Respectful Voice chart from AhaParenting.com/RespectfulVoiceChart.

**2.** Talk to your family about the chart. For example: "*You know how I yell sometimes? I don't want to yell so much. It doesn't help things. It's not a good way to solve problems with people you love. And no one deserves to be yelled at, no matter what. Will you help me with this? See this star chart? I want you to draw a star (or give me a sticker) every day that I don't yell. I will ask you every day how I did in using a respectful voice. Will you help me with this?*"

**3.** Make a list below of ways you can support yourself so you're less stressed and able to stay more patient with your child. Which of these can you begin today?

_____

_____

_____

## Practice: **When You Get Triggered**

As you go through your week, notice when you get triggered. Write down how you feel in your emotions and in your body.

*Example*

| My child is being defiant | I have been constantly picking up after my children today | My children are being too wild before bedtime |
|---|---|---|
| I feel so angry I want to slap her. My mouth feels tight and my hands are in fists. | I feel exhausted and resentful. My body feels heavy, weighed down. | I'm getting more and more tense and worried that someone will get hurt and there will be tears. My throat feels tight and I feel short of breath. |

*Your Turn*

|  |  |  |
|---|---|---|
|  |  |  |

## Reflection After Practice: Working with Your Triggers

Later, as you consider each situation, breathe and notice any lingering feelings in your body. Simply breathing into those tense places in your body helps to heal the emotions that are causing you to get triggered. (You're emptying your emotional backpack!)

In each case, consider what past experiences or beliefs might be causing you to get triggered in that situation. Then, explore what you could say or do to lessen your upset next time this situation comes up.

*Example*

| What triggered you today? | How did your body and emotions feel? | What past experiences or beliefs might be causing this trigger? | What could you do or say next time to lessen your upset? |
|---|---|---|---|
| My child is being defiant. | I feel so angry I want to slap her. My mouth feels tight and my hands are in fists. | If I talked back to my parents, I was physically punished, so when my child talks back to me, all that rage comes up. It feels like an emergency. I just want to lash out, because I feel so terrible. | Next time I could stop, drop, and breathe. I could remind myself that my rage is not actually about her, that her defiance is not actually a threat to my authority. I could try empathizing about how upset she must be to speak to me in that way. I could listen to her problem and help her solve it. |

| What triggered you today? | How did your body and emotions feel? | What past experiences or beliefs might be causing this trigger? | What could you do or say next time to lessen your upset? |
|---|---|---|---|
| I have been constantly picking up after my children today. | I feel exhausted and resentful. My body feels heavy, weighed down. | When I have to pick up after everyone, I feel like my needs don't matter and will never be met. I feel uncared about—devalued and hopeless and invisible, like I'm carrying such a heavy weight. I just wish someone would take care of me once in a while. I don't know if anything in my childhood explains this, but I sure get tired of having to be the grown-up all the time. I wish I could get away with being irresponsible like my kids do. | I am going to set up more routines for the kids to put their things away. But also, I am going to take better care of me. They're kids: they are bound to make messes. If I didn't feel so depleted, it wouldn't bother me so much. I need to make sure I feel good, so I'm not so impatient with them when I ask them to pick up. I think they would respond more positively. |
| My children are being too wild before bedtime. | I'm getting more and more tense and worried that someone will get hurt and there will be tears. My throat feels tight and I feel short of breath. | I'm just beat by bedtime. I don't have any patience left. But really, it's because I don't want anyone to get hurt and cry. It's hard enough during the day, but at night when I'm tired, I just can't stand it. I remember that when I cried, my parents told me to stop, and if I didn't, I had to go to my room. I hated that I couldn't stop crying and got sent away. And I realize that I do try everything I can to stop my children from crying. | Next time I could roughhouse with the kids before bath to get some of that wildness out well before bedtime. And I need to remember that it's not bad for people to cry! |

## *Your Turn*

For each situation when you got triggered this week, what past experiences or beliefs might be causing you to get triggered in that situation? What could you say or do to lessen your upset next time this situation comes up? As you write, notice any lingering feelings in your body and breathe into them. Notice how they change.

| What triggered you today? | How did your body and emotions feel? | What past experiences or beliefs might be causing this trigger? | What could you do or say next time to lessen your upset? |
|---|---|---|---|
| | | | |
| | | | |
| | | | |

# Practice: **Self-Regulation Growth Grid**

Use this space to write about your self-regulation experiences. Include both the times you are successful and the times you aren't. It's not a mistake if you learn from it!

Date and time:

_____

Describe the situation:

_____

_____

_____

What triggered you?

_____

_____

_____

How you responded:

_____

_____

_____

What you learned about how to support yourself better next time:

_____

_____

_____

. . . . . . . . . . . . . . . . . . . . . . . . . . . . . .

Date and time:

_____

Describe the situation:

_____

_____

_____

What triggered you?

_____

_____

_____

How you responded:

_____

_____

_____

What you learned about how to support yourself better next time:

_____

_____

_____

. . . . . . . . . . . . . . . . . . . . . . . . . . . . .

Date and time:

_____

Describe the situation:

_____

_____

_____

What triggered you?

_____

_____

_____

How you responded:

_____

_____

_____

What you learned about how to support yourself better next time:

_____

_____

_____

# WORKING WITH BIG EMOTIONS

Emotions are part of living a rich human life. But when we feel swamped by big emotions and don't know how to deal with them, it can become a struggle to stay patient with our children when they're having a hard time. In this section, we'll briefly cover the big emotions that most often cause us problems, so you have some tools to work through them.

## *Working With Fear*

> Here's something that fear will never tell you. You don't have to feel this way. Fear only tells you about fight or flight. It never tells you that the mountain in front of you is of your own making.
>
> — Guy Finley[38]

Fear keeps us alive. It alerts us to pay attention, to mobilize, to be ready to fight, flee, or freeze. If you're lucky, you've only felt terror in nightmares. But all of us experience mild fear on a daily basis. It isn't pleasant, but we take it for granted. We think of it as feeling stressed or mildly anxious.

Often, we don't even notice the fear; we just react to it with a defensive edge by collecting grievances in our minds, or lashing out at others with blame or annoyance.

When we do notice fear, we often make the mistake of believing it. Sometimes, fear has a useful message for us. If you step into the path of a moving car, you might die. But often we're worried about the wrong things. For some of us, our four-year-old screaming at us feels like an emergency. Before we know it, we're plunged into fight, flight, or freeze mode.

Leadership coach Robert Gass calls this the "elevator shaft." In his leadership trainings, he describes it as stepping onto an elevator on the 10th floor of a building. Everything's good. But suddenly something happens that's upsetting. It's as if the elevator starts plummeting toward the basement, where all the old, dark shadows loom. You might not even be aware of what's getting triggered. All you know is that something terrible is about to happen.

We all have different triggers. But for every one of us, at the bottom of the elevator shaft is the fear of death. That sounds crazy, I know. But whether the fear is that we would be left alone and unprotected, or that someone would hurt us, the ultimate fear is that we would not survive.

It might seem odd that you would be angry at your child because you're worried about surviving. But here's how it works. Your four-year-old begins to scream at you. At that moment, seeing his angry face and clenched fists, old experiences of your parent or someone else screaming at you get triggered. Those are primal feelings of terror. If you follow them to their source, you're at the bottom of the elevator shaft, where you're terrified of this huge person with the fierce face, looming over you, screaming at you threateningly. You're shaking with terror, or frozen inside ("playing dead"), which are normal reactions to help us survive terrifying situations. Suddenly, in this situation with your four-year-old, you're gripped with the feeling that something terrible is about to happen, unless you can immediately get control of this situation. That's why you lash out at your child—to prevent disaster. So you overreact.

# Practice: **Elevator Shaft Exercise**

We might start with a vague worry. Then, one thought leads to the next in quick succession, and before we know it, we're plunging down the elevator shaft into the basement, where our very survival seems at stake.

## *Example*

| 10th floor: | "My son is often mean to his sister." |
|---|---|
| 9th floor: | "He seems like an unhappy person." |
| 8th floor: | "I feel powerless to change this ... Maybe he'll be this way his whole life." |
| 7th floor: | "What did I do wrong as a parent to make him this way?" |
| 6th floor: | "What if I've ruined my son?" |
| 5th floor: | "I'm a failure as a parent." |
| 4th floor: | "I'm a failure as a person." |
| 3rd floor: | "I'm so ashamed ... If people knew, they wouldn't love me." |
| 2nd floor: | "I'm not worthy of love. I'm unlovable." |
| 1st floor: | "I'm all alone... I'm unprotected" |
| Basement: | "I could die." |

## *Your Turn*

Take a moment to consider what issues are most likely to send you on a fast slide down the elevator shaft.

1 _____

2 _____

3 _____

Now, pick one of those issues. See whether you can identify some of the thoughts that send you plummeting to the basement.

Triggering thought (10th floor): _____

9th floor: _____

8th floor: _____

7th floor: _____

6th floor: _____

5th floor: _____

4th floor: _____

3rd floor: _____

2nd floor: _____

1st floor: _____

Basement: _____

## Practice: **Living with Fear**

Even when we don't plunge all the way into a state of emergency, fear has a way of disabling us and sabotaging our relationships. As parents, most of the decisions and actions we end up regretting come from fear. Research shows that when we bow to anxiety (which is mild fear) and let it govern our choices, it seems to gain a foothold.[39] Then, it starts to undermine us in other areas of our life.

You can expect fear to show up in some way every day for the rest of your life. That's normal; it's part of having a human brain and physiology. Our nervous systems are wired to overestimate threat, which is part of how the human race has survived. But you can handle fear.

Don't fight with fear—you can't win. Fighting with fear just convinces you that fear is something to be taken seriously and to be frightened of. From the perspective of fear, no defense is sufficient. But, on the flipside, from the perspective of love, no defense is necessary.

So the antidote to fear is love. We can't feel both love and fear at the same time. While love feels like the ultimate expansion, fear feels like the ultimate contraction.

The best way to begin working with fear is to simply do something that scares you a little, every single day. How, if you're scared? Try this: the more love you feel, the less fear you feel, so love yourself through it. Or, as Susan Jeffers famously said, *"Feel the fear and do it anyway."*[40] As she wrote in her wonderful book with that title, fear is the worry that you won't be able to handle something. But, if the thing that scares you happens, you will in fact handle it, somehow. Every time you face your fear and go forward anyway, you lessen the hold that fear has on you. You claim more courage and aliveness with each brave action. Give it a try in your own life.

## Practice: **Cultivate Courage**

This is a great exercise for a family. Announce that you're launching a "courage project." Every day, you will try to do one thing that scares you. Ask if anyone else in your family wants to join you.

Brainstorm about things that might take courage. Trying something you've never done? Taking the training wheels off the bike? Apologizing?

Reassure your child that everyone gets frightened. Courage is feeling the fear and doing the scary thing anyway. Of course, sometimes it's important to listen to fear. You might discuss some times when that's true, such as not jumping into water until you know it's safe.

Then, every night at dinner, invite everyone in the family to share their courageous acts of the day. Celebrate the bravery and ask questions. What was scary about the act? How did they summon up their courage? Did it turn out to be scary after the fact?

## *Working With Shame*

> Shame is…the fear of disconnection; the fear that something we have done or failed to do, something about who we are or where we come from, has made us unlovable and unworthy of connection.
>
> — Brené Brown[41]

Let's start by experiencing mild shame. Try this:

1. **Say "yes" aloud several times.** What do you feel? I smile and feel excited, happy.

2. **Now say "no" aloud several times.** What do you feel? My smile dies. My body feels tight, closed in. I feel a sense of dread. Some people (usually those whose parents were punitive) also feel anger.

That's mild shame, which is nature's way of helping us rein in our impulses so we can stay safe, live well with others, and even attain our goals. Dan Siegel calls it the "prefrontal cortex clutch,"[42] because it allows us to shift from something we want, to something we want more—for instance, not to disappoint our parent, or not to be stared at in church because we're making inappropriate noise. All of us need to develop that clutch in childhood, so we can self-regulate enough to live with others.

Think of one of our ancestral tribes. The excited three-year-old rushes into the serious gathering of adults, shouting about his discovery of a cool bug. The chief looks askance at him. His internal "brakes" rein in his excitement. Inside, he feels a sinking feeling, a heaviness in his chest. He turns his eyes away.

That's shame. The "forbidden" behaviors that trigger shame vary across cultures, so we know they are learned, not innate. But that feeling of mild shame, that mechanism for learning to regulate behavior so that we can live communally, is universal. In its mild form, that feeling of shame is nature's way of ensuring that young humans learn to live with other humans and follow the rules of the tribe.

So there is nothing wrong with this instinctive response to correction that happens inside all children, *if*—and it's a big *if*—the child continues to feel connected and loved. We can do this by reassuring rather than punishing, so he can integrate the teaching and still feel like a good person.

Watch what happens next, as the three-year-old's mother or father intervenes. They gently scoop the child into their arms and smile reassuringly. They take him out of the hut and admire his bug. They explain that the adults are too focused on their concerns at the moment to be interrupted, and suggest that maybe he can show his grandfather later. If they think the child can handle it, they might suggest that he make a repair to the adults, simply by returning to the meeting in the parent's arms and listening respectfully for a short time to show that he understands what is appropriate behavior.

So the child learns from his instinctive reaction what is appropriate behavior in the context of his tribe. Because his parent understands, he doesn't feel like he is a bad person. He still feels connected. He even learns that he can make a repair when he makes a mistake.

But what if the parent had instead scolded him, or even punished him? That appropriate, instinctive, mild embarrassment reaction would get mixed up with the emotions we all have when we're punished—feelings of not being understood, of not being good enough, of being rejected. Because the child can't bear the pain of being cut off from those whose love he needs, he defends against that pain by blaming himself and seeing himself as flawed. In other words, shame is a defense against the pain and fear of separation. The child is left feeling like there's something wrong with him that makes him unlovable, and hating himself for it. Unworthy and alone, with no help to cope.

So, if a child's "transgression" is followed by punishment or isolation—or even stern lecturing that makes the child feel like a bad person—it creates shame. If these interactions are repeated throughout childhood, the shame can become toxic—the beginning of a fear of being defective that can shadow us throughout life. That's why conventional parenting, which doesn't help children with emotions and relies on punishment, often raises children with what Brené Brown, the leading U.S. expert on shame, calls "toxic shame."[43] That shame will flare up throughout the child's life, undermining his confidence whenever he hits a bump in the road.

You can see that shame develops when we worry as children that the love we receive is conditional on us meeting parental expectations. The child concludes that he's too flawed to ensure his parents'—and the tribe's—love and protection. This brings us to the public nature of shame, where we feel somehow as if we're embarrassed in front of all humankind. Shame feels like everyone is staring at us and finding us lacking.

In primitive cultures, being banished from a tribe meant that you weren't protected, and, if you got hurt or sick, you wouldn't be taken care of, so you would almost certainly die. A child without the protection of a tribe wouldn't survive. Of course, that's why shame exists, as a warning signal: "Danger!" That's why Brené Brown calls shame "the fear of disconnection."[44]

> Think of yourself as a child. In those moments of anger and punishment, it may have felt like your parents withdrew their love. Maybe they thought that was the right way to teach you to be a good person. So, like the rest of us, you constructed a "good" self, which you tried hard to be, and you pushed any unacceptable parts of yourself deep down inside and tried to hide them from everyone. You know that feeling that you're faking it, that you could be found out and exposed as a fake? That's shame.

Brené Brown says shame makes us hide, not take healthy risks, not realize our full potential. John Bradshaw, who wrote *Healing the Shame that Binds You*, agrees: "*Toxically shamed people tend to become more and more stagnant as life goes on. They try to be super human (perfect, and controlling) or become less than human (losing interest in life or stagnated in some addictive behavior).*"[45]

We do everything possible to keep our shame out of our conscious awareness, hidden away in our emotional backpack. We work so very hard to be good, to hide our secret fear that we aren't worthy of love, that we're broken. But every so often, especially when we fear that others are judging us or when we know we've acted so badly that everyone would judge us if only they knew, we're overcome with shame. We feel worthless.

Shame feels awful, and it doesn't make us behave better or correct our mistakes. It just terrifies us. This is different from when we feel guilty for doing something wrong—let's say, something big like lying to our partner. When we feel guilty, it's because that action conflicts with something else that's important to us, such as, in this case, our caring for our partner and our desire for an intimate relationship. Our guilt says to us, "*That action isn't something I want to do. That's not who I want to be.*" Our guilt alerts us when we're out of integrity and can help us choose a different course of action. But shame doesn't do that. Shame says, "*I'm a bad person.*" Shame tells us we're deeply flawed and that we're not fixable.

> Shame is so scary to us that we can't even take responsibility for what we've done wrong. Have you noticed that when your child feels shame, they blame everyone else around them, and they can't bear to talk about what they might be able to do differently next time?

We can sometimes see our child's shame, but we have a harder time recognizing our own feelings of shame. We push them down out of awareness, but we still feel them, so we soothe ourselves with overeating, screen time, or overwork. But often the feelings are so unbearable to us that we develop a repertoire of ways to fend them off when they get triggered— everything from avoiding any risk to substance abuse to passing the shame on to our own children.

**How do we pass shame on?** There are many ways. But just imagine for a moment that your child is ramping up into a tantrum at the market. You feel everyone staring at you. If you're like most parents, you feel on the spot, criticized, unsupported, alone. You might even feel worthless, like you're secretly defective and now everyone will know. That's shame.

So, if you're like most humans, at that moment you try to deflect that intolerable feeling in any way you can. You make it your child's fault. You hiss a threat or a reprimand. In that moment, your child shifts from the problem she was having—being tired, or hungry, or simply needing to run around. Now, she feels cut off from her connection with you. She feels alone, all eyes on her. She feels shame.

That's one way we pass shame on to our children. Is that the end of the world? No, not if it's an isolated occurrence and you make a repair afterward. No parent is perfect. Every one of us has sometimes let our own issues spill over onto our children. Kids are resilient; they can handle those isolated incidents, and even learn from our repairs. We'll talk more in Part 3 of this book about how to break the cycle so you don't pass shame on to your child. **For now, what you need to know is that it is possible to heal any shame you carry.**

One foolproof antidote is self-love. Since shame is the opposite of unconditional love, noticing those moments gives us an opportunity to heal the shame by choosing to love ourselves, even though we aren't perfect.

And because shame so often includes fear that others will reject us, another foolproof antidote is authenticity. If we take the risk to show our true selves to others and they accept us, we overcome the fear that we'll be rejected because we aren't good enough. The cure for shame comes from the heart. When we love ourselves unconditionally—without conditions—our imperfections no longer seem shameful, because we realize we're worthy of love, exactly as we are.

## Practice: **Meditation for Healing Shame**

This exercise to heal shame is best done as a guided meditation. The audio is on the Aha! Parenting website at AhaParenting.com/Workbook. Every time you do this exercise, you will either experience love, which transforms you, or (and this is just as valuable) you will experience "not love" or the feeling that you're not lovable. That's shame. As you allow those feelings and hold yourself with compassion while you breathe through them, they begin to evaporate.

In this exercise, as well as others in this book, I suggest putting your hand on your heart and breathing into your heart. This technique, known as "heart-focused breathing," has been shown by researchers to have a calming effect on the nervous system. It also shifts your brain away from our usual intense focus on incoming perceptions and into the open neural circuitry that allows you to unlearn old, automatic responses and relearn new, healthier responses. You might think of it as activating your heart perceptions so you can see beyond the fears and judgments of the mind. As Antoine de Saint-Exupéry said, "*It is only with the heart that one can see rightly. What is essential is invisible to the eye.*"[46]

In this meditation, we invoke both love and compassion. You might think of love as the ultimate connection of warmth, affection, and opening. You might think of compassion as the willingness to be present with suffering. Each time you do this meditation, go slowly. Notice how your experience changes over time.

## Practice: **Journaling**

In the previous meditation, you were asked to tell yourself that you love you. As you said "*I love you*" to yourself, how would you rate the love you felt on a scale of 1 to 10?

**1**      **2**      **3**      **4**      **5**      **6**      **7**      **8**      **9**      **10**

That's your baseline.
Keep repeating this meditation throughout the week.
Then, bring your heart healing into your conscious daily life. Every time you're in the bathroom this week, look lovingly in the mirror. Say to yourself, "*You are more than enough. I love you.*"

How did you feel when you spoke lovingly to yourself in the mirror?

_____

_____

_____

Did your feelings change over the course of the day, or the week, as you continued to push through your discomfort and speak lovingly to yourself?

_____

_____

_____

One of the reasons this exercise is so powerful is that eyes really are the windows to the soul. When you look in your own eyes, you see your deepest, truest, most vulnerable self, and you know that shame is a lie, so the shame begins to lose power over you. Every time you do this, you're surfacing any old shame that's in your emotional backpack, and you're healing it.

You can do this exercise as often as you want. As long as you feel something, some shift, as you do the process, then it's valuable to you, so keep doing it.

After a week of doing this, how would you rate the love you feel on a scale of 1 to 10?

**1      2      3      4      5      6      7      8      9      10**

How does that feel inside? How can you continue and maintain this shift?

_____

_____

_____

# Practice: **Sharing Shame**

> "
> If we can share our story with someone who responds with empathy
> and understanding, shame can't survive.
> — Brené Brown[47]

Because shame includes the public element of fearing that others will reject us for being ourselves, it can be very healing to share things we're ashamed of with others. We learn that we're not alone. Everyone has things they're ashamed of. We also learn that we're good enough as we are and that no one will reject us for being ourselves.

To do this exercise, I suggest you recruit a friend or loved one with whom you have a strong bond of trust. Decide who will be Partner 1 and who will be Partner 2. Do the dialogue, and then switch places. You can repeat the dialogue over and over, recounting anything that you feel ashamed of. Notice all the feelings that come up along the way. Love yourself and your partner with compassion throughout this exercise.

### Partner 1

"*I want to share something with you. I worry that once you know this about me, you will find me unlovable and shameful, and reject me. I once* _____ [name something you did or experienced]. *Can you still accept me and love me?*"

### Partner 2

"*Thank you for your courage in sharing that with me. I hear that you once* _____. *I accept that human part of you, along with all the other human parts of you. You don't have to be perfect. I accept you as the wonderful human you are, and I love you.*"

> Most of us wish we had more love in our lives. We wish someone else would love us, or that the people we love would love us more, better, differently. But we can only take in love from others when we've patched up the hole in our hearts that tells us we're not fully lovable. When we deeply love ourselves, we realize that we don't need to be perfect. We're more than enough, exactly as we are. That lens of love softens our judgment of ourselves. Shame starts to melt away.

## Working With Grief

Learning to mourn, and to be comfortable with the grieving process, might not seem like a parenting skill. But, if we can't allow ourselves to grieve our losses, walls harden around our hearts and our ability to love contracts. So to be the loving parents we aspire to be requires that we grieve our losses along the way.

Parents also have a unique relationship with everyday grief. As our children grow, every exciting new development includes a measure of loss for us as parents. Yes, as our child leaves each stage behind, we receive the solace of the next, often wonderful, stage. But that doesn't erase the profound loss of the infant's earliest milky smiles, the toddler's adoring gaze, the preschooler's unmatched exuberance, the six-year-old who once climbed onto our lap for bedtime stories.

Part of loving our child is grieving each stage as she moves on into the future. We need to honor that grief, because if we don't allow ourselves to grieve, we sometimes give our child the message to stop growing up so fast. Kids can't learn to fly if we are, even unconsciously, clutching at their ankles. Our willingness to honor our mixed feelings about our children growing up is part of what frees them to try their wings.

Some of us, of course, have deeper grief to work through. Loss visits every one of us, and how we handle loss has a huge impact on the richness of our family's emotional life. If we fend it off like an unwelcome visitor, grief doesn't leave. It takes up residence like a shadow in our psyches and we become stuck in its bitter influence. Unresolved grief compromises resiliency, threatening to burst out at even minor provocations, leaving us fragile and prone to depression.

Thankfully, grief is never interminable. Like all feelings, if we let ourselves feel it, grief swamps us, and then, eventually, fades away. Not that grief ever disappears, but we can think of it as a slice of the pie of our lives: at first an important loss pervades the entire circle of our life, but gradually the slice of our life in shadow becomes smaller and smaller. Eventually, we can go on with our lives in a healthy way, although we are forever changed and may always revisit the pain of our loss.

Our comfort level with loss also gives our children an important role model. In our society, we usually distract ourselves from pain or self-medicate. But healing requires us to accept pain, to sit with it, to love ourselves through it. At times, there will be nothing we can do for our child except to sit with him and let him experience his grief: over a sports defeat, an inconsiderate peer, a dead pet, or even an ill or deceased loved one. To work through his grief, our child needs what therapists call a "holding environment," and we are the ones who do the holding, both physically and emotionally.

If we're so uncomfortable with loss that we cannot allow our child to mourn, we give a destructive message that can reach far into his life. So accepting loss as a normal part of life is important for optimal mental health for all of us. The more we allow ourselves to grieve when necessary, the more joy we can feel.

## Practice: Meditation for Healing Grief

I recommend that you try this guided meditation even if you don't have anything in particular to grieve except the small losses of daily life.

As with all deep emotions, we heal grief by bringing our conscious attention to the feeling and holding ourselves with compassion while we experience it. One of the best ways to do this is through guided meditation. I first learned a version of this meditation for healing grief from mindfulness teacher Stephen Levine when I had the good fortune to attend one of his workshops 30 years ago. I've taken the liberty of adapting it here. You can download this meditation from the Aha! Parenting website at AhaParenting.com/Workbook. Each time you do this meditation, go slowly. Notice how your experience changes over time.

## BREAKING THE CYCLE: HEALING YOURSELF

It may surprise you to think that your childhood, so long ago, is still having an effect on you today. But what we learn before the age of six shapes who we are and how we respond to our adult experiences on deep, unconscious levels. And, because the way we were treated as children is our blueprint for how children "should" be treated, your relationship with your child is profoundly influenced by the way you were parented.

**You can't change how you were parented, but you can change how you understand and view your childhood.** Research shows that as you come to terms with your childhood experience and are able to integrate it into a positive understanding of yourself, the way you "tell the story" of your childhood changes.[48] That changes the way you see yourself, and it changes the way you act toward your child. In fact, research shows that this is one of the most valuable gifts you can give your child, because it breaks the cycle of any pain you're carrying. Even those of us who feel we had wonderful childhoods usually carry some scars from the past.

> The experience of remembering your childhood and considering how you "tell your story" will bring up tender feelings for most of us. The secret to healing is to allow yourself to accept those feelings at the same time that you hold yourself with compassion and resist taking action. That allows you to integrate the experiences without being triggered by them in the future. It's a bit like detonating the experiences' emotional charge.

Reflecting and journaling have been proven to help develop the self-reflection capacity of your prefrontal cortex.[49] So, in this section, I ask you to journal about your past self. Doing this work will change your understanding so that you see your childhood from a more adult perspective, deepening your compassion for yourself and others and helping you see the past in a more empowering way.

## Practice: Reclaiming Your Whole Self by Sitting with Your Discomfort

No matter how loving our parents were, most of us got the message in childhood that we were too needy, too greedy, too self-centered, too loud, too shy, too *something*. Our self or our needs were too big and we somehow were not quite good enough. These messages might not even have come from our parents. Men in our society often get the message to disown their vulnerability, needs, and emotions. Women often get the message that their bodies are not their own, that what they look like is more important than what they feel like, that good girls don't get angry and can't protect themselves.

The pain of feeling not good enough hurts. Naturally, we try to avoid that discomfort. It's only human. We develop little (and sometimes big) addictions to numb and distract ourselves—food, screens, sex, shopping, liquor, drugs, porn. But that doesn't get rid of the emotions we're carrying. It just cuts off our awareness of parts of our bodies, or our emotional lives, or our souls. Unfortunately, if we don't reclaim the parts of ourselves that we've cut off, we can't live fully. And we end up passing our brokenness on to our children.

Luckily, our bodies know how to heal all of this hurt. The body, which holds the emotions that have been pushed away, will always help us become aware. All we have to do is show up and stay present, holding ourselves with compassion, while we become conscious of those buried parts of ourselves. Once we're able to stop resisting and simply accept, those disowned parts reintegrate. We heal.

**Use this practice when you're upset, to work through challenging emotions.** You can also use it to explore emotional baggage from past events, such as when you're journaling.

1. **Notice your breathing.** Take a few breaths into your belly and blow them slowly out through your mouth.

2. **Become aware of the sensations in your body.** You may recognize particular emotions, or you may simply notice physical tightness or discomfort. If you feel emotion, just breathe into it and let it go. Notice how some part of you wants to push those feelings away, or numb them, or distract yourself.

3. **Stay present.** This takes courage. You may sweat, shake, or yawn. You may want to vomit. You will certainly feel the urge to jump up and do something, anything, besides sitting with what you're feeling. Just tell yourself that your only job is to sit and bring light into the dark places.

4. **Imagine yourself flooded with light**, surrounded by light, breathing light in and out. You feel safe and loved, filled with compassion.

5. **Keep welcoming those uncomfortable sensations in your body or emotions.** If you feel resistance, remind yourself that you are safe and loved. Just keep soothing yourself so you can sit with the discomfort.

That's all there is to it. Scientists say that every time you do this, you're training your mind so that it isn't overwhelmed by difficult emotions so easily.[50] I think of it as emptying your backpack, so you aren't as prone to getting triggered. You could also think of it as bringing conscious awareness to those dark places, welcoming them into the light—so the shadows vanish.

## What Negative Beliefs Do You Carry From Childhood?

Most of us don't even notice the unconscious beliefs we formed in early childhood, even though they shape the way we treat our child. For instance:

- If our parents reacted harshly when we got upset, we may have concluded that getting emotional is an emergency, so we go into fight or flight mode when our child gets upset—and our child looks like the enemy.
- If we weren't treated with respect when we were young, we may grow into adults who perceive others as disrespecting us—so we may react with anger to the slightest defiance.
- If we never felt really seen and heard and appreciated for who we are, we may think that children who are being emotional or acting out "just want attention"—as if that's a bad thing!

- If we concluded as children that we simply weren't good enough, then we may set impossibly-high standards for ourselves and torment ourselves with self-criticism—and, even if we try not to visit that perfectionism on our children, they may always feel they aren't quite good enough.

We often talk about thoughts and beliefs as if they're interchangeable. Actually, beliefs, or story lines, are more like a subconscious worldview that shapes how we perceive our experiences. We aren't always aware of our beliefs, but, if we pay attention to our thoughts, we can often figure out the underlying belief system, since our belief systems give rise to our thoughts.

| Beliefs... | ...Give Rise to Thoughts |
|---|---|
| I'm not good enough unless I'm perfect. | I'm so ashamed that I messed this up. |
| | If I were a better parent, my children wouldn't fight. |
| | If I can just keep things under control, things will be okay. |
| When someone gets upset, it's an emergency. | When my children get upset, I bribe them, and if that doesn't work, I threaten them. I can't bear it. |
| | When my children fight, I can't stop myself from yelling. |
| People may love you but they leave you. | I wish my husband wasn't so friendly to everyone—or at least to other women! |
| | I don't want my child out of my sight. |
| | I don't like being alone. |

Are you aware of any beliefs from your childhood that cause you to overreact now? Write them down below. What thoughts do those beliefs give rise to?

_____

_____

_____

_____

_____

## Practice: Heal Your Negative Beliefs About Yourself

This practice has six easy steps. (Okay, not so easy, but simple. You can do this.)

1. **Say aloud, "*I have to be perfect to be loved.*"** Notice your emotional and/or physical reaction. (For me, this phrase makes me crumple.) This is what we're going to heal. Now just put that aside for a moment.

2. **How did your parents react when you displeased them?** Imagine a particular incident from your childhood. Play the scene out in your mind with you as the observer. Notice their reactions. Notice your reactions. What did you feel? How did you act on the outside? What did you conclude?

3. **Can you see why you concluded that you weren't "good enough"** to be lovable, from this interaction and others? After you "learned" this belief, you applied it to many other situations. Thoughts derived from this belief can influence your feelings in interactions even today.

4. **Imagine a compassionate observer.** Might someone watching have formed a different interpretation than you did? For instance, might they have concluded that:

- Your parents were well-intentioned and loved you, but were misinformed about bringing up emotionally healthy children.

- Your parents' expectations were unreasonable.

- Even if you had been perfect, your parents might have found fault with you just because they were human and hadn't been unconditionally loved themselves.

- Humans are by definition imperfect, but you were then and are now "more than enough" and completely lovable.

5. **Now, let's give your younger self that alternative explanation for your parents' behavior. Tell yourself, "*You are lovable and more than enough, just the way you are.*"** Say it aloud. (Yes, aloud. That's an important part of reprogramming your subconscious. We need to hear the words.) How does that feel? Say it again. Let that good feeling sink in. Say it again: "*I am more than enough.*"

6. **Now say aloud again, "*I have to be perfect to be loved.*"** Notice your emotional reaction. Are you indignant now, rather than hopeless? That's a good sign. If the words just feel flat, with no emotional resonance, they're no longer true for you. If they feel even a bit true, just keep repeating this exercise until the belief is gone. A deep belief like this one can take some daily reflection to "reprogram," maybe even a few minutes daily for a month. But, since this belief is behind so much of our inner criticism, it's worth it—even, potentially, miraculous.

**Aside to self-critical parents:** Are you feeling a bit nervous about the beliefs your child is forming? You don't have to be perfect. Deep beliefs don't derive from a single incident but from the accumulation of repeated parent–child interactions. Just keep supporting yourself to stay emotionally regulated and connected, and your child's beliefs will keep evolving as you do. I promise.

## Practice: Talk to Yourself Like Someone You Love

> The brain is like a computer. Your success or failure in anything, large or small, will depend on your programming—what you say when you talk to yourself.
>
> — Shad Helmstetter[51]

Every day you have thousands of thoughts. Experts tell us that for the average person, most of those thoughts are negative: "*Not again!... I knew this wouldn't work... I am so clumsy... That was a dumb thing to do... I certainly screwed that up... Can't you do anything right?... We'll never make it in time now... I just can't handle this...*"

Imagine if you had a loving parent in your head, nurturing you through your day: "*Good try... Wouldn't it be nice if this worked out?... It's okay, don't worry... You don't have to be perfect... Nobody bats 1000... I love you just the way you are... Practice makes perfect... Just breathe... Don't take it personally... It's never too late to make things better... Every journey starts with the first step... You're a hero for everything you do... Two steps forward, one step back still takes you to where you're headed... Sooner or later this will work out... You are more than enough!*"

Today, come to your defense as your nurturing parent would, and reframe every negative thing you say to yourself. Really soak in that terrific parenting. You deserve it. See if a little of that self-nurturing doesn't rub off on your kids.

- "*I blew it!*" becomes "*Nobody's perfect.*"
- "*I'm so stupid*" becomes "*Let's pay attention and try that again.*"
- "*I can't get through to that child!*" becomes "*The more I listen to her and connect, the more she listens to me.*"
- "*I'm just not good at that*" becomes "*Practice makes perfect.*"
- "*I wish I had more time!*" becomes "*I make time and I take time for what I need to do.*"
- "*This is impossible!*" becomes "*The impossible just takes a little longer. What do I need to do to make this happen?*"

## Your Turn

| Original Thought | Reframed |
|---|---|
|  |  |
|  |  |
|  |  |
|  |  |
|  |  |
|  |  |

## Healing Trauma

Researchers think that the human mind regularly processes our life experiences during dream states. The hippocampus orchestrates a process during REM (or "rapid eye movement") sleep in which recent events are reviewed, the attached emotions are deactivated, and the learning is stored as a memory. It's well known that our eyes move during this process, but researchers are still working to understand what the eye movements of REM sleep have to do with this emotional processing.

We do know that when recent memories are processed during REM sleep, they lose their emotional power. That's why most of us can recall incidents that upset us when they happened but are actually funny as we look back on them. The rapid eye movements of the dream state "facilitate the transfer of episodic memory, which includes emotions, physical sensations and beliefs associated with the original event, into semantic memory networks, in which the meaning of the event has been extracted and negative associations are no longer present."[52] This feature of our brain design allows us to learn life lessons without being crushed under the weight of a lifetime of emotions.

However, when an experience is too traumatic to process—meaning that we aren't able to tolerate the emotions associated with the experience—the event is not processed normally. Instead, it is split off into a separate holding pen of unprocessed experiences. Since we haven't processed the event in our usual way, these experiences have raw emotions attached that are as powerful as when they first occurred—even if we don't have a conscious memory of the event. When an unprocessed traumatic memory is triggered by current experience, we re-experience it as if it were happening in the moment, complete with the raw terror (or whatever the emotions were).

Most of us think trauma is caused by big events, such as a rape, war, or the difficult death of a loved one. But traumas aren't measured by what happened on the outside. Trauma simply means that we weren't able to handle the processing of that event at the time, so it still affects us. The result is that intense childhood experiences that damaged our sense of self can continue to affect us as any trauma would.

You've already learned how to heal emotional patterns that no longer serve you by rewiring your neural circuits (see page 18). But, when the original experience was especially upsetting, we need to give ourselves special support to work through those triggers. After all, those emotions are there because they were too overwhelming for us to work through when we first felt them.

Counselors can be invaluable in this process. I especially recommend treatments that help you tap into the wisdom of the body, because, as trauma expert Bessel van der Kolk says, "*The body keeps the score.*"[53]

Empirical research shows that EMDR, or "eye movement desensitization and reprocessing," is one effective treatment for trauma.[54]  While we don't fully understand how EMDR works, the eye movements that are the foundation of EMDR therapy seem to mimic the eye movements of REM sleep, so that the traumatic memories can be accessed and processed, with new, appropriate neural connections. Be sure to find an EMDR practitioner who is certified by EMDRIA, the EMDR International Association (there is a directory of therapists on its website[55]).

If you have milder memories and would like to experiment with processing them yourself, you can follow the same basic strategy without the eye movements. Some neuroscientists call this "memory reconsolidation"[56] or neural "reconditioning."[57] The basic idea is that first we summon up the old memory, belief, or emotion that continues to trigger us. Then, while that neural pattern is activated, we create a contradictory positive experience. That contradiction stimulates the brain to take into account this new, contradictory information, so it creates new neural connections. What fires together, wires together, so we create a new, more positive neural association.

Notice that the human mind is perfectly capable of holding two contradictory beliefs, as long as they aren't thrown into sharp relief. For instance, you might have had a tough childhood but have had many experiences since then of people loving you. Those contradictory experiences, though, may still not be sufficient to convince you on a deep level that you're completely lovable, because the old experience is still triggering beliefs that you aren't, at least under some circumstances.

> For brain rewiring, it's essential that the old distressing experience be activated at the same time that the new contradictory experience is felt. Research shows that as the old experience is activated, the neural network associated with it will spontaneously reconsolidate and then, only a fraction of a second later, rewire. When you've paired that old experience with a new, contradictory experience, "the simultaneous firing of neurons encoding both strategies allows them to...rewire together"[58] so the new information becomes part of the old neural pathway, changing the conclusion.

Notice also that summoning up the distressing memory, by itself, does not rewire the brain. In fact, repeatedly revisiting distressing memories without an antidote simply reinforces that neural wiring—like etching them more deeply into your brain. It is crucial that the brain experiences something that contradicts the upsetting experience, in order to rewire it. So, when your child has a big scare and sobs in your arms, she is not simply "venting" her upset. She is also having a contradictory or corrective experience. She had a moment of terror, but now while she "relives" it, she is safe and loved. That's why simply reliving our distress is not enough to heal it and can even be re-traumatizing, strengthening those original neural networks—*if* we don't have support. We need to feel that we—complete with our upsetting emotions—are accepted by a loving witness. This offers us the connection that heals, the contradictory experience that allows us to rewire our painful memories to come to a more positive conclusion, using the context of love.

## Practice: Healing Trauma by Rewiring Your Brain

Let's look at an example of how you might rewire your own brain to deal with an early upsetting experience. Maybe you know that when your children fight with each other, you yell. Maybe you've figured out that this is a reaction to growing up in a home where your parents fought a lot. But knowing that hasn't helped you to stop yelling. So you decide to go directly to your neural wiring.

1. **First, rate the distress you feel** from the old memory or experience on a scale of 1 to 10. Maybe when you think about your parents fighting all the time and how it made you feel as a child, you would rate that distress as a 6.

2. **Use a guided meditation** to shift from your busy mind to your healing heart, which provides a buffer of love. (For instance, use the basic three-minute meditation from the Aha! Parenting website at AhaParenting.com/Workbook.)

3. **Shift yourself into a state of well-being.** You can do this simply by meditating and filling yourself with love, or by summoning up a memory that stimulates positive emotions.

4. **Now, from this place of well-being, summon up the upsetting memory or feeling.** Don't get caught up in the story line. Just notice the sensations in your body. What do you see, hear, smell, feel? You're re-activating the neural pattern of the upsetting experience.

5. **Instead of getting swamped by this old experience, simply observe it.** While the pattern is activated, we want to interrupt the established neural circuitry that causes you to react in the old pre-programmed ways (in this case by yelling). First, you need to resist acting on the previously programmed responses that no longer serve you (in this case, yelling at your kids). Those habits reinforce the pattern.

6. **Now, to rewire the neural circuitry, let's give you an experience that contradicts the old, upsetting experience.** First, shift yourself back into well-being again, and hold yourself in love and compassion. Now, summon up a memory that directly contradicts the upsetting one. For instance, even if your parents fought a lot, you can probably remember one incident when your family felt peaceful and you felt safe. Step into that memory and let yourself soak in that peace and safety. If you can't find a strong contradictory memory, don't worry. Your imagination can create one for you. The imagination is so powerful that the brain will take that image at face value and use it as reality. So simply summon up an image of your family happily connected, and flesh that out. What do you see, hear, smell, feel? Notice all the accompanying sensations. Savor them.

7. **Hold these two contradictory memories in your conscious awareness at the same time**—this is the key to rewiring the brain. It's usually easiest to begin by alternating, attending to each of them in turn. Spend more time on the positive image, strengthening that one repeatedly. Then, every time you return to the distressing image and start to notice those feelings getting activated, immediately substitute the corrective image.

8. **To finish, rate again the distress you feel from the old memory or experience**, on a scale of 1 to 10. You will probably notice that your distress has diminished.

You can repeat this exercise multiple times, always strengthening the positive memory. At some point, you're likely to notice that the emotional charge from this old experience has simply vanished. You'll also notice that the actions that were triggered by this experience—in this case, responding to your children's fighting by lashing out—have vanished too. That doesn't mean you'll enjoy it when your kids fight. But it does mean you won't get hijacked by distress and come out swinging. Instead, you'll be able to take a deep breath and intervene constructively to calm the storm.

### *Reparenting Yourself*

The questions in the following two exercises aim to help you reflect on your childhood relationship with your parents. Psychologists have found that thinking and writing about questions like these[59] can help you integrate and heal those essential relationships, which will change how you relate to your child.

## Practice: **Healing Your Relationship with Your Mother**

How would you describe your childhood relationship with your mother? What *specific* experiences come to mind that characterize that relationship?

(1) _____
_____
_____

(2) _____
_____
_____

(3) _____
_____
_____

(4) _____
_____
_____

(5) _____
_____
_____

How do you think these experiences, and your overall relationship with your mother, affect you today?

_____
_____
_____

What was positive about the way your mother interacted with you?

_____
_____
_____

In what ways would you like to be a different kind of parent than your mother was?

_____

_____

_____

Can you imagine your mother as a child? What was she like? What was her childhood like?

_____

_____

_____

If you could write a letter to your mother *when she was a child*, what would you say? Obviously, your mother's own childhood experiences do not excuse any ways in which she was not able to be the parent you needed. Still, understanding what shaped her can be very healing for you, as it helps you to realize that her behavior toward you actually had little to do with you personally, no matter how you behaved. This letter is worth writing because it is another step in helping you come to terms with your own childhood. Do so now on a separate piece of paper.

## Practice: **Healing Your Relationship with Your Father**

How would you describe your childhood relationship with your father? What *specific* experiences come to mind that characterize that relationship?

**(1)** _____

_____

_____

**(2)** _____

_____

_____

**(3)** _____

_____

_____

**(4)** _____

_____

_____

**(5)** _____

_____

How do you think these experiences, and your overall relationship with your father, affect you today?

_____

_____

_____

What was positive about the way your father interacted with you?

_____

_____

_____

In what ways would you like to be a different kind of parent than your father was?

_____

_____

_____

Can you imagine your father as a child? What was he like? What was his childhood like?

_____

_____

_____

If you could write a letter to your father _when he was a child_, what would you say? Obviously, your father's own childhood experiences do not excuse any ways in which he was not able to be the parent you needed. Still, understanding what shaped him can be very healing for you, as it helps you to realize that his behavior toward you actually had little to do with you personally, no matter how you behaved. This letter is worth writing because it is another step in helping you come to terms with your own childhood. Do so now on a separate piece of paper.

## Practice: Say What You Need to Hear

Imagine yourself as a small child. You were _so_ cute. You weren't perfect. Sometimes you made mistakes. Sometimes you intentionally misbehaved. But your heart was so big. You wanted so much to be loved. You wanted to be a good person, to make a contribution, to make your parents proud. And you tried so hard!

What helped you on that path? Do you remember when an adult was kind to you? Do you remember when an adult listened to you? When you felt like an adult really saw you and appreciated you—valued you just for exactly who you were? Do you remember how that made you feel? Maybe that adult was one of your parents. Maybe that adult was a teacher, a coach, a next-door neighbor, or even someone you met only once. Put your hand on your heart right now and send that person love and gratitude for the way they helped that young person who was you.

Now, think about the most helpful things that anyone ever said to you. List them here. Notice that sometimes it was the feelings behind the words, more than even the wisdom of them, that helped you.

_____

_____

_____

Now, think about the words you wish someone had said to you when you were a child. What words did you need to hear from the adults in your life? Write them here.

_____

_____

_____

Notice the love behind these words that you needed to hear. You can still give yourself that love. In fact, you can give yourself these words. Go ahead and say those words aloud, to yourself. Notice how that feels.

Why not do that daily? You deserve a cheerleader who knows exactly what you need to hear! Write down what you need to hear on sticky notes and stick them all over your house and car. Every time you read one, pause and let it fully sink in. As neuroscientist Rick Hanson says, "*By taking just a few extra seconds to stay with a positive experience—even the comfort in a single breath—you'll help turn a passing mental state into lasting neural structure.*"[60] In other words, when you say loving things to yourself and savor how that makes you feel, you're rewiring your brain to be happier!

## Practice: **Journaling to Develop the Prefrontal Cortex**

Research has repeatedly shown that journaling is an effective way to process emotions, build insight, and stay on track with personal growth programs. You could think of this workbook as a journal with specific prompts. But you might also want to start another journal, where you have the unstructured space to record and reflect on your experiences.

Journaling is a form of "reflective investigation" in which we focus our awareness on our own experience. This develops what psychologists call "the observing ego," which is the part of our mind that is self-aware and able to observe ourselves. Modern researchers would probably locate the observing ego in the prefrontal cortex, so strengthening it gives us more insight and self-control.

Linda Graham, the author of the wonderful book *Bouncing Back*, says that "*the key to investigating what is and isn't working is to ask ourselves the question, 'What story am I believing right now?*"[61]

The story we believe about our current circumstance is always creating our response to that circumstance. If we want to change that response, we need to see those beliefs more objectively. The following exercise, which is adapted from Linda Graham's work, is designed to strengthen your prefrontal cortex so that it can see more options and solve problems more flexibly. It can also help you resolve problems that might seem unsolvable.

**Identify a particular problem with your child that has remained unresolved**, despite your best efforts.

_____

_____

_____

**Put on your "observer" hat and reflect on the problem.** Become aware of the sensations in your body as you consider this issue. Notice any feelings or thoughts (for example, "*I notice I feel a tightness in my chest… I feel trapped… I notice I keep thinking that my son will never change*"). Write down what you observe.

_____

_____

_____

**As you observe your own process of trying to solve the problem, ask yourself, "What story am I believing right now?"** about your child, about the situation, about yourself.

_____

_____

_____

**Reflect on what you've noticed.** Notice any new perspectives or options that arise as you consider this.

_____

_____

_____

## MINDFULNESS: YOUR TRANSFORMATIONAL PARENTING TOOL

How can you stay centered, so you can keep from getting triggered and thrown off balance by strong emotions? The truth is, you probably can't! Life is constant flow, so you can't stay in any one state, even being centered. What you _can_ do is notice when you get off kilter, so you can regain your balance. This is also known as mindfulness.

What does mindfulness mean? It means that you heighten your attention toward what's happening inside you, instead of allowing strong emotions to hijack you. You really notice what you're experiencing. Every time you take a deep breath and feel the sensations in your body, you're practicing mindfulness. Meditators call this bringing your conscious attention to your experience. Psychologists call it strengthening your observing ego. One nine-year-old called it "just not hitting someone in the mouth."

> Mindfulness is what gives you the awareness and self-control to enable you to slow down and use your Pause Button. Wise teachers throughout the ages have observed that the moment between perception and action is where we have the choice not to get hijacked by our automatic emotional response. By observing, you give yourself the power to choose your response to a situation.

Mindfulness is also what helps you to recover when you're upset, in two ways. First, you don't get swamped so easily by strong feelings because mindfulness helps heal your triggers and diminishes your volatility. Second, by becoming more conscious of upsets as you feel them, you develop a new relationship with them. You're more able to step out of them, to let them go and move on. The more you cultivate mindfulness, the more you can show up as the patient, emotionally generous parent every child deserves.

All of us have the ability to stop and become more aware at any time, but, if we want the tools to use mindfulness in those tough moments, we need to practice them. Over time, mindfulness practices actually change our brain's structure, making us more aware, more regulated, and happier.

**Any regular habit in which you stop and bring your conscious awareness to the present moment is a mindfulness practice.** You can even invent your own daily mindfulness practices, and these can take less than a minute. In this section, I'll introduce you to some basic practices and point you toward more resources. There are thousands of mindfulness resources available to you online, at no charge.

## *Your Brain On Meditation*

Imagine that scientists have discovered a new medicine that measurably:[62]

- improves immune function
- reduces inflammation
- reduces blood pressure
- reduces premenstrual and menopausal symptoms
- reduces anxiety
- improves depression
- improves distractibility and impulsivity related to ADHD (attention-deficit hyperactivity disorder)
- makes it easier to stop smoking
- decreases emotional eating
- increases emotional intelligence, insight and self-regulation
- decreases feelings of stress
- decreases pain associated with chronic illness
- improves memory and concentration
- improves decision making and creative thinking
- protects the brain against the effects of aging
- increases happiness and compassion

In sum, this medicine measurably increases health, happiness, and mental function in everyone who takes it, with zero negative side effects. There is only one drawback to this medicine. You have to sit quietly for 20 minutes while you take it.

I realize that for parents, 20 minutes is hard to come by. However, five or 10 minutes is a perfect place to start. You can even begin with two minutes, as you fall asleep at night. Really! The important thing is to begin, and to practice daily. You'll like the results so much, you'll keep finding new ways to fit meditation, even for a few minutes a day, into your life.

The best news is that all of those measurable changes in your physical, emotional, and mental well-being are accompanied by permanent physical changes in your brain structure. For instance, as mentioned earlier in this book (see page 22) even eight weeks of regular meditation will measurably shrink the size of the amygdala while simultaneously increasing the connections between the limbic system and the prefrontal cortex,[63,64,65] all of which make it easier to calm yourself.

One last point. Most people struggle to "quiet their mind" during meditation. But please don't worry about that. That isn't your goal. Your goal is to be present with whatever is happening. When you notice that your mind has gone off on a tangent, lovingly bring yourself back to stillness. That might happen 60 times in a minute, and guess what that gives you? Sixty opportunities to become more aware. Sixty opportunities to improve your concentration and focus. Sixty opportunities to increase your ability to love, by loving yourself more, even though you aren't perfect!

## Practice: **Basic Meditation**

The first time you do this, don't plan to do it for more than five minutes. Even two minutes is a good place to start. Just find a time when you can practice daily, and keep practicing at the same time every day. As you notice how good this feels, you'll keep doing it for longer.

1.  Sit comfortably in any position, but don't lie down or you'll find it harder to concentrate. A straight spine makes it easier to concentrate. (You don't get extra points for discomfort.)

2.  Notice your breath going in and out. Don't try to control it. Just notice.

3.  Greet yourself with love. How are you feeling? Whatever you feel is okay; just accept it.

4.  Become aware of the sensations in your body. Emotions will also show up as sensations in your body.

5.  Don't try to empty your mind or stop your thoughts. Just notice any thoughts and let them go. Don't follow the thoughts or the story lines. Notice that the thoughts are not necessarily even true. Some meditators simply notice and label what's happening "Thinking."

6.  You will notice that your mind has wandered. Just keep bringing yourself back to your body in the present moment. If it makes it easier to stay attentive, focus on your breath.

7.  It's okay if it isn't super-quiet. Just notice the sounds and let them go.

8.  You can also experiment with a mantra that inspires or soothes you.

9.  You will notice little itches or other sensations. It's fine to scratch, but resisting the urge to scratch helps you develop the ability not to respond automatically to triggers.

10.  At the end of your meditation, stretch and give yourself a big hug.

## Practice: **Just Breathe**

This is a deceptively simple practice. Simply remind yourself to pay attention to breathing, calmly and deeply, as often as you remember, all day long.

Put sticky notes up all over your house and in your car that say "BREATHE." When you see one, take three deep breaths. This practice will make it easier to remember to breathe and stay calm when you have one of those inevitable stress-inducing moments.

Remembering to breathe may sound simple, but it will change your life. Late for an appointment? Breathe. Kids just dump their toys in the toilet? Breathe. Taking deep breaths so you get more oxygen actually reduces the level of stress hormones circulating in your body and helps you think more clearly.

Remember, noticing your breath is your Pause Button. It brings you back into the moment, so you have a choice. Do you really want to get hijacked by the stress and end up yelling at your kid, or could you choose a better way to handle things?

Sometimes when we bring more mindfulness to our bodies, we begin to release stored-up tears. If this happens for you, welcome those tears. You're bringing more spaciousness to your life by healing those old hurt places.

## Practice: **Guided Meditation**

If you're just beginning to meditate, the easiest way is probably to listen to guided meditations. There are many resources online. There's a page of my favorites on my website at AhaParenting.com/Workbook.

While guided meditations offer many benefits, once you establish the habit, you'll want to move on to unguided meditation, in which you simply sit with your own mind. This is a bit harder for you, but because it asks your brain to function in a new way, it also means the brain develops new capacities.

## Practice: **15-Second Check-In**

1. Stop.
2. Drop what you're doing.
3. Breathe deeply a few times.
4. Bring yourself fully present.

5. Ask yourself: *"How are you?"*
6. Whatever the answer, it's okay.
7. Accept yourself exactly as you are in this moment.
8. Give yourself a big hug.

## Practice: **The One-Minute Pause that Refreshes**

Stop.
Drop what you're doing.
Breathe deeply a few times.
Notice the sensations in your body.
Your feet touching the floor. Your hungry stomach growling.
Notice what your senses are taking in.
The sounds around you. The breeze on your cheek.
If any emotions are present, notice how they show up.
Are they linked to sensations in your body?
Are they linked to thoughts?
Let any thoughts that arise simply pass away.
Don't follow the story line.
Just stay with your physical experience.
Observe without trying to change anything.
Keep breathing deeply.
Wrap yourself in love.

## Practice: **Three-Minute Blessing**

You can do this anytime, anywhere. Just stop, take a deep breath, and send love throughout your whole self: your body, your emotions, your mind. Imagine yourself filled, surrounded, and protected by love and light. Then, direct that love toward your child (or any other person). Imagine your child filled with love, surrounded by love, protected by love. Does this affect your child? The scientific research isn't conclusive, but in my opinion, the answer is yes. But, even if not, the research is very clear that sending love improves the health and happiness of the sender.[66] The more often you feel love and send it to others, and the longer you do it, the better, but even three minutes can shift your mood, especially if you do it regularly.

## Practice: **The Body Scan**

We know that if we allow ourselves to feel our emotions, they begin to dissipate. And we know that emotions are stored in our bodies. That's why body scans are a wonderful way to clear emotions and keep your emotional backpack light. Because you have to concentrate as you move through your body to stay with each new experience, body scans also strengthen concentration. You can find a body scan meditation that I've recorded for you at AhaParenting.com/Workbook.

## Practice: **Chanting**

Have a few minutes while you're doing dishes or sitting in traffic? Chanting is a time-honored mindfulness practice that distracts your mind with something constructive to do while you sit in a state of grace for a few minutes. Think of it as a micro-vacation for your mind, to give your being more access to the spaciousness beyond your mind.

My personal chanting favorites are the Hawaiian "Ho'oponopono" forgiveness meditation and the Buddhist Loving-Kindness meditation. The Hawaiian meditation[67] seems to clear blocks between us and other people (without them even knowing why), but it's also powerful at creating self-acceptance when spoken toward oneself. Just keep repeating it. The Loving-Kindness meditation[68] has been linked to many beneficial effects. Don't be surprised if you start loving traffic jams.

### Ho'oponopono Meditation

I'm sorry.
Please forgive me.
I love you.
Thank you.

### Loving-Kindness Meditation

May I be happy.
May I be well.
May I be peaceful.
May my heart be filled with love.
May you be happy.
May you be well.

May you be peaceful.
May your heart be filled with love.
May everyone be happy.
May everyone be well.
May everyone be peaceful.
May everyone's heart be filled with love.

## Practice: **Staying Conscious Throughout Your Day**

We all tend to go on autopilot as we rush through the day. Instead of noticing what's actually happening, our mind's default mode is to ruminate on the same repetitive thought patterns. But that increases your stress level and disconnects you from your own current experience, from other people, and from life.

There are a number of advantages to bringing more conscious awareness to your experience throughout your day:

- You process your emotions as they come up, rather than stuffing them in your emotional backpack.
- You feel more connection with your child (or whoever you're interacting with) and they feel more connection with you.

- You don't get hijacked so easily when big emotions get triggered.
- You savor the little moments of life so it feels more meaningful. You feel more alive.

Here are some ideas to return yourself to a state of more conscious presence during your day:

1.  As you do those "mindless" tasks with your child, bring mindful attention to them. As you change that diaper, notice your little one's soft skin and beautiful eyes. As you carry him up the stairs, notice the weight of his little head on your shoulder, his arms clasped around your neck.

2.  Take every opportunity to notice the sensations in your body, instead of following your mind with its endless chatter. As you scrub the oatmeal pan, notice the feeling of the water against your skin. As you drive, really notice the passing scenery instead of going on automatic pilot.

3.  Create rituals that remind you to be present, pegged to something that is already a habit. For instance, every morning when you wake, stretch your body and find something to be grateful for. Drink herbal tea often to nourish yourself throughout your day, and, as you savor the first sip of each cup, bring yourself back into conscious presence. As you step out of the door of your house every day, make it a habit to take a moment to breathe in the morning air and feel it against your face. Whenever you're reunited with a loved one during the day, give them a long hug and really drink in their presence.

4.  Put little sticky notes around your house with reminders to breathe and short mantras that inspire you.

5.  Set a bell alarm tone on your phone to ring every hour. When it goes off, check in with yourself. Send yourself some love. Ask yourself if there's anything you need, and either give it to yourself at that moment or put it on your schedule to do later in the day.

## Using Gratitude To Transform Your Family Life

A whole body of research shows that regularly experiencing gratitude makes us happier and healthier.[69] When we're struggling emotionally, gratitude heals. And gratitude somehow seems to open the door to the life we want. The deeper our gratitude, the greater our ability to receive and the more we get out of life. But why is gratitude so effective?

- **The state of gratitude is very similar to love.** Scientists say that gratitude shifts our heart into a more "coherent" (healthier) rhythm.[70] Meditators might say it opens our hearts so we can take in the blessings that surround us. No matter how difficult the day, there is always something for which to be grateful. And the better you feel, the more effectively you can respond to any challenge.

- **Focusing on the positive makes us happy.** Savoring positive emotions actually rewires the brain. Feeling gratitude lifts us out of the mind's usual restless feeling of "not enough" into the joy of sufficiency. When we dwell on a "good" feeling, our body chemistry changes to make us feel better. And our neural wiring shifts from the mind's usual negativity bias—watching out for threats—to a positivity bias—noticing all the good things surrounding us.

- **We program our subconscious to create more of what we're appreciating**, especially when we hold a picture in our mind that triggers a feeling of gratitude.

# Practice: **Gratitude**

Let's do an experiment. Right now. Name 10 things for which you're grateful. Actually do this, and name at least 10.

(1) _____

(2) _____

(3) _____

(4) _____

(5) _____

(6) _____

(7) _____

(8) _____

(9) _____

(10) _____

Even in hard times, there's so much to be grateful for.
Savor that gratitude.

What do you notice after doing this practice? Research shows that you can shift a bad mood simply with an avalanche of appreciation. You can use small variations on this practice all day long to upgrade your mood, any time.
Following are a few more quick practices that will change your life—and your relationship with your child!

# Practice: **Gratitude Journal**

Every night before you go to sleep, write down at least three things you're grateful for (it's okay to write the same things on different days). Research shows that people who do this get happier almost immediately, and they stay happier for as long as they continue this practice.[71] If one day you've had a hard time with your child, be sure to find three things to appreciate about your child.

# Practice: **Gratitude for Your Child**

Every day, find a moment to sit with each of your kids and feel gratitude for them. How did you get lucky enough to have this child put into your arms? Don't let your worries steal this precious moment. Instead, remind yourself of how much you love this child. Let gratitude wash over you. Pour your love and appreciation into your child. You just changed your physiology, and your child's, to make both of you happier and healthier.

## Practice: **Express Appreciation to Your Child**

Express appreciation to your child throughout your day, as specifically as you can.

- *"Wow! You picked up your toys! I love how orderly this room looks now!"*
- *"Thank you for getting your chore done with only one reminder!"*

Notice that your child doesn't have to be perfect to deserve your appreciation. The more you appreciate steps in the right direction, the more motivated your child will be to get there.

And notice this doesn't take any extra time out of your day. All it takes is for you to notice anything positive and express it to your child. In fact, if you really want to see a child blossom, try an avalanche of appreciation. Why stop at three things? Why not acknowledge your child throughout the day with as much enthusiasm as you can? Instead of evaluating your child or giving general praise (*"You're my good girl"*), be as specific as possible about what she's doing or about the positive effects including how you feel.

- *"I notice you got your pajamas on all by yourself!"*
- *"Thank you for helping your sister with that—she loved having you show her."*
- *"I appreciate how you took care of that."*
- *"You two kids figured out how to share that cookie fairly all by yourselves!"*
- *"I love how you help me find things in the grocery store. It's so much fun to work with you!"*

Just express your appreciation as many times as you can, every day for a week, accompanying it frequently with an affectionate hug. Watch your child's happiness—and your relationship with your child—transform.

## Practice: **Train Yourself to Find Something Positive in the Situation**

Throughout your day, stop, breathe deeply, and express gratitude for life having brought you to this moment. What if that moment happens to be a hard one? All the more important to empower yourself by noticing any ways that challenge is serving you. (And you might find that your perspective completely shifts, so instead of feeling annoyed at your child's jacket on the floor, you're grateful that your child came into your life.) This may feel artificial at first, but you'll quickly notice that your attitude really does depend on your perspective.

- *"Thank goodness she had this meltdown at home instead of in the store."*
- *"I'm getting better and better at dealing with his anger calmly."*
- *"This is a chance for him to get out all the tension from starting the new school."*
- *"At least this came up now, so I can see how upset he is about it and address it."*
- *"She cries with me because she trusts me."*
- *"How I handle my child's emotions will make a difference for the rest of his life."*
- *"This isn't a disaster. It's an opportunity for growth."*
- *"Being a parent is a chance to be a hero."*
- *"True, my child sometimes drives me crazy. But what about those people who so desperately want a child and can't have one? Or who mourn a child? I am lucky, lucky, lucky to have this child, upsets and all."*

Gratitude doesn't mean that you don't take action to change things that aren't working. But you'll do that better from the feeling of goodness that gratitude gives us.

Can't find your gratitude? Life can be hard, even heartbreaking. Yet, even during tough times, there is so much to be grateful for. Remind yourself of what you already know: you are truly blessed.

# Teaching Gratitude to Your Child

When you experience the benefits of gratitude, you'll want to share them with your child. Just remember that children don't have the context to understand their many blessings, and guilt is not an effective teacher. Modeling is the best strategy, simply noting aloud, frequently, how lucky we are to have this beautiful day, this bountiful meal, this reliable car, such a terrific teacher or neighbor, and, of course, each other. Information is also useful, given judiciously and matter-of-factly in an age-appropriate manner and without guilt or shame:

- *"Some kids don't have a back yard to play in like we do—that's why we cherish it and take good care of it."*
- *"Grandma is getting older and won't be with us forever, so we take advantage of every chance we can to visit her, even though it's sometimes not so interesting for you."*

And, of course, adopting a daily gratitude practice as a family will give your child the experience of how wonderful gratitude feels. For instance, have your family count blessings by listing things everyone is grateful for every night at dinner or bedtime. In one study,[72] a group of middle-school students were asked to count their blessings for two weeks by listing five things every day that they felt grateful for. Another group were asked to list complaints about hassles in their lives. The kids who focused on blessings for just two weeks felt more gratitude, more life satisfaction, and more optimism, and were also more positive in general—even several months later.

## *Using Mindfulness To Manage Stress*

We all know that it's those times when we're stressed that we're more likely to snap at our child. It's impossible to be emotionally generous when we're tense. That's because we're already halfway to fight, flight, or freeze mode, so any childish behavior pushes us over the edge. But life with children will always include childish behavior, and life is full of triggers that make us stressed.

Of course, those triggers, be they tantrums or traffic jams, don't actually make us stressed. We make ourselves stressed in response to them. It's a choice. It may be hard to believe, but it's entirely possible to breathe deeply and feel at peace during a traffic jam—or even a tantrum.

In fact, your attitude toward stress and stressful events determines how they affect you. Research[73] shows that if you think stress is exciting, you don't react to it in ways that are bad for you. It's when we "resist" stressful events that our health and well-being suffer.

So it's true that modern life creates a ton of stress, and that when we get overwhelmed, stress is bad for us. But it's also true that what stresses out one person may just roll off the back of another, and our attitude largely determines how overwhelmed we will get. So stress is partly what happens to us, but mostly our reaction to it.

Each of us has a responsibility as a parent to manage our own stress. Stress-inviting events are inevitable, but stress is not.

I'm stressed, we're rushing, and before I know it, I'm yelling. When I see the look on his face, I feel awful. He was just being a kid. And I was just stressed out.

— Dana, mother of five
and eight-year-olds

**A three-pronged approach works best:**

1. Cultivate daily mindfulness practices so you notice as you slip into stress mode and can make the choice to shift gears.

2. Practice radical self-care, so you have more internal resources to deal with stress.

3. Pare down the stressors in your life.

The practices in this section on mindfulness and in the following section on self-care will help you with numbers one and two. But right now, let's tackle what's often the toughest: number three. Most of us resist the idea of paring down the stressors in our lives. After all, what would you give up? Sometimes, that's because we're perfectionists, bullying ourselves to take on more than we can gracefully handle. Sometimes, it's because we need to keep ourselves exhausted to feel good enough. And sometimes, it's because we've become addicted to adrenaline.

If that sounds familiar, you'll be interested to know that stress hormones such as adrenaline and cortisol may seem to give you energy, but they also wear out your body. They signal your metabolism to put on pounds. They fray your patience. They dull your ability to relax into the joy of each moment. They keep sleep from fully renewing your body. And they compromise what you can offer your child, because it's impossible to be fully present and patient when you're stressed.

## Practice: **Does Your Schedule Keep You Stressed?**

Much of the stress we feel comes from routinely over-scheduling. But that's a choice we make. We think it's helpful to squeeze more in, but it always costs us. Kids thrive on connection, so when we get too busy to lovingly connect with them, they act out. Prioritize your kids and your relationship with your partner or spouse. Then drop anything else you can. Your house can stay a mess a little longer. Your children need you in a good mood *much* more than they need a tidy house.

**What could you pare back to cut down on the amount of stress in your schedule?**

1 _____

2 _____

3 _____

4 _____

5 _____

## Practice: **Solve Those Stressful Times of Day**

Are there certain parts of your daily routine that always feel stressful? For example, is it impossible to get out of the house on time in the morning, or does bedtime drive you crazy?

**Which parts of your day stress you out?**

(1) _____

(2) _____

(3) _____

It's your life and you're in charge, whether it feels that way or not. Letting yourself feel victimized doesn't help your kids. Consider how you could make these times of day better, either through better scheduling or by nurturing yourself through necessary tasks. If mornings are impossible, maybe you need to be self-disciplined enough to go to bed earlier. Do you find it excruciating to take your child to the playground and push the swing? Find a way to make it fun for yourself by connecting more with your child or using the activity as a sort of moving meditation. Do you find diaper changing unpleasant? Use this time to look into your baby's eyes and tell her how adored she is. Or just stop fighting with your toddler and change his diaper standing up.

**Pick a stressful time of your day. What ideas do you have to de-stress it?**

(1) _____

(2) _____

(3) _____

If the whole family needs a better routine for a certain time of day, write one out that works for both you and your child. Post it, complete with photos of your child doing his activities. Keep refining the new schedule until you can enjoy it stress-free. Make sure you include something you *love* doing in that part of the routine, whether that's the bedtime snuggle or a family hug or a blessing in the morning before you head out the door.

## PREVENTIVE MAINTENANCE: SELF-CARE

Parenting is hard. It requires extreme emotional generosity. But you can't be emotionally generous when you're stressed out or depleted. You can't even regulate your own emotions, and your whole family ends up in the emotional equivalent of the breakdown lane. That's why your number-one responsibility as a parent is doing whatever preventive maintenance is necessary to maintain your own well-being at a high level.

Of course, you're human, so sometimes, no matter how hard you try, you'll take your upset out on your child. You may have noticed that no matter how remorseful you feel later, it doesn't help much the next time you get upset. That's because you're actually doing the best you can with the resources you have. Beating yourself up won't help you do better. Truly. What you need is more support. And it's your job to get that support and give it to yourself.

So every time you lose it, that's a learning opportunity. What might have helped you notice that you were getting cranky? What did you need at that moment to restore your sense of well-being? What could you have done instead of taking your upset out on your child? What would have allowed you to calm the storm instead of escalating it? What could you do to give that support to yourself in the future, both on an ongoing basis and in the next tough moment?

This is hard. Most parents have real-life pressures that make support a scarce commodity, and our society doesn't offer parents much support. But remember that the support you need is both internal and external. Once you start giving yourself support, external support has a way of becoming more available. That's why the first step is always to find a way to give yourself support. For instance, you might choose to begin by trying one or more of the following:

- Use the practices in the previous sections of this book to help yourself develop and maintain a sense of well-being.

- Work through old issues that have been dragging you down.

- Practice talking to yourself like someone you love.

- Find another parent to talk to on a regular basis. (Patty Wipfler of Hand-in-Hand Parenting has pioneered the practice of trading "listening time" with other parents. The Hand-in-Hand website is a treasure of information on this and other parenting topics.)

- Get more sleep. Go to bed when the kids do. (You won't be surprised to hear that research has now proven what every parent already knows: we're better parents when we get more sleep![74])

- Find a way to exercise, with your child if necessary.

## Practice: Jump-Start Your Self-Care

What one step can you take today to take care of yourself so that you feel more energized and emotionally generous?

_____

_____

_____

### Self-Care Means Caring For Yourself

> I read a lot about self-care, but just have trouble fitting it into my life. I am breastfeeding and it's just not practical to leave my child for a whole day to take care of myself. He is not a great sleeper, so I don't get great sleep.
>
> — Clara, mother of a baby and a toddler

If you've been reading this section and getting frustrated, thinking that self-care does not apply to you, I urge you to stop and reconsider. I understand how hard it is to have your sleep interrupted. But you, even more than other parents, need to give yourself whatever care you can. Remember, the "self" in self-care is not just the receiver. It's the giver. Self-care is what you give to yourself. And that is not easy, but it is possible.

You don't have to leave your baby all day. You don't have to spend a dime. You just have to talk to yourself tenderly, like someone you love. That really is the most important thing. Then, extend that to treating yourself tenderly, and look for ways to nurture yourself all day long.

So, if you're feeling a bit frustrated or demoralized with this section of the book, that's your signal that you need self-care and that you feel trapped and unable to give it to yourself because of the needs of your family. My challenge to you is to find ways to nurture yourself anyway. Start small and move toward big. What's one way can you nurture yourself today?

### Cultivating Your Own Well-Being

> If nothing else, when you model good self-care to your children, you teach them the importance of dealing with life's challenges rather than numbing ourselves to them.
>
> — Susan Stiffelman[75]

Well-being could be defined as a state of physical, emotional, mental, and spiritual wellness. It doesn't mean that your life is perfect. Instead, it means that you usually feel you have the inner and outer resources to cope with life, and when you don't, you take steps to replenish them. You feel aware and alive. That well-being allows you to tap into more optimism and emotional generosity.

**Well-being doesn't mean you don't experience discomfort.** In general, discomfort is a teacher, and it's an important part of growth. That's why when your baby is struggling to turn over, you don't turn her over. You let her develop her muscles and learn how to do it for herself. If she doesn't get to do that, she'll be delayed in learning to crawl. So well-being means you feel you have the inner resources, most of the time, to tolerate discomfort, rise to the occasion, and reach for growth.

**Well-being doesn't mean you're always happy.** In fact, constant happiness isn't our goal. It isn't possible. Our goal is awareness, which allows us to notice when we're uncomfortable. But instead of just reaching for something to numb the discomfort (such as a screen or food), if we allow ourselves to sit with the discomfort and actually feel it, we'll notice the deeper cause.

Because we accept the reality of what's happening, we find ourselves better able to cope with it. If we take action, it's to address the actual cause, not just numb the feelings. Because we solve problems at their source, our lives work better. Because we're willing to accept our emotions, we work through them and let them go. You'll find that greater awareness brings you a deeper level of joy, meaning, and aliveness. That's what I mean by a sense of well-being.

> Most of us find that when we can stay connected to our internal fountain of well-being, it overflows onto our children and we're more patient, loving, joyful parents.

To love our children unconditionally, we need to keep our own pitchers full so we can keep pouring as needed. Quite simply, we can only give what we have inside. And, even if parenting is the most meaningful part of your life, it still requires a whole lot of giving.

And yet, most of us live in constant stress, which means we're often running on empty. Many days we wake up wishing life could be different. Small wonder we lose patience with our children. And then we feel even worse.

Sadly, remorse and self-blame after we lose patience don't change anything. Actually, they make things worse, because you can't be emotionally generous when you're feeling like a bad person.

What if, instead, you could find a way to stay in a positive state more often? You can. Not all the time, of course—into every life some stress must fall. But most of us can find a way to be more positive more often. It starts with finding ways to nurture and nourish ourselves, so we can stay more centered. But if you're like most parents, that's not so easy.

**The secret is radical self-care.** What do I mean by radical? I mean not just tending to yourself after everyone else's needs are met. I mean actually moving self-care high up on your priority list. I mean overwhelming yourself with love and appreciation.

Because that's the only way you can be the happy, patient, unconditionally-loving parent your child deserves. And because you deserve it! Wouldn't that be a radical act? Here's how to do it.

1. **Nurture yourself as you would your beloved child.** Treat yourself as you would your child—do you need a snack or a break right now so you don't have a meltdown? Find a way to help yourself feel better. Maybe that means finding a way for your child to occupy himself, or maybe it means giving him a snack, too.

   - Do you need to go to bed when your child does tonight so you get a really good night's sleep? Why not do that routinely while your child is still waking up at night? It won't last forever (even though it seems like it will!).

- Do you need to take Sunday off and just enjoy being alive? You can't stop being a parent, but you don't have to do laundry, you can leave the dishes in the sink, and you can have peanut butter sandwiches and carrots out of the bag for dinner. If you feel like you're playing hooky, ask yourself: Whose life is it, anyway? And, at the end of it, who will have been responsible for how you felt during it?

- What if your child needs you at this moment? I'm not suggesting that you shouldn't take care of your child. I'm suggesting that there is usually a way to take care of yourself at the same time, even if it's just being present with yourself and treating yourself tenderly.

- Sometimes we simply can't give ourselves what we need, just as we can't always fix whatever is wrong for our child. In those cases, self-care means listening with compassion, whether to our child or to our own distress. In other words, just notice what's happening in the present moment. "*The baby is screaming… my jaw is tight… my shoulders are clenched…*" You don't have to change anything. Just "witnessing" with compassion is a huge gift to yourself. Often, it shifts your experience. And, of course, make a promise to yourself to do more self-care as soon as you can manage it.

2. **Take responsibility for meeting your own needs and solving the problems life presents to you.**

   - What needs do you have that weren't met when you were little? That's what you have to give to yourself now. Maybe you felt you were never quite good enough. Can you start reassuring yourself, every time you look in the mirror, that you're more than enough and are deeply loved? Every time you feel "bad" in any way, just notice that contracted feeling, breathe into it, and love yourself through it. You'll notice that love is bigger than any bad feelings, and often melts them right away. Once we've taken care of that old unfinished business, it gets much easier to find ways to take care of ourselves in the present.

   - Do you need some appreciation? Give it to yourself! Some of us have a hard time feeling appreciated by others. If that's the case for you, daily practice with giving yourself appreciation will increase your ability to receive that love and give it to your children.

   - And what if your problem is in the now? Fights with your partner? A job you hate? A life on constant overwhelm? Challenges like these are tough, but when we leave them unaddressed, they demoralize us. Can you take a step, any step, toward solving that problem now? It may not solve everything overnight, but moving in the right direction will help you increase your sense of well-being and stop you from spilling tension onto your child.

3. **Don't postpone joy!** We're all guilty of taking the joy that pours into our lives for granted. We let it slip right through our fingers in the name of efficiency and responsibility. But what if reveling in that joy is part of what allows you to love unconditionally, because it grows your heart? What if enjoying your daughter's dancing on the sidewalk helps her start the day basking in your love? What if that water fight is just what you need to defuse tension and reconnect with your kid? What if those bedtime stories give your child the message that you'll always be there for a snuggle, no matter how old he gets? What if you and your partner need those kisses to stay connected so you're a better parenting team? What if that bubble bath would help you be a more patient parent tomorrow? What if you never know which sunset is your last?

**Don't wait. Commit to radical self-care.**

# Self-Care Ideas from Parents

Many parents, especially mothers, say that they need ideas on how to bring short moments of self-care into their day, so I've compiled suggestions for you—from other parents! The key is to give yourself explicit permission to take a few minutes several times a day to re-charge and re-center. Remember, you can't give your children the emotional generosity they deserve if you're running on empty. Most of these are ideas you can do while with your children.

**BREATHE**

- "Just regular deep breathing for a few minutes throughout the day has made a huge improvement to my mood and well-being!"
- "If I close my eyes and breathe even once a day for five minutes, I feel better and I parent better."
- "Just a few moments of deep breathing and visualizing something positive."

**MOVE**

- Exercise increases endorphins, which make us happy, and serotonin, which calms us, so it's an effective treatment for depression and anxiety. Moving your body is the fastest route to shifting your mood and enhancing your sense of well-being.
- "Find a gym with a nursery and go there often."
- "Get your kids out of the house and run around with them at the park."
- "Take your baby with you to a 'Baby and Me' exercise class."
- "Take my dog for a run."
- "Work out, even if it's just for 15 minutes."
- "Take walks during lunch at work."
- "Lay on a yoga ball and roll back gently to stretch out your neck and upper back."

**SLEEP**

- "Go to bed when the children do."
- "Nap with your kids."

**MUSIC**

- "Put on music you like to lift your mood."
- "Put on dance music and move with your kids."
- "Put on your favorite music and sing along loudly."

**NATURE**

- "Wear your baby, put your child in a stroller, and get outside."
- "When I need a minute or two, I step out back and enjoy looking at my plants."
- "Pulling a few weeds is a good mindless activity that makes me feel great."
- "Just stand in the sunshine for a minute and drink it in."

- "Plant flowers. If the kids are big enough to play outside, they can plant with you, or they can play while you plant."
- "Smell flowers."
- "If you can't get outside, play nature sounds on your phone or computer. It may sound silly, but it helps me."

## MEDITATE

- "Even five minutes a day helps."
- "I do guided meditation, so the kids hear what I'm doing. I invite them to do it with me or give me space to do it alone."
- "Part of my practice is learning that it doesn't have to be perfect (or perfectly quiet) for meditation to be worthwhile."

## YOGA

- "Put on a 15-minute yoga video and let the kids join in. Kids love 'Silly to Calm' or 'Cosmic Kids' yoga on YouTube."
- "I retreat to my yoga mat when I need to reset. I diffuse essential oils, fold into child's pose, and focus on my breathing. My two-year-old usually comes with me, but she knows the yoga area is a place for calmness."

## SELF-NURTURE

- "When the kids are busy playing, stop working. Just sit down by yourself for a few minutes."
- "A hot bubble bath alone."
- "Washing my face and/or hands and putting on lotion."
- "I put ice and lemon in my water and use a pretty glass instead of some cartoon cup."
- "I make sure I have fast, high-protein stuff around to eat."

## MORNING MIRACLE

- "I wake up half an hour before my kids and have coffee in the stillness of the morning. When they wake up, I'm in a good mood."
- "I wake up one hour before my kids. It's my time. I use it for Bible study, writing in my journal, and yoga. The energy I get outweighs the sleep I lose."

## BE PRESENT, SAVOR, APPRECIATE

- "I keep an appreciation journal and make sure that every day I write at least three things."
- "Notice moments throughout the day and drink from them. Like noticing your child's smile or an act of affection or hearing birds singing or the sweet sound of silence for just a moment."
- "I offer a big hug to my son and just sink into it and stay there for a while."
- "I do small, mental check-ins with myself."

## Practice: **Joy List**

Taking care of ourselves has to include learning how to tap into joy. Otherwise, parenting becomes one long burden (and so does life!). Kids need to know they're a source of joy for us. If they sense that we find life with them to be drudgery, what can they conclude about themselves?

Of course, there are times when parenting *can* feel burdensome. But we can minimize those times by finding the joy that sings silently in the ordinary moments of our lives.

Our ability to choose to feel the joy in spite of the burdens depends also on keeping our own personal cups full. All humans need the replenishment that comes from tapping into something greater than ourselves, whether that's a walk in nature, singing, meditation, or simply the sensual solitude of a bubble bath.

Make a list of things you can do to keep yourself replenished and feel joy on a regular basis. List as many things as you can. Be sure that at least half of the things on this list can be done even when you are *with* your child. Post your list and do at least two things every day. Life is not a dress rehearsal. You deserve joy!

(1) _____

(2) _____

(3) _____

(4) _____

(5) _____

(6) _____

(7) _____

(8) _____

(9) _____

(10) _____

(11) _____

(12) _____

## Practice: **Your Current Level of Well-Being**

What would you say is your current level of well-being on a scale of 1 to 10?

1        2        3        4        5        6        7        8        9        10

When you imagine yourself in a state of well-being, what images come to you?

_____

_____

_____

Savor those images. Revisit them several times each day. You're programming your subconscious to create them more often.

What do you already do to take care of yourself that helps you maintain a higher level of well-being? Give yourself a pat on the back for each one of these things.

**1** _____

_____

**2** _____

_____

**3** _____

_____

**4** _____

_____

**5** _____

_____

**6** _____

_____

What decreases your level of well-being? For each of these, what would it take to resolve this issue so it ceases to be a negative factor in your life?

**1** _____

_____

_____

**2** _____

_____

_____

**(3)** _____

_____

_____

**(4)** _____

_____

_____

**(5)** _____

_____

_____

**(6)** _____

_____

_____

## Practice: **Checking-In with Yourself**

1. Set the alarm on your phone to go off every hour.

2. Each time your alarm sounds, ask yourself: "*What do I need right now to stay in balance?*"

3. Then, give it to yourself—whether your child is there or not. (Five minutes to sit on the back steps and listen to the birds? A glass of water? Five minutes of dancing?)

4. If you really can't do it right now, make a date with yourself for later. (How about a bath after the kids go to bed? Trading shoulder massages with your partner? More sleep tonight?)

You won't be able to do what you "need" every time—maybe you're rushing to pick up your child from school or in a meeting with your boss. But whenever possible, just do it. When it's not possible, promise yourself that you'll do it soon.

## Reflection After Practice: **Meeting Your Own Needs**

Your alarm probably sounded about 12–15 times yesterday. What were some of the things you found that you needed?

_____

_____

_____

How often were you able to give yourself what you needed?

_____

_____

_____

How did it feel to take care of yourself?

_____

_____

_____

What got in the way of you taking care of yourself?

_____

_____

_____

Did you feel any different at the end of the day than before you began this practice?

_____

_____

_____

What have you learned today that will help you take better care of yourself when you repeat this practice tomorrow?

_____

_____

_____

Repeat this practice for a week. Notice how your feeling of well-being increases as you put yourself back on your priority list.

_____

_____

_____

# Practice: **Your Self-Care Plan**

Now, let's work together to create a self-care plan to maintain your sense of well-being, both because you deserve it and so that you can be emotionally generous with your child. Notice this isn't self-care as we often think of it, meaning things that cost money (such as manicures) or even things that take you away from your child for long periods of time. It's about caring for yourself while you care for your child; nurturing your body, mind, emotions, and spirit to increase your sense of well-being.

What are the most important ways that you could take better care of yourself physically, to maintain a high level of well-being and energize you? (Examples include taking vitamins, working out, and getting more sleep.)

_____

_____

_____

What are the most important ways that you could take better care of yourself emotionally, so you can give yourself more support to stay emotionally generous? Focus less on what you want from others (since you can't control them) and more on what you can give yourself. For instance, what are some ways in which you could increase the amount of love and compassion you give yourself? How could you feel more nurtured?

_____

_____

_____

What are the most important ways that you could take better care of yourself spiritually, to maintain a high level of well-being? For instance, how could you support yourself to feel more grateful, more joyful, more connected to your own inner wisdom, or more trusting in the goodness of the universe?

_____

_____

_____

Now, list below the things you could do on a regular basis that would increase your emotional well-being rating from page 84. Include on this list the most important answers you've written above about how you can nurture yourself, decrease your stress level, love yourself more, and take better care of yourself physically, emotionally, and spiritually.

(1) _____

(2) _____

(3) _____

(4) _____

(5) _____

(6) _____

You can't do everything at once. But you *can* tackle one habit at a time. Remember, this might be starting something new (such as exercising) or stopping something (such as staying up late to feed your Instagram addiction). It might take you six months to master the previous six practices. But just think how different your life will be in six months!

Now, which of these self-care strategies do you think would make the most difference in your life? Pick the change you'd like to begin with, out of your six ideas, and circle it. This is your new top self-care goal.

Next complete the information on the next page to make your goal a reality.

**Describe what it will look like once you begin to do this self-care habit.** For instance, "*I now listen to a guided meditation each day while the children nap.*" This helps you create a picture of yourself doing this new habit, which re-programs your subconscious.

_____

_____

_____

**Describe the effect you hope this self-care practice will have on you.** For instance, "*Now that I meditate every day, I find that I am calmer and more energetic.*" Seeing the positive effect helps motivate you.

_____

_____

_____

**List the necessary steps to create this habit.** For instance, if you want to start meditating, you might write, "*Find and download a good guided meditation,*" "*Find another time to return phone calls instead of once the children fall asleep, so I can meditate then,*" and "*Come up with a plan for those days when one of the kids has a hard time falling asleep at naptime, so I have another time to meditate.*" This is your map to developing this new habit. If you don't have a map, you won't get where you want to go.

**(1)** _____

**(2)** _____

**(3)** _____

**(4)** _____

**(5)** _____

**Describe what might get in the way of your making this a habit.** For instance, "*If I go to check my email or Facebook, I might not start meditating.*"

_____

_____

_____

**Describe how you could support yourself to avoid that pitfall.** For instance, "*Once the children are asleep, I go right to my meditation spot. I do not look at my computer for any reason. I listen to the guided meditation on my phone, but I put the phone on airplane mode and turn off all other apps so I am not tempted. I check my meditation off every day on my calendar and give myself a star!*"

_____

_____

_____

Now, just start doing this one thing. Do it today or make a sacred promise to begin tomorrow and put it on your calendar for a certain time. You can do this. You deserve it. And your family will benefit.

Put on your calendar every day for a month to come back to this section of this book to evaluate how your new habit is going. (Yes, do that now. I'll wait.) Once you feel like you've made this a habit, you can repeat these steps to start your next self-care strategy.

## Practice: Daily Dozen Self-Care Reminders

Make a list of the daily self-care habits that you think will be most important for you to achieve your new top self-care goal. Post this list where you'll see it several times a day until these practices become habits. Here's an example.

My top self-care goal: *I want to stay more calm, patient and emotionally generous with my children. To begin, I now listen to a guided meditation each day while the children nap.*

My daily habits to support this goal:

| | |
|---|---|
| 1 | Once the children are asleep, I go right to my meditation spot. I do not look at my computer for any reason. I don't do household chores at this time. |
| 2 | I listen to the guided meditation on my phone, but I put the phone on airplane mode and turn off all other apps so I am not tempted. |
| 3 | I check my meditation off every day on my calendar and give myself a star! |
| 4 | I get enough sleep so I won't fall asleep while meditating. (Go directly to bed once the kids are asleep and the dishes are done. Do not look at computer or phone!) |
| 5 | I also listen to inspiring audiobooks and parenting podcasts in the car. |
| 6 | I eat protein throughout the day so I stay in a better, more energized mood and can tackle meditation even when it seems hard. |
| 7 | I do dance parties with the kids daily so I stay more energized and positive and so do they. |
| 8 | I set my phone to do a check-in every hour and monitor my mood throughout the day, so I keep my cup full. |
| 9 | I notice when I'm gathering kindling and take action to address the issue and restore my well-being before I start yelling. |
| 10 | I get my partner to agree to watch the kids every Saturday for a couple of hours so I can take a yoga class. |
| 11 | I take hot baths at least a few times a week because they make me feel cared for! |
| 12 | I forgive myself when I make mistakes. I talk to myself like someone I love. |

## *Your Turn*

My top self-care goal: _____

My daily habits to support this goal:

| | |
|---|---|
| 1 | |
| 2 | |
| 3 | |
| 4 | |
| 5 | |
| 6 | |
| 7 | |
| 8 | |
| 9 | |
| 10 | |
| 11 | |
| 12 | |

Repeat daily. Watch your life transform.

## Part 2
# Connection Is the Secret to Happy Parenting

> Recently my four-year-old dug his heels in and refused to enter the house after exiting the car in the pouring rain. He began stomping and screaming at me. I got down on his level and simply opened my arms to him. It took a minute of me waiting silently, but then he seemed to melt and folded himself into me and started crying. We stayed that way for a good few minutes, until we were soaked and could hear the baby crying in the back seat of the car. We giggled and were very close the rest of the day after that. Reminding myself and him of our soaking cuddle can bring us back to that moment of love whenever things get a bit strained!
>
> — Oriana, mother of a four-year-old and a seven-month-old

## WHAT IS CONNECTION?

How we humans build connections with each other, how we deepen them, and how we repair them when they fray can be as simple as a warm smile, or as mysterious as the way the ground lurches when we see a picture of someone we have loved and lost. So much of this intimate process happens below the level of consciousness. But John Gottman, who is probably the foremost researcher on family dynamics in the United States, has distilled the creation of intimate relationships down to their practical essence. It turns out that the building blocks of connection are the small overtures we make to each other every day, and the way our loved ones respond. Gottman calls these "bids," as in "bids for attention."[76] We could also call them "overtures," as in the opening movement of a piece of music.

In happy relationships—whether between romantic partners, parents and children, friends, or coworkers—bids are made and responded to warmly. It almost doesn't matter what the bid is about; the process of reaching out and receiving a response builds the relationship. It also increases the trust level so that we're likely to reach out to that person again, with more and more vulnerable bids—which deepens the intimacy.

If we begin with *I'm worried about…* and receive an empathic response, we're likely to elaborate and may ask the other person for support. Our trust in reaching out is rewarded with caring. We both end the interaction feeling closer. Trust is built. If, on the other hand, our comment is ignored or greeted with anything that doesn't feel empathic, we're unlikely to make ourselves vulnerable, and the relationship loses a chance to deepen. In fact, we're hurt, so we build a little wall against more vulnerability.

The same process is enacted with our children in hundreds of daily interactions. If we respond with compassion to our child's distress or anger, we build trust and strengthen the relationship. If we respond with something other than compassion, our child feels less safe with us and adds a brick to his defensive wall. And, of course, this goes both ways. If we ask our middle-schooler about the upcoming school dance and receive an engaged response, we might venture further and ask whether she's nervous. If, on the other hand, her response is surly—which means she's already defensive—most of us will back off.

That's why your best connection tool is to train yourself to notice the tone of your interactions with your child. Then, take every opportunity to add a little more warmth to the interactions, even if your child isn't welcoming. Gradually, you'll notice that your child is responding with more openness to your bids and that your relationship feels sweeter and closer.

## *Your Magic Wand For Less Drama, More Love*

It used to be so difficult as a working parent to get my daughter ready in the mornings. However, since I started to spend 10 minutes as soon as she wakes up hugging and kissing her and getting her laughing, it's much easier to get her to do things.

— Shika, mother of a four-year-old daughter

Life, with its infinite distractions and constant separations, has a way of eroding connection. So all parents need to repeatedly reconnect with their children just to repair the daily erosion created by life's normal separations and distractions.

Have you had a moment of connection with your child today that made your heart melt? You need that kind of moment every day to motivate you to be a peaceful parent. Daily life with children can feel like a thankless, endless grind. But when you create more sweetness with your child, suddenly it becomes the most rewarding, meaningful thing you could be doing. Connection is what reminds us that our child is a young human doing the best she can, even when we wish she'd act differently, and that guiding her and loving her is an honor. And, when we have the (admittedly not always pleasant) privilege of seeing our kids at their worst, that connection renews our faith so we can keep seeing our child's best potential, even when they can't.

Our kids need those heart-melting moments too, to trust us. That's when our love really sinks in to create the secure connection that allows children to feel safe, so they can take risks, learn, and rise to age-appropriate developmental challenges. When kids feel unconditionally loved, they become convinced that they're lovable and they're more likely to act lovable.

By contrast, when children start to feel disconnected, they don't feel safe, so they "act out"—which just means they have feelings they don't know how to express, so they act those angry, upset feelings out with angry, resistant behavior.

When kids act out, most of us reach for threats or bribes to get cooperation. But those don't work long term, because all humans rebel against feeling manipulated and controlled. Even if it helped your child to behave—which research shows it doesn't[77]—you wouldn't actually want to control your child, because then he would never develop his own inner compass and learn to take responsibility for himself. It would also be a violation of the sacred contract all parents make to nurture the unique essence of their children, to help them develop into autonomous, self-actualized adults.

So the only real influence we have with our children comes from our relationship with them. Luckily, that's enough. The more kids feel a warm, responsive connection from their parents, the more they're open to our guidance—now and as they move into the teen years. By contrast, until children feel connected, they don't accept our guidance. They resist, or even rebel. That's why I always say that connection is 80 percent of parenting.

If you're feeling a bit worried that your family isn't in constant harmony, let me reassure you. No relationship is constantly connected, and your child will feel disconnected from you on a regular basis, no matter how wonderful a parent you are. When your child is away from you during the day, he can't stay connected, so he connects to his teacher or peers. When she's upset or angry, that overrides her feeling of connection. When you're super-busy and just trying to move him through the schedule, he disconnects. So our job as parents is to become experts at noticing when there's a disconnection and then to reconnect. Effective parenting is almost impossible until a positive connection with your child has been re-established, so think of connection as preventive maintenance, before there's a problem.

The easiest antidote to the disconnections of daily life is simply to build connection rituals into your day. I know you have a full plate of things to do already and you aren't looking to add more things to your to-do list. But many of my suggestions for connection won't take you extra time; they'll just help you make the most of the interactions you're already having with your child.

> I've stopped prioritizing the rush to get my own agenda done and am taking the time to be in the moment—and really see and hear and join in his play. Instead of my standard platitudes that were vague and inattentive ('good job' or 'that's nice'), I have been actually engaging and enjoying his play. My commentary is now sincere! We are both happier after school, and strangely enough I end up with more time to do 'my things' because after a good play session he will go off and happily do his own thing!
>
> — Tanya, mother of six-year-old

Please consider this your official reminder that your in-box will never be empty, but your children will definitely grow up. Sooner than you think, you'll be the last person they'll want to spend time with. (That's even if you're a great parent and they adore you. It's their job to connect with people their own age as they get older.) I know, that seems a long way off. But your child has only about 900 weeks of childhood with you before he leaves your home. And that assumes you'll spend every week together between now and the time your child turns 18, which is highly unlikely. What's much more likely is that by the time your child is 14, you'll rank pretty low on her priority list. So if your child is still young enough to want your time in the evening, why not give it to him or her in a whole-hearted way? Why not turn off your computer and phone while you're with your child? Why not chase your toddler around the house with a diaper on your head, roaring like a tiger? Why not have an extra-long story hour tonight with your six-year-old? Why not ask your pre-teen to play you a few of her favorite songs? I guarantee you'll see the benefits in the form of more closeness and cooperation tomorrow.

What if you could create a deep, loving connection as your (almost) constant way of being with your child? It would be like giving yourself a magic wand. There would be no more yelling in your home. Some heart-felt tears, maybe. Lots of hugging, smiling, laughing, fun. And lots of moments that will make your heart melt.

## What Every Parent Needs To Know About Attachment

Think about all the "bids"—for attention, food, comfort, play, connection—a baby makes to her parents during her first year of life. By the time babies are 13 months old, they have a lot of experience with each of their significant caretakers, so even a baby who can't speak a word yet can predict how each of his significant adults will respond if the baby is distressed, gets angry, or wants to "do it myself."

Attachment theorists have developed strategies to help us see a toddler's assumptions about whether their parent can be counted on to help them when they're in distress. Using those methods, researchers can evaluate whether children's relationships with their parents (the relationships with each parent are rated independently) are securely attached. About 60 percent of toddlers in the English-speaking world are considered securely attached. The other 40 percent are either anxious about whether their parent will meet their needs, or they've concluded that their parent won't meet their needs, so they don't express them.

What does that mean? It means the securely-attached children believe they can count on their parents to respond warmly to their distress and with understanding to their anger and upsets. Notice that the most important factor in creating secure attachment is the parent's responsiveness to the baby's emotions. Wearing your baby, nursing your baby, and co-sleeping may increase the likelihood that you'll notice his bids and respond warmly, but by themselves those "attachment practices" won't guarantee secure attachment—they're a means to an end. I used these practices with my own children and recommend them if they work for you. But if they don't, please don't worry. Long before these were common practices in western culture, the majority of toddlers were securely attached to their parents. What matters is that you're responsive to your child's needs and emotions.

> Why is secure attachment so important? Because it gives the child a foundation of feeling lovable—of believing that she is valuable enough to inspire her significant people to adore her. She learns trust: the world is a safe place where her needs can be met. As you know from Part 1 of this book, any repeated experience rewires the brain. So children who experience early secure attachments have brains that are wired for trust, connection, and confidence.

In comparison, children who don't feel secure that their needs will be met build brains that are wired to respond to other people with drama: wariness, neediness, or demandingness. Not surprisingly, longitudinal studies show that securely-attached children do better in relationships—with friends, teachers, colleagues, and partners—throughout life. They're also more accomplished academically and professionally, more able to manage their emotions, and happier.

What's more, attachment security is often passed on to our children. For example, research shows that parents who are uncomfortable with their child's neediness will often raise a child who is uncomfortable with her own needs and thus, eventually, with her child's needs.[78]

> The good news, though, is that even when your relationship with your parents was insecure, you can "earn" a secure attachment by working on yourself: reflecting on your past, becoming more comfortable with your emotions, and learning to love yourself unconditionally.[79]

As you do this work, you're "reparenting" yourself. You become more comfortable with your child's emotions and needs, so you're more responsive, and your child is likely to develop a secure attachment with you. This is part of "breaking the cycle" to meet your child's needs, even if your own weren't met.

If you're wondering whether your child's attachment to you is secure, ask yourself these questions:

- Does your child share her distress with you?
- Does your child share her anger with you?
- Does your child share her fears with you?

If the answer is yes, your child probably trusts you as a safe haven. If not, please don't panic. In this part of the book (on connection) and in Part 3 (which covers emotion-coaching), you'll learn many skills and strategies to strengthen your connection with your child. Even if your child concluded as a toddler that he couldn't trust you with some of his emotions, you can choose now to offer him new, better experiences that will transform that belief. Not only will that strengthen your relationship with your child, but you'll also be giving him a priceless gift that will improve every relationship he has for the rest of his life.

And please don't blame yourself. Yes, parental responsiveness is the most important factor in attachment security. But every relationship is a two-way street and some children are just more difficult to connect with. And some children who are insecurely attached had special circumstances—early hospitalizations, sensory issues, anxiety, and so on—that made bonding harder.

Often, frayed parent–child connections begin early. For instance, a mother who is depressed following her child's birth may find it hard to bond with her baby. This distance can persist into toddlerhood, when she may find herself less patient and more reactive to her toddler's age-appropriate challenging behavior. In fact, often parent–child relationship issues stem from an insecure infant attachment, which therapeutic intervention can heal.

Other parents bond easily with their baby, but find that their toddler's defiance pushes all their buttons, particularly if a new baby enters the picture and their connection with their toddler becomes strained. Mismatches between parent and child can also make appreciating each other more challenging, as when a boisterous, super-active child is born to a highly-sensitive parent who needs time alone to recharge her energy.

If you recognize yourself in these scenarios, this book is designed to help you create new patterns of connection with your child. But if you find yourself frustrated as you try to connect, I recommend that you schedule a few sessions with a parenting coach who can help you build on the work in this book to develop a personalized program to strengthen your relationship with your child. Please don't hesitate to do this if you feel your connection could be stronger. No amount of "parenting skills" can make up for a strained parent–child bond. Parenting when your child doesn't feel connected is like riding a bike up a very steep hill—it's almost impossible to keep peddling! By contrast, parenting with a good relationship is like coasting downhill—you still have to pay attention and steer, and twists and turns certainly arise, but the momentum is with you.

## Practice: Taking Stock of Your Connection with Your Child

You know your relationship with your child needs some support any time you repeatedly notice that:

- You aren't enjoying your child. You may feel distant or resentful or constantly annoyed.
- Your child often does not cooperate with your requests.

Be honest with yourself. (This will be your baseline, against which you measure progress.) How connected would you say you feel to your child most days?

1     2     3     4     5     6     7     8     9     10

How connected do you think your child feels with you most days? Remember, just because *we* feel connected doesn't mean *they* feel connected.

1     2     3     4     5     6     7     8     9     10

If there is a difference in how you and your child would rate your level of closeness, what do you think causes that?

_____

_____

_____

If you feel your child is challenging, or your relationship with your child is not as rewarding as you would like it to be, do you have any ideas on why that might be?

_____

_____

_____

In what ways do you encourage connection with your child?

_____

_____

_____

What gets in the way of connecting with your child?

_____

_____

_____

What could you do to deepen your connection with your child?

_____

_____

_____

## Practice: **Reprogram Your Subconscious for Connection**

1. **Right now, imagine yourself connecting to your child, feeling deep love.** Your child is responding with affection and joy. Maybe you're having that good-morning snuggle with him. Or you're twirling her around, both of you laughing. Hold that picture for a full 60 seconds. Watch it like a movie. How are you feeling and acting? How is your child responding? Let that heart-melting, connected feeling soak in. You're programming your subconscious, so you can create more of these moments in your life.

2. **As you go through your day today, notice each time you start to get irritated at your child. Now, give yourself an antidote.** Before you correct your child, show yourself that warm picture and feel that love again. Is that hard? Keep practicing. It gets easier. It helps tremendously if you can see things from your child's perspective instead of getting stuck in yours. There's always more than one way to interpret a situation.

3. **Take at least one action *today* to make that loving image happen.** Even a small action moves you in the right direction. Humans connect most quickly through physical touch. Play is also foolproof. But it doesn't happen without slowing down, letting go of distractions, and bringing yourself completely into the interaction with your child. Snuggle on the couch, give a foot rub, or start some roughhousing that gets everyone laughing. Or encourage sibling bonding with a "kids against parents" pillow fight. (Let the kids win.)

4. **Repeat every day.** You'll be amazed at the transformation in your home within a week. Love never fails.

## EMPATHY

> I had just read Dr. Laura's blog about staying calm and acknowledging his desires. When the screaming and stomping began, I stopped what I was doing and sat down next to my toddler. I made eye contact, listened to his complaint, and did not let the screaming anger me. I calmly explained that I heard him. I said, 'I know those are so tasty and I love them too, but you will have to wait half an hour until dinnertime.' He blubbered briefly, collapsed into my arms for a minute, and then went to play with his toys. My husband congratulated me on keeping my cool. The best part? My son was perfectly pleasant the rest of the evening. Wow!
>
> — Aimee, mother of a three-year-old

Empathy is both a visceral understanding of what another person is feeling and the expression of that understanding. Empathy is one of the most powerful tools you have to connect with your child, or any other person.

Your empathy helps your child feel understood and less alone in her suffering, whether she's feeling disappointment because her team lost the soccer game, irritation at her annoying younger brother, or anger that you won't let her stay up to finish her art project. You don't have to change your limit about bedtime, and you may think she should be kinder to her brother, but you can still offer understanding about how she feels. Feeling understood helps your child accept your limit more gracefully. It may even help her be kinder to her brother, because she feels validated and has had a chance to blow off steam.

> Empathy is your most effective tool to help your child work through and manage her own emotions.

Giving and receiving empathy changes the body chemistry of both people by stimulating the release of the neurotransmitter oxytocin, which reduces stress and produces a sense of connection and well-being.[80] Finally, research shows that when children have the experience of receiving empathy from others, it helps them develop empathy themselves.[81] (The experience of feeling empathy for your child also changes your brain and body chemistry to make *you* happier, healthier, and less stressed.[82])

While we often express our empathy in words, empathy is only partially communicated by what we say. It's an emotional resonance that's transmitted between the nervous systems of two people,[83] largely through tone, facial expression, and body language. In other words, empathy is physical. First, our mirror neurons—an aptly-named part of our sensory system—pick up the physical and facial signals of the other person and give us a taste of how it would feel if we were giving off those signals. Then, our insula[84] and right supramarginal gyrus[85] (both involved in empathy) work with other brain areas to help us imagine what the person is feeling by suggesting the bodily sensations associated with those emotions. Finally, we communicate back to the other person, through our own facial expression, body language, and words, that we understand how they feel and that we have compassion for them, which literally means the willingness to "suffer with" them.

So given all that, how can you as a parent use the power of empathy to connect with your child and support him emotionally? Here's how:

1. **Center yourself as much as possible.** If you're in an emotionally-charged state, it's much harder to read someone else's emotions and to communicate your understanding.

2. **Slow down and tune in to your child.** Notice the "feeling" of her facial and body language as well as the words. Let yourself resonate with the emotions your child is feeling.

3. **Communicate your understanding.** Do your best to describe your child's perspective as well as her feelings. You might also express your own feelings.

   - *"How disappointing to lose the game, especially when your team practiced so hard and you all played your hearts out. I'm so sorry, Max."*

   - *"It sounds like you're getting pretty annoyed at your brother. You don't like how he keeps interrupting you when you're concentrating."*

   - *"Nate, I hear how much you wish you could finish your art project. I'm sorry you can't stay up later, but it's a school night."*

**Notice that:**

- You don't have to agree with your child to express understanding about how he feels.
- Empathy doesn't mean you're going to change your limit.
- You don't have to "label" your child's feelings. You can simply describe your perception of what she wants or what she wishes. So if you don't know what she's feeling, you can still describe the situation and try to acknowledge her perspective.
- You aren't trying to talk your child out of his emotions. He can't move past them until he feels heard.

Once you've empathized, you might move on to problem solving, for instance by engaging with her brother so that he stops annoying her, or by coaching her on what to say to him. But coaching and problem solving are a later step, not effective until after you've empathized. (We'll look at coaching and problem solving more closely in Part 3 of this book.)

## Practice: Cultivating Empathy by Broadening Your Perspective

Think about the last time you were angry at your child. Describe why you were angry.

_____

_____

_____

The description you've written is the story line that frames your reaction to your child in this instance. It isn't right or wrong, but it's by definition incomplete. In that story, the focus is on you, so you're viewing your child through the lens of what you want and need.

Now, pull back the camera to see a broader perspective. You can still see yourself there, trying so hard. Now, though, your child becomes a protagonist, too. As you look at your child, you realize that she's actually hurting. There's something she needs that she doesn't know how to get, or even how to articulate. She loves you, but she feels a gulf between you. She doesn't know how to even begin to communicate what she's feeling. So she's acting out.

Now, describe the same situation from your child's perspective.

_____

_____

_____

Notice how different the situation looks now that you see the broader perspective, including your child's point of view. From this perspective, you'd probably intervene very differently.

It's difficult to find empathy for our children when we're angry. We get righteously attached to our own story line, so it's very hard to stop and see our child's point of view. But when you can reach out to resonate with your child, empathy will help you talk yourself down from the cliff of anger.

Let's say your three-year-old gets mad because his favorite crayon breaks. He's so mad that he breaks every other crayon in the box. Naturally, you're angry. Crayons cost money. But if you remind yourself to Stop, Drop, and Breathe, you can empathize with your child's frustration. Then you immediately see that your child is acting like a three-year-old because he *is* a three-year old. As soon as you see it from his perspective, your anger lessens. The broken crayons just don't seem so important in the context of a little person struggling with the big drama of loss, disappointment, and rage. You realize that he needs your help to manage these emotions much more than he needs a lecture about money not growing on trees. "*Wow. You must have been so mad when your crayon broke because that's your very favorite color crayon in the whole world, right? It made you so mad you wanted to break all the crayons. Is that what happened?*"

He feels understood, and your "telling him the story" of what happened helps him develop reflective capacity, which is a first step in developing judgment. Your empathy doesn't mean that you're going to go buy new crayons, and it doesn't mean that you think this was an okay way for him to handle his anger. But, after all, he is only three. Your first job is to reconnect with him before you can do problem solving or teaching of any kind. In fact, once he masters those emotions, he'll come to the desired conclusion himself, so breaking the crayons won't be a choice he'll make again.

## Practice: Using Empathy, What Will You Say and Do?

Many of us didn't grow up experiencing empathy, and this can make it hard to give empathy to our children. Even loving parents often shut down their children's emotions by saying things like, "*Oh, don't be a baby*" or "*You don't need to be upset about that. Come on, get over it.*" This exercise will help you think about how you could express empathy to your child in everyday situations.

Read the situations below. Under each scenario, write what you could say and do that would help your child to feel your empathic understanding—without you necessarily compromising your limit to do what your child is asking.

### *Example: Your Child Is Disappointed That It's Raining*

What you say:

- "*Oh Zack, it's raining, and you wanted to go out and play!*"

What you do:

- Connect physically with my hand on his arm.
- Make eye contact, with my face reflecting his disappointment (mirroring his feelings).
- Let the moment of empathy sink in to see how he responds.
- If he cries, hold him and continue to mirror his disappointment.
- If he's angry, acknowledge his anger, and also the sadness under it: "*You wish it wasn't raining. You wanted to play in the sandbox.*"
- After this, I might use playfulness or problem solving to shift the mood and help him adapt to the situation.

### *Your Turn*

( 1 ) **Your child says she can't sleep because she's afraid of the dark.**

What you say:

_____

_____

_____

What you do:

_____

_____

_____

**(2)** **Your child is angry at his sibling.**

What you say:

_____

_____

_____

What you do:

_____

_____

_____

**(3)** **Your toddler has a tantrum.**

What you say:

_____

_____

_____

What you do:

_____

_____

_____

**(4)** **Your child misses her other parent, who is on a business trip.**

What you say:

_____

_____

_____

What you do:

_____

_____

_____

**(5)** **Your pre-teen doesn't get the part she wanted in the school play.**

What you say:

_____

_____

_____

What you do:

_____

_____

_____

Many parents ask, "*What's the right answer to these?*" There is no right answer. But you can find examples of possible answers to these scenarios at AhaParenting.com/empathy. You'll learn more if you wait to read them until after you've already done your best to answer them on your own.

## Empathic Listening

> As a child, I was conditioned to think children crying and expressing emotions was bad and irresponsible. Now, with a four-year-old child of my own, it was difficult to reset my way of thinking but my heart would break every time she became distraught during a tantrum, or simply when she felt things didn't go well in any given situation. Starting to acknowledge her feelings was a magic formula. She started to look at me. Really look into my eyes. And when I followed this with compassion about her experience, she started to open up and elaborate on what she perceived and how she felt. I want her to know she can come to me any time and I'll always be supportive. Even if it's a situation where she didn't feel at her best.
>
> — Cindy, mother of a four-year-old daughter

Since empathy starts with understanding what the other person is feeling, learning how to listen is an essential empathy tool. We all think we know how to listen, but most of us don't listen very much. For example:

- We "listen" to our child chatter on about her morning at school while we think about the email we have to return.
- When our child begins to tell us about a problem he's having, we get anxious and start telling him what he should do to solve it.
- We demand an explanation from our child about her behavior—"*What were you thinking?!*"—but instead of listening to her halting explanation we jump into lecture and scold.

Then, as our child gets older, we wish he would talk with us!

Empathic listening is listening for the emotion behind the words. It begins with a commitment to be fully present and take in what our child is saying. Don't feel you have to solve the problem, whatever it is. In fact, it's much better to bite your tongue than to jump in with an opinion or solution. Every time you give advice, you're implying that your child is unable to handle the problem. Kids learn most from the opportunity to hear themselves talk and come to their own conclusions. If you give in to the temptation to lecture, your child will clam up. If you want to let your child know you're listening, make short sounds:

- *"Mmmm…"*
- *"Really?"*
- *"What happened then?"*
- *"My goodness!"*

- *"Oh…"*
- *"Wow!"*
- *"Tell me more."*

Empathize. Re-state what you heard to be sure you understood. Ask questions that begin with *"I wonder."*

- *"I wonder what would happen if you did that?"*
- *"It sounds like what he said really hurt your feelings."*
- *"So you think next time he says that, you're going to tell him you don't want to be his friend? I can certainly understand why you would want to say that!"*

## Practice: **Empathic Listening**

> Listen. People start to heal the moment they feel heard.
> — Cheryl Richardson, bestselling author

Think about the last time your child spoke with you about something. How would you rate your listening?

1    2    3    4    5    6    7    8    9    10

Were you able to resist jumping in with advice?

_____

_____

_____

Are there any ways that you can see to become a better listener?

_____

_____

_____

> To listen fully means to pay close attention to what is being said beneath the words.
> You listen not only to the 'music,' but to the essence of the person speaking. Generative listening
> is the art of developing deeper silences in yourself, so you can slow your mind's hearing to
> your ears' natural speed, and hear beneath the words to their meaning.
> — Peter Senge[87]

## Practice: **Slow Down So You Can Connect**

Many children say they wish they could talk to their parents more, but their parents don't listen. Or they overreact. Or they just wouldn't understand. Most of all, they're too busy, moving too fast.

Moving more slowly might be an essential part of connecting with our children. You could try emulating Zen master Thich Nhat Hanh, who has been described as a cross between a snail, a cloud, and a piece of heavy machinery.[88] Might slowing down be a precondition for that lightness of touch and depth of presence? Today, try this powerful little experiment and see what kind of difference it makes in your family.

First, find a deeper silence and stillness within yourself.

Notice the sensations in your body.

Look your child in the eye when he speaks.

Savor the light glinting on your child's hair. Pause before you answer.

Breathe deeply and consciously. Listen for the meaning under the words.

Notice that an upset tone is a plea to be heard.

Linger longer with each hug.

**Notice that everything your child says is code for "Please love me."**

## Reflection After Practice: **Deepening Your Listening**

After this experiment, consider these questions.

How does your child's behavior change when you slow down and really listen?

_____

_____

_____

What do you need to do for yourself each day so that you can slow down enough to really hear your child?

_____

_____

_____

What happens if you just sit for three minutes with the intention to feel a state of peace?

_____

_____

_____

# How to Help Your Child Open Up and Talk to You About What Matters

Use "conversation openers" rather than direct questions, which put kids on the spot. "*Tell me how you feel*" is not empathy. Empathy is mirroring whatever your child is already showing you. "*You seem sad this morning*" or "*You're very quiet tonight*" followed by a warm smile will encourage him to open up more than badgering him with questions.

When your child shares something with you that makes you anxious, use your Pause Button to Stop, Drop your anxiety, and Breathe. This is not about you. Your anxiety comes from the fact your child is also anxious and needs your help at this moment. So, for instance, if your child comes home and yells, "*I hate that, teacher! She yelled at me in front of everyone!*" you might well *want* to respond, "*What did you do to make her yell?*" or "*Kylie! Don't say you hate people.*" But what your child needs to hear is, "*Wow! That must have been so embarrassing. No wonder you feel so angry at her!*"

**Do:**

- Notice your own emotional reactions and just breathe through them, instead of trying to make yourself feel better by jumping in with opinions, lectures, pronouncements, or attempts to change or blame your child.

- Allow your child to be emotional and angry. If he can talk about what he's feeling, he won't have to act it out. This is your opportunity to help him "befriend" those emotions so that he can manage them.

- Sit next to your child so you aren't looking right at him, which takes the pressure off. This is why car rides often help children (and adults) talk.

- Turn off technology when you interact with your child. Your child will remember for the rest of her life that she was important enough to her parents that they turned off their phones for time with her.

**Don't:**

- Try to change how your child feels, with comments such as "*Of course you have friends!*" or "*You're overreacting, Julia*" or "*You'll see, they'll come around.*" That makes her feel invalidated instead of heard.

- Blame your child or make it his fault with comments such as "*I told you not to…*" or "*Why didn't you tell me about this?!*" or "*You know better than that!*"

- Rush to problem solve while your child is still expressing feelings.

If your child is older and resistant to talking with you, try this suggestion from Heather Forbes, an expert on connecting with children, including kids who have trauma histories.[89] Help your child begin to feel more comfortable being vulnerable by playing "two truths and a lie." Invite your child to tell you three things about his life, two of which are true and one that is not. You guess which two are true. You may have to go first, or even try this yourself without his participation a few times, before your child is ready to share his experience. Use your self-regulation skills so that you can respond to your child's sharing without overreacting and with empathy. Remember your child is giving you a window into his experience. Proceed with caring.

## *When Empathy Doesn't Work*

When parents begin using gentle guidance, they're often amazed by how well empathy "works" to calm their child. For most people, just having our views and feelings acknowledged makes us feel better, so we're more cooperative. So, once parents get past their fear of "agreeing" with their child's "negative emotions"—a common fear, though empathy doesn't mean you agree—they quickly learn to empathize when their child is having a hard time:

- *"Nothing's going right for you today, huh?"*
- *"You wish you could have ice cream now—I hear you."*
- *"You sound very angry!"*

In fact, empathy is so effective in reconnecting with our upset child and helping her calm down that it takes us by surprise when it "doesn't work."

But empathy isn't a trick to control the other person. It's a means of *connection* and of *helping your child process emotion.* So, when empathy doesn't "work," consider whether you're really connecting and whether you're helping your child with her emotions.

Here are the problems I hear most often from parents about using empathy:

1. **"Empathy makes my child cry harder."** Yes, when we validate kids' feelings, the emotions often intensify. But we aren't creating those bad feelings. They're in there anyway. Think about a time when you had some big feelings locked up inside you. Maybe something bad happened. You were holding it together. Then someone arrived with whom you felt safe, and they hugged you or said something compassionate, and you burst into tears. It's the same with kids: when they have big feelings and we empathize, they get more in touch with the feelings. But that's a good thing. Because once they feel those emotions, the emotions begin to evaporate. That's how emotions work.

2. **"Empathy doesn't stop the tantrum."** Once your child is swept into "fight or flight" mode, words don't help. So instead of labeling the emotions, communicate safety so your child can show you all those feelings. The fewer words the better—just enough so she hears your compassion and knows you're standing by with a hug. Empathy won't stop the tantrum, but it will help your child let all those feelings up and out. That's what's healing.

3. **"I keep repeating *'You are very sad and frustrated'* but my child gets mad and tells me not to say it."** How we acknowledge feelings depends on how old the other person is. With an angry toddler, you might get down on his level and say *"You're so mad!"* in a voice that makes it clear that you understand how passionately he feels. The toddler is often reassured: Mom and Dad don't think it's an emergency, and he learns that there's even a name ("mad") for this tidal wave that's swamping him.

   But, as kids get older, naming the emotion often makes them feel analyzed and managed, rather than understood. Imagine if you were upset and your partner just kept repeating, *"You are very sad and frustrated."* It would probably make you angrier!

   Your goal here is for your child to feel understood. So use a tone of voice that matches how he feels. Labeling the emotion is fine if that helps him feel understood,[90] but otherwise, there's no reason to do it while your child is upset. (Please see "Do You Have To Name It To Tame It" on page 163 for more discussion on this issue.) And of course, while your child is in the middle of a tantrum, the only thing they need to know is that they're safe, that you understand, and that you're ready with a hug when they're ready.

**4. "I say 'You are mad, but we don't hit' and he hits again 10 minutes later."** Often when we use the word "but" the other person doesn't feel like their feelings are actually being acknowledged. (There's an old saying: "*Everything before the 'but' is a lie.*")

You might try the word "and" instead of "but" to see whether there's a difference: "*You're feeling really mad, aren't you? I understand! AND it's not okay to hit, no matter what. Tell me in words.*" Of course, your tone has to make it clear that you really do understand how upset your child is.

But the big reason that empathic reminders don't prevent more hitting is that you simply can't expect "talk" of any kind to solve the problem. Kids who hit have big fear locked inside. They need you to create safety and set a compassionate limit so they can cry and show you that fear. Only then does hitting usually stop.

**5. "I empathize with her emotions, but then she's still upset."** If you're truly empathizing, you feel some of what your child is feeling. One test of this is whether you have tears in your eyes. If you can see the situation from her perspective and feel that deep level of empathy, your child will feel cared about and understood. Often, that's enough to help her begin to move through her emotions. If it doesn't, that's because empathy by itself doesn't necessarily address what your child is upset about. Often we need to go a step further and help her solve the problem: "*You're so upset that your little sister keeps knocking down your tower. Let's find a place for you to build that is out of her reach.*"

Sometimes she needs our support to solve it herself: "*You're so mad at your brother. I think he needs to hear how you feel. Let's go find your brother, and I will stay with you while you tell him.*" And sometimes she simply can't have what she wants, but you can give her what she wants with a wish: "*Do you want me to write this here on your birthday list so when it comes time you can see if you still want it?*"

Sometimes, though, wish fulfillment isn't enough and there's no solving the problem. The disappointment is so great—or it triggers some earlier hurt that's still lurking and waiting to be expressed—that only tears will do. In that case, your empathy "worked" perfectly. Your child now feels safe enough to show you her upset. That's how kids build resilience: they feel safe enough to let themselves feel their disappointment fully, and they learn they can come out on the other side feeling okay. She's crying? That's a *good* thing.

In fact, if you're truly feeling the empathy, it will *always* work to help your child feel understood. (Sometimes that means the emotions come gushing out, which is ultimately healing.)

So, if your empathy doesn't seem to be "working," maybe words are getting in your way. Stop trying to come up with the right words. Instead, imagine yourself as a child feeling what your child is feeling at this moment. If you were your child, what would you wish your parent would do right now to love you through this? Do that.

## Practice: Rewiring Your Brain for Empathy

You can see why empathy is such a powerful tool to strengthen your relationship with your child. And yet most of us find that there are times when it's a struggle to find our empathy. Maybe we're angry, or simply stressed and moving too fast.[91] Or maybe we didn't grow up feeling understood, so empathy doesn't come naturally. Wouldn't it be wonderful if you could find a magic formula that would increase your ability to feel empathy and compassion for your child?

You can! Loving-Kindness meditation practice has been proven to engage and strengthen the neural pathways linked to empathy[92] in addition to shifting the meditator into a more positive mental state. Every time you do it, you're activating the parts of the brain that enable you to experience empathy and also building the neural connections that make it easier to feel empathy.[93] Luckily, Loving-Kindness meditation is one of the easiest meditations to do:

**1.** Sit comfortably, close your eyes, and take a few deep breaths to center yourself.

**2.** Imagine someone you find easy to love. Send love, compassion, and wishes for health, safety, well-being, and happiness to that person.

**3.** Now imagine a stranger or acquaintance who is suffering. Send love, compassion, and wishes for health, safety, well-being, and happiness to that person.

**4.** Now imagine someone you find it more difficult to love. This might be someone with whom you have a conflict or who you find annoying. Send love, compassion, and wishes for health, safety, well-being, and happiness to that person.

**5.** Now send love, compassion, and wishes for health, safety, well-being, and happiness to yourself.

Different empathy "muscles" are exercised when we send compassion to people we can't immediately identify with, so this practice stretches your heart. You can do this meditation for a few minutes any time you want, or you can do a full "workout" for 30 minutes or an hour daily, to grow your empathy. You can also try shorter versions of this meditation any time you have a few minutes and want to shift into a more positive emotional state. For instance, you might try sending loving wishes to the people around you next time you're in a slow-moving line, in traffic, or on the subway. I've never seen any research on this, but my anecdotal report is that this practice immediately shifts my mood so that I have a greater sense of well-being, and the people around me seem more friendly!

## PLAY AND LAUGHTER

From the infectious release of side-splitting giddiness to the exuberance of an impromptu pillow fight, playfulness and laughter are one of the easiest and most powerful paths to connection. This isn't surprising, since when we laugh our brain releases oxytocin, the bonding hormone, into our bodies. That means that when you're laughing with someone, you're bonding. Laughter also transforms bad moods by decreasing the stress hormones circulating in our bodies and increasing our beta-endorphin and serotonin levels.[94] You might visualize this as laughter siphoning off the whole top layer of mild fear and anxiety from your emotional backpack.

# Why Not Tickle?

"My dad used to tickle me when I was a little girl. I now know it was his way of connecting but I hated being powerless when tickled. The weird thing was that I laughed so much that I could not even shout 'stop!' This made my dad think that I was enjoying it when actually I felt trapped and hated it."

— Mari, mother of four-year-old and one-year-old

While most adults immediately think of tickling as the easiest way to get kids laughing, I don't recommend tickling. It robs the child of control, which can create anxiety and an experience of powerlessness. The physiological response to tickling seems to involve a different part of the brain from the part that lights up when we laugh at a joke, which is more of a psychological release—and in roughhousing we're hoping for that psychological release.

I hear from most parents that when they start doing other kinds of roughhousing, their children stop asking for tickling. If your child begs for tickling, that's probably because he's learned that tickling is a reliable way for you to laugh together. Try "air tickles," where you threaten to tickle by wiggling your fingers close to her neck or tummy without touching. Your child will usually burst out laughing, especially if you're laughing.

"Roughhousing"—a term coined by Lawrence Cohen, author of *Playful Parenting*[95]—also builds self-esteem as kids experience their own physical strength. This is especially helpful for children who are less assertive or smaller than other kids their age. And, like other young mammals, when kids "play" fight, they learn to manage aggression, which makes them less likely to lash out when they're angry.

That's why playing together is one of the fastest ways to heal minor relationship stress, help people drop grudges, and bring your family into sync. In fact, if you want to make one easy change in your family that will be transformational, I recommend you begin with 10 minutes a day of roughhousing. That's because children build up all kinds of feelings in the course of a day, and laughter is a great way to heal those minor upsets. The disappointment when you say "no," the frustration of learning to use scissors, the jealousy when you smile at her brother, the fear of a barking dog, the sense of insignificance when you send just one more important text while she's talking, the powerlessness when she can't reach the light switch in the dark bedroom, the panic when she calls and you don't answer immediately—throughout the course of your child's day, every stressful experience that isn't accompanied by a release can build up cortisol, adrenaline, norepinephrine, and other stress hormones.

These stress hormones make kids more cranky, demanding, even explosive. Crying helps the body restore regulation, but when children can't quite get to tears, they get angry instead. The stress hormones that affect kids are the same ones that soar in your own body in a challenging traffic situation. Just as they affect you in traffic, they keep children on edge, so the slightest disappointment can trigger a tantrum. These biochemicals stay in the body for hours and can even prevent children from falling asleep easily at night.

That's why roughhousing is the place to begin. Laughter works almost as well as tears to discharge tension and built-up anxieties. Even if the laughter doesn't fully release the upsets in the emotional backpack, it siphons off the top layer of anxiety and builds trust, so the tears become more accessible. So the most effective way to help children process upset feelings, decrease anxiety, and dissolve that chip on their shoulder is to get them laughing. (Just remember that once someone is expressing upset, it's too late for laughter. Promise yourself to do some roughhousing with your child once he calms down, and shift into empathy.)

> Tantrums are nature's way of helping kids release all those feelings and down-regulate their body. Emotional tears contain ACTH (adrenocorticotropic hormone, which stimulates the production of cortisol), adrenaline, and other stress-related chemicals. So tears clear those chemicals so they don't overload the body with toxins. But this only works when kids feel safe while crying—usually they need to be in your arms or hear your soothing voice. Kids left to cry it out alone end up with higher levels of stress hormones in their bloodstreams. And, since the emotions that come with the tears don't feel good, most children try to push those feelings away with anger. To let the tears flow, children need to feel safe.

Our intention with roughhousing is playfulness and laughter, so it isn't actually "rough," but it is often rambunctious. Physical movement bypasses the rational mind and helps the child express unconscious feelings that are stored in the body. Your goal is to help your child release pent-up anxiety—another word for fear—using laughter. That usually means the child faces something that scares them a bit, but just enough to let them master it. Maybe the parent is the bucking bronco while the child screams with laughter, and the parent eventually bucks the child onto the bed. The child on some level is wondering, *"Is Daddy going to drop me?"* However, because he trusts Daddy and feels safe, he's able to laugh. (If he's screaming with fear, you're obviously taking the game too far.)

Roughhousing probably sounds like a lot of energy for a tired parent, but you'll find that it energizes you because you'll be laughing and offloading stress hormones that were making you tired. You don't need a lot of extra time to be playful. Just find ways to connect warmly and be silly as you go through your daily routine. And, if you incorporate even 10 minutes of actual roughhousing into your routine on a daily basis, you'll notice that it helps your child *want* to cooperate with you, which makes everything go more smoothly.

# Should You Let Your Child Win?

In all the games in this book, the parent bumbles ineffectually, blusters, and hams it up, but they just can't catch the strong, fast, smart child. If you're the scary witch chasing your child, be just scary enough to get your child laughing. Be sure to trip or just miss grabbing your child, and then lament how she always gets away. If you play basketball with your child, let her dominate the court. I understand that you want to teach him to "win fair and square," but there is nothing fair about an adult playing against a child. Besides, your child will suffer plenty of losses at the hands of his peers. If you want him to feel like a winner, he needs to regularly experience winning. Don't worry, you won't be letting him win forever. As his confidence increases, he'll ask suspiciously if you're really trying, so you can say, "You don't think I'm trying? Okay, I'm going to try even harder!" At that point, do so, and once in a while you'll even win. Before you know it, he'll be winning fair and square. Just take your cues from your child as you ease into playing a harder game.

## *Games To Strengthen Your Relationship With Your Child*

Roughhousing games are like having a secret weapon.
The mood shifts from grumpy to giggly in seconds. My kids laugh uncontrollably, and, although they resist stopping, they are more cooperative for the rest of the evening.

— Lauren, mother of twin seven-year-olds

I've separated the games in this section into love games (which convince kids they're loved), separation and reunion games (which help with the anxiety of goodbyes), courage games (which help kids work through fear), power games (which help kids feel more powerful and therefore less resistant to cooperating), wrestling and escape games (which enable kids to claim their power), and three types of games for specific situations: low-energy-parent games, games for siblings, and non-physical games. But in reality, these are arbitrary distinctions, and many games blur these lines. Any physical game that gets your child laughing will strengthen your relationship and help your child feel, and act, better.

### • *LOVE GAMES* •

These games are all variations on the theme of how much you want and need your child. They're designed to transform a child's doubt about whether he's truly loved (and any child who is "misbehaving" harbors that doubt). These games are especially helpful with sibling rivalry, clinginess, and separation anxiety (including nighttime fears), but all kids love them. As one parent told me: "*I'm kind of shocked how much my son is loving the Fix Game! I don't think I've ever heard my son say 'Let's do it again!' so many times.*"

- **Kissing Game.** Try to kiss your child but keep missing her, so that most of your kisses land in the air or on the wall or couch. Lament loudly, wondering where she went, and keep proclaiming your determination to kiss her because you love her so much.

- **Fix Game.** I call this the Fix Game because it fixes whatever's wrong. Convince your child on a very deep level that you love him by chasing him, hugging him, kissing him, and then letting him get away and repeating the whole thing—again and again. For example: *"I need my Michael... You can't get away... I have to hug you and cover you with kisses... Oh, no, you got away... I'm coming after you... I just have to kiss you more and hug you more... You're too fast for me... But I'll never give up... I love you too much... I've got you... Now I'll kiss your toes... Oh, no, you're too strong for me... But I will always want more Michael hugs..."*

- **Fight Over Him.** A version of the Fix Game involving both parents. Fight over your child (jokingly), vying to see who can snatch her up and hug her. *"I want her!"* *"No, I want her!"* *"But I NEED her so much!"* *"No, I need her! You ALWAYS get her!"* (Be mindful, though, that kids are very sensitive to parental conflict. Be sure it's obvious that this is a game, not a serious struggle!)

- **I'll Save You!** *"My three-year-old lies on me, with his belly on my belly. I roll back and forth, pretending I might drop him on each side. I act silly and exaggeratedly say, 'Oh, I can't drop my boy, I love him very much. Nooo, I can't do this, he is my precious... I'll save you!"*—Natalia, mother of three-year-old.

## • SEPARATION AND REUNION GAMES •

Many of the games that children love most are actually about separation, which is a source of great fear for children. Peek-a-boo, one of the earliest games that gets babies laughing, is a separation and reconnection game. Hide and seek is just a more advanced version of peek-a-boo.

- **Chase.** Toddlers especially love chase games, which are about both power and separation. Simply chase your child around, eventually catching him. If he doesn't like it when you catch him, then narrowly miss, lament it, and express your determination to eventually catch him.

- **I Neeeed You.** Cling to your child, being super-exaggerated and silly. *"I know you want me to let go so you can go play, but I NEED you! I only want to be with you. PLEASE be with me now?"* Keep holding your child's hand or clinging to her dress. Keep your voice light and playful rather than needy so she feels free to pull away, and keep scooping her back to you and begging her to stay. She'll like the feeling that *she* is the one in charge of letting go, rather than feeling pushed away. If you act silly enough, she will also giggle and let off some of the tension around goodbyes. When she definitively pushes you away, say, *"It's okay. I know you will come back. We always come back to each other."*

- **Bye-Bye Game.** This is a simple version of hide and seek that triggers just a little separation anxiety, just enough to get kids giggling. Say, *"Let's play bye-bye. If you want me, yell 'Abracadabra!'"* (or another magic word that they pick). Then hide behind the couch or the door for just a moment before *you* yell *"Abracadabra!"* Then run out and hug your child. Say, *"I missed you! I just had to use our magic word so I could see you again! Okay, let me try that again... I'll be brave."* Then go hide again. Once more, come back out before he yells for you, which should get him giggling, especially if you play-act being silly and excessively worried. Keep playing in this way for as long as he's giggling, with you trying to yell first—and not really leaving—to work through his anxieties about you leaving him.

- **Search Game.** *"I pretend as if my kids are invisible and search all around the room, under the cot, inside the cupboard, under silly places like the carpet or even a cup (which always gets them to giggle) and then I turn toward the direction of the sounds pretending I heard something from there. Then in a few seconds they will make a sound to distract me and I'll catch them and hug them, saying, 'There you are, I was searching all over for you!'"* —Arthi, mother of a six-year-old and an eleven-month-old.

- **Magnetic Hands.** *"I pretend my hands are magnetic and I can't get them off her. She'll push me off, but they just keep pushing back to her. This works quite nicely at bedtime with separation anxiety."*—Kate, mother of four-year-old.

## • COURAGE GAMES •

These games provoke laughter because they allow kids to dance on the edge of their fears by being vulnerable while being manhandled by a safe parent. Give the child as much control as he wants. These games are great for any child dealing with physical fear, for instance with swimming lessons or potty learning.

- **Bucking Bronco.** Let your child hang onto your back (and hold his legs to keep him on) while you careen around the house madly like you're about to knock him off, finally bucking him onto the couch. In an alternative version, you simply get on your hands and knees on a bed, let your child climb on, and then buck him off.
- **Pizza.** Your child lies defenseless and giggling on the bed or rug while you make her into a pizza: kneading, applying sauce and toppings, baking, slicing, and nibbling.
- **Boingo.** Push your child over onto the bed and let them keep springing back up, to your great surprise.
- **Race Car.** *"My son sits on my lap and we pretend we're driving in a car with lots of turns and sudden stops."*—Emily, mother of four-year-old.
- **Elevator.** *"I open my arms to let my daughter into the elevator, than 'start' the elevator and do whatever action she chooses—I can be the hugging elevator, the kissing elevator, or the broken, shaking one."*—Corina, mother of seven-year-old.
- **Laundry Pretzel.** *"When my daughter is 'helping' to sort out the clean washing, we sometimes pretend that she's a T-shirt that needs folding and she ends up with her limbs in all sorts of wonderful configurations, which she finds hilarious."*—Anna, mother of three-year-old.

## • POWER GAMES •

Children often feel powerless and pushed around, as well as not yet able to cope with a big, scary world. Give your child the chance to be the more powerful one and to outsmart and overpower a terrible monster—you! Swagger and strut and roar at your child about how you'll catch him and show him who's boss, but when you chase him, trip and bumble and let him outsmart you or overpower you and get away. When you fail in your attempts to be powerful, your child gets to laugh at your incompetence, which helps her feel better about her own abilities. These games are especially good for strong-willed kids who want more control or who love to be right.

- **Push Over.** When she high-fives you, pretend she almost knocked you over. Another version of this is giving your child a feather or a pillow to hit you with. Every time he hits you, fall over! Acknowledge your child's formidable power: *"You are so strong! You pushed me right over!"* Another variation is to put your palms against your child's palms and let them push you across the room while you resist and lament how strong they are. In yet another variation, kids run from one room to another to tackle the parent, who is sitting down and rolls backward, hugging the child in their arms.
- **Remote Control.** Give your child a remote and pretend he can make you stop, start, move forward, and move backward.
- **Scary Monster.** Chase your children all over the house, letting them work together to outwit you. Scare them by coming close to catching them, but then miss, lamenting about how fast and strong and smart they are.
- **Animal Chase.** *"My daughter loves to play animal chase. She's usually the larger animal (for example, she is the cat while I am the mouse) and we make animal sounds as we chase one another. I let her 'catch' me after we run around for quite a while, laughing."*—Kelsey, mother of six-year-old.
- **Who's Stronger?** *"I try hard to lift my kids' arms, threatening to tickle their armpits. I'll comment about how strong they are and how hard it is to lift their arms. Eventually I'll get one arm up and try to tickle before they can pull it down again. The anticipation of me finally getting an arm lifted is enough to create infectious laughter."*—Jennifer, mother of four-year-old and seven-year-old.

## • *WRESTLING AND ESCAPE GAMES* •

Children often like to push against us and struggle free, which helps them to work through fear and claim their power. The child is less passive than in the courage games (see page 113). As with all of these games, the child should laugh and giggle, which means that he's releasing his fears and anxieties. If he gets very serious and fixated on "winning," it means the game is too threatening to him, and you need to ease off so he wins easily.

> Our bright, energetic, connected boys often have a lot of feelings to get out every day. We began a game called 'Escape,' almost by accident, when the boys were under three. We hold them and cackle, 'I won't let you go until all those feelings come out… you can try to escape, but you won't… ha ha ha!' They squirm and wriggle and arch and push and slither and I hold them tight. They laugh and yell and love it. The game ends with them cuddling up for a chat or escaping—which is always followed by crawling back on our laps for cuddles or another round of Escape. They now ask for Escape when they have a lot of feelings inside that they can't express. This activity can turn an ugly day right around! [96]
>
> — Lawrence Cohen

- **Escape.**
- **Pillow Fight.** Even teens will respond with laughter and reciprocate when you start whacking them gently with a pillow. One variation is to give your child a pillow to hold and then try to steal it from her.
- **Water Fight.** Make sure everyone feels safe (so no hose spraying in the face) and that it's a fair fight.
- **Take Off Each Other's Socks.** On the bed or a soft rug, compete to see who can get each other's socks off first.
- **You Can't Get to Mommy/Daddy!** This is a great game for when your child goes through a stage of only wanting Mommy or Daddy. Let the preferred parent sit on the couch. The other parent gets between the child and the preferred parent and boasts, *"You can't get to Mommy! You are all mine! Only I get to be with you! I will keep you from getting to Mommy!"* As he tries to get to Mommy, grab at him, but bumble and be unsuccessful. When he reaches Mommy, she laughs, cheers, hugs him, and then lets him go. You lament that he got through but continue to boast and challenge him and try to grab him. Exaggerate your boasting—*"You can't push around me to get to Mommy!"*—and then repeatedly bemoan how he gets past you. The child laughs as he works through his fears of being kept from his preferred parent, which helps him to accept the other parent instead of needing to defend his time with the parent he wants to be with. Very often, once you've played this game a few times, the child starts requesting to spend time with the formerly non-preferred parent.

## • *LOW-ENERGY-PARENT GAMES* •

These games are for those times when you want to get your child laughing, but need to sit or lie down.

- **Snore.** Lie down on the rug and—you guessed it—pretend to be asleep. Your kids will be hysterical trying to wake you up.
- **What's This Lump?** Sit lightly on top of your child on the couch, bed, or floor, and then wonder aloud why it's so lumpy. Let your child push you off so you fall down in surprise as she struggles to freedom.
- **Roly Poly.** Lie on the bed, hugging your child, and roll lightly over your child, first one way and then the other.

- **Gonna Catch You.** An easy version of Scary Monster (see page 113) for those days when you can't summon up the energy for a chase. Lie on the bed with a pillow on top of you and have your child jump over you as you try (not very hard) to catch her.
- **Briar Patch.** Like Brer Rabbit, announce to your kids that they can do whatever they want to you, as long as they don't do a certain thing that you specify, such as take off your shoes, pile pillows on top of you, or push you off the couch. Of course, they'll work together to do exactly that, while you get to do nothing, except occasionally protest, while they laugh as they manhandle you.
- **Asteroid.** *"When I was pregnant with number three, the kids made up a game called Asteroid where I could simply sit down in a chair. They would run toward me through 'space' one at a time and I'd shove them, so they would spin all crazy back toward the couch. Over and over again. Sounds stupid, but they love it and will still play it."*—Kelley, mother of three.
- **Be Very Afraid.** *"Notice the scary things under the covers (which are actually your feet) and pretend to be terrified of them. Let your child be the expert on how they are your feet and not something scary, but you keep being confused and scared anyway, so your child laughs and laughs at how incompetent and scared you are compared to her."*—Emily, mother of two.
- **Pillow.** *"I lie down with my head on my little 'pillow' (my daughter's tummy) while she sings a lullaby to help me fall asleep. She then tries to wiggle out from under my head (which I let her, after playfully grabbing and hugging her in my sleep as I would a real pillow). She then plays the role of a 'naughty little pillow' that jumps on me and wakes me up, while I pretend to be very surprised."*—Corina, mother of seven-year-old.

## • GAMES FOR SIBLINGS •

Since laughter releases oxytocin into the bloodstream, siblings who laugh together are bonding. On the other hand, it's easy for an older child to accidentally (or even intentionally) hurt a younger child. In general, it's best to keep games more gentle if your children are mismatched in age or strength. Here are a few ideas for games for different-age siblings:

- **Silly Dancing.** Put on music and dance together in silly ways. Practice giving everyone their own space or bubble while still coaxing each other into laughter. If one of your children is a baby or toddler, you may want to hold them and dance them around.
- **Pile of Pups.** *"Put the children on the bed and let them lie, roll, and bounce all over you and each other, while they pretend to be puppies. They always laugh and get some snuggles in with Mom and even with each other. My four-year-old holds back a bit to keep the one-year-old safe."*—Coralee, mother of four-year-old and one-year-old.
- **Ventriloquist.** Be the voice for a baby who can't talk yet, and have him say all kinds of funny things to his siblings to get them laughing. Be sure that he also says tender, grateful, and admiring things.
- **Chase.** *"I play a game where I hold our baby and we chase her big sisters until we catch them for a cuddle. The baby starts giggling in anticipation and always smiles at her sisters, which in turn gets her sisters giggling as well. The big girls know they have to be very gentle with the baby."*—Jessica, mother of three-year-old twins and a three-month-old.
- **Touchdown.** Pretend the baby is a football and run her around your other children into the end zone.
- **Pile Up.** *"My three children pile one at a time on top of Daddy and Mommy. The person on top is usually laughing because of the thrill of balancing and wobbling, and everyone in the middle gets their laughter squeezed right out. Plus the kids get to feel powerful in squashing their parents."*—Courtney, mother of seven-, five-, and three-year-olds.
- **Blind Bear.** *"Our kids love it when we crawl around on our hands and knees with our eyes closed and try to catch the kids as they run all around. The big ones help the little ones."*—Shannon, mother of ten-, eight-, five-, and two-year-olds.

- **Mouse in the House.** "*I pretend I'm busy in the kitchen while my kids stand right outside of the kitchen and they make scratching sounds on the wall. I keep wondering aloud what I'm hearing until I start running after them down the hall. They giggle crazily outside the kitchen in anticipation of when I'll take off after them, then throw themselves on their bed while I smother them with hugs and kisses, saying, 'I caught the mice!' I remember playing this with my mom growing up and it's now my kids' favorite game!*"—Barbara, mother of two.

### • NON-PHYSICAL GAMES •

- Make up funny song lyrics in the car.
- Rhyme with silly words.
- Trade roles at the dinner table so that each family member acts as someone else (kids' portrayals of adults can be hilarious).
- Sternly proclaim, "*No smiling, no laughing!*" and keep admonishing the kids to stop smiling and laughing as they erupt in giggles.
- Communicate with crazy animal sounds, silly rhymes, funny faces, and voices.

# Keeping Games Fun

- Agree on (and practice) safety rules, such as "When anyone says 'Stop!' we all freeze."
- Sometimes children get very focused on the physical struggle and become tense and serious. If they stay stuck in that struggle, they aren't offloading anxiety. The goal is to break through to giggling or laughter. See if you can shift the mood with silliness and by letting the child win. Whatever gets your child giggling, do more of it.
- Competition in itself is not bad, but valuing winning above the game is. For many children—and even some fathers and sons—noncompetitive games work best. (See the box on page 111 on "Should You Let Your Child Win?")
- Be sure opponents are well matched by handicapping adults and older siblings. When roughhousing with more than one child, try having teams of kids against grown-ups, to be sure the children don't use the opportunity to beat up on each other.
- You'll find that children will request a game over and over and laugh hysterically, which means it's touching some fear in them so they're finding it useful. But then, often fairly suddenly, they won't find it interesting any more, which means they've worked through that issue and it's time to experiment with other games.

## *When Roughhousing Ends In Tears*

When kids wrestle, pillow fight, and roughhouse, it's terrific for them. But it isn't always so good for our houses. And parents often worry that sooner or later, someone will get hurt.

Luckily, we can usually find a way to keep things safe. But that takes some attention on our part, and some teaching, over time. We can't just hope for the best; we need to help our kids learn how to roughhouse safely. It's our job to give kids the tools to stay safe, and to notice when the game stops feeling fun.

1. **Set limits *before* you get angry.** The minute you start getting worried that someone will get hurt, it's a signal to do something. (No, not yell.) It's time to intervene in a positive way to make sure things are safe. Many

parents try so hard to be patient that they let things get out of hand. Next thing you know, someone's crying, and someone (you!) is yelling. That's not the emotional regulation you want to model.

2.  **Assess the danger.** Is it actually dangerous? Maybe the kids are being loud and exuberant, but they're having a great time and there's no actual danger to anyone or to your home. Or maybe a small change would make a difference, such as moving the bed closer to the dresser so the kids can jump onto the bed safely, or substituting stuffed animals for blocks in their throwing game.

3.  **Connect before you correct.** Yelling across the room will just add to the frenzy. Instead, go physically to your children. When a child is spinning out of control, you can't get through to her unless you move in close in a friendly way. Make a positive connection with your child *before* you ask her to do something different. "*You two are having lots of fun with this roughhousing, aren't you?*"

4.  **Set limits.** State your rule or expectation, firmly and kindly: "*This kind of play doesn't belong in this room. I'm worried that you might roll into the lamp or the TV.*"

5.  **Empathize as you offer an alternative, and maybe a choice.** "*I know it's hard to stop, but this kind of play belongs in the basement on the tumbling mat, or outside. Outside? Okay, let's go!*"

6.  **Check in with all participants to be sure everyone is enjoying the activity.** "*Is everyone still having fun with this?*" If one of your kids is getting into a frenzy and the other seems a bit tense, you can help them check in with each other. "*Jaden, do you see that your brother isn't laughing? Let's stop for a minute and be sure everyone feels safe... Henry, you can tell Jaden to stop whenever you want. Let's practice that right now.*"

7.  **Help kids create safety rules.** If you're worried that someone's about to get hurt, try to resist just shutting down the action out of your own anxiety. Instead, help your kids make rules to keep everyone safe: "*Play wrestling is great, as long as you have rules to stay safe. What are your rules? Oh, when someone yells 'Stop!' both people have to stop? And no hitting? Those sound like great rules! How are they working so far? Do you need any other rules?*"

8.  **Tears aren't the end of the world.** Often, kids begin to cry when they get a big bump while roughhousing. Sometimes those tears are appropriate to the injury and your child is ready to get back into the action after a quick hug from you. Sometimes, though, kids sob wildly, clearly overreacting. That's a good thing; it means all of that laughter has loosened up the feelings stuffed in their emotional backpack, and they're taking advantage of this owie to share the deeper wounds they can't verbalize. After a good cry, your child will be so much more relaxed and happy.

    So instead of feeling like a bad parent because someone got hurt, relax. Take the opportunity to help your child with her feelings, and be glad she got a chance to cry. Afterward, ask both kids if they think they need to add any new rules to keep everyone safer next time. You might even write the rules down, have the kids sign them and put them up somewhere, so you can easily remind everyone of the agreed-upon roughhousing rules next time they start getting wild. (Written agreements have extra power even for kids who can't read.)

9.  **Help them wind down.** Sometimes you do need to redirect to a calmer activity. But often when kids are really wound up, they're about to meltdown. If you sense a meltdown brewing, test it by moving in close and setting a limit: "*Okay, Jacob, time to calm down now. That's enough rowdiness.*" If he calms down, great! If he bursts into tears, great! Better those feelings should come out by crying in your arms than by his hurting his little brother.

10. **Make sure your kids have a safe place to be wild.** Like puppies or bear cubs, kids need to roll around, wrestle, climb, and jump. Our modern lives don't always offer them those opportunities. If you don't have a yard, or a basement with a tumbling mat, make the kids' room safe for roughhousing, and make sure they get plenty of playtime at the playground or park. If you don't, your couch will start to look a lot like a trampoline and your lamps will be living dangerously.

## SPECIAL TIME

> He adores one-on-one time, really likes to be in charge of what we do, and is eager for the time without his brother interrupting. I get to know him better during this time and see glimpses of situations and phrases he's exposed to at preschool.
>
> — Bip, mother of four-year-old and one-year-old

Special Time is simply time that you spend *one on one*, focusing solely on your child. You turn off your phone and let your child take the lead in the interaction, asking your child to decide what the two of you will do.

- **Avoid structured activities** such as screens, books, or making cookies when having Special Time with young children. They don't offer as much opportunity for intimacy and imagination, and both the adult and the child often get more caught up in the activity than the connection. If you're worried about how much salt your child is putting into the cookies, you won't be able to simply adore your child as she takes the lead. And while reading to children is my favorite activity in the world, it puts the focus on the book instead of the child; there are plenty of other opportunities to read to your child, but usually not enough opportunities to let her take the lead in playing with you. And if you let your child do screens for Special Time, he'll never choose anything else. Of course, if your toddler wants to read you a book or your eight-year-old wants you to watch him ace his game on the tablet, it's fine to make an exception. And these guidelines no longer hold for tweens and teens who no longer "play." Letting them take the lead may well mean structured activities such as basketball, making cookies, or using a screen for them to introduce you to their music.

- **Say "yes."** If your child wants to do something that's impossible, such as going on a picnic by yourselves without the little sibling, find an approximation. Maybe you can have a picnic in her room while the sibling is napping. Sometimes children want "forbidden fruit" during Special Time—things that are usually off limits. Is there a way to make an exception for Special Time since you're present to help him stay safe? If you hold him while he slides down the banister during Special Time, it stops being "forbidden fruit" and he's less likely to try it when you're not around.

- **Let your child lead.** Resist your impulse to suggest improvements. Think of yourself as your child's assistant or his play therapist. Your job is to show up with all your heart, stay focused and emotionally generous, and enjoy your child. If you've ever felt truly seen, heard, and appreciated, then you know just how great a gift this is.

- **Learn instead of teaching.** Let your child show you his world and teach you whatever he wants, even if he insists that the grass is a raging ocean and dogs are fire-breathing dragons. Resist any impulse to teach your child anything during Special Time.

- **Don't ask questions.** It can feel intrusive to the child and forces her to shift from the wide world of imagination back to the world of logic and adult rules.

- **Stay present.** Many parents find Special Time excruciating at first. That's because most of us aren't experienced in simply being present. If you get bored, that's a signal to bring yourself more fully present into the moment with your child. (Time flies when you're having fun!) You can do this by becoming conscious of your breathing and your senses. Note the sounds in the room. Appreciate your child's enthusiasm, the delight in his smile. You may also need to stop evaluating yourself based on how much you've crossed off your list, and instead appreciate how much love you're bringing into the world by spending this time with your child.

Every parent I know who has started having regular Special Time with their child has told me that they see significant positive changes in their child's behavior. Parents often say that their child begs for Special Time, as if they've been missing an essential nutrient. In a way, they have.

Why? Because Special Time is a tangible expression of the parent's love, and an antidote to the disconnections of daily modern life.

Some parents tell me that they expected Special Time to "cure" their child's jealousy of a sibling but it hasn't worked. In those cases, the relationship repair is only part of what the child needs. He probably also needs a chance to work through his tangled feelings about his sibling. Otherwise, he'll carry them around and they'll drive his behavior. But at least starting Special Time will motivate him to *want* to follow the parent's lead, even if he can't always do it until he gets help with those emotions.

Other parents say, "*I only have one child and I'm home with her all day. I don't need Special Time.*" But I have heard from so many parents in this position that starting Special Time, where the parent sets aside time that the child knows is *hers*, makes a qualitative difference in the connection.

Bottom line: I've never seen Special Time, when the parent is really present with the child for 10 minutes a day minimum, fail to strengthen the parent–child relationship.

## *The Transition From Special Time: When Your Child Wants More, More, More!*

> My five-year-old daughter seems to have a difficult time having her 'cup filled.' Even after five minutes of Special Time (games where I'm doing what she wants, whether it's the tickle monster game or a game of cards with her—something that I consider quality time) she is still needy and can't turn it off. Even if I've given the two-minute warning, she will continue to jump all over me and then when I've clearly stated it's time for bath, she stomps off. Her attitude negates the fun time we just had. Even when I try to validate her feelings by saying that I know it's hard to stop the fun, I can't get through to her. I do understand that she is probably trying to tell me that we need to do this more often and I am working harder at making sure we get that quality time together, but when I'm just spent at the end of the day, I don't know how to respond to her need for more, more, more when I feel I've just given all I can.
>
> — Katrina, mother of five-year-old

We can all relate to this, right? After all, the parent has just spent time focusing intensely on her child, "filling her cup." It's the end of a long day, and it isn't easy to summon up our patience and presence to spend Special Time with our child, even for a few minutes. At this point, any sane parent is moving kids toward bath and bed. After this nice interaction, shouldn't the kid go off to her bath with a smile?

*Yes*, or at least that's what we hope for! And sometimes, some children will. But many kids won't, at least some of the time. And if we want to get through the evening without a rupture in our relationship, it helps to understand what's happening. Here are some reasons kids might struggle when you end Special Time:

1. **Her cup isn't yet full.** I'm sorry to be the bearer of bad tidings, but when kids are away from us all day, they need us intensely in the evening. Five minutes of one-on-one "quality time" may not be enough for your child, especially if she can't count on it daily. She's finally got your undivided attention; why should she let you go? Imagine you've been waiting for a few days for quality time with your partner. After five minutes of a lovely connection, your partner says, "*Sorry, we have to stop now.*" You might have a hard time transitioning, too. You might even feel hurt.

2. **It wasn't what he needed.** Maybe the activity was fun, and maybe your child even chose it, but maybe it didn't fill his deeper hunger to be held, adored, and wholly accepted. Those needs are best filled through physical play, not card games, reading, or other "structured" activities. So if you're having a hard time fitting in daily roughhousing as well as Special Time, try combining them. Let your child choose what to do with his Special Time every other day (except that screen time and reading are off limits). Then, on alternate days, you (the parent) reserve the right to choose, and always opt for physical games that get your child laughing. Depending on your child's age, chasing him around the house, the Fix Game (see page 111), or a contest to take off each other's socks (see page 114) will work like magic.

3. **It did fill her cup, but she doesn't make transitions easily.** All kids have a hard time with transitions, which is why we give them two-minute warnings. But some kids need extra help to get themselves from one activity to the next, especially when they're physically wound up from playing with us and the next activity moves them closer to bedtime. So don't take your child's upset as a reflection on your playtime. When you see it from her perspective—she was just getting going!—it's a reasonable response. Don't let the tough transition negate the nice connection you just made. Keep your own attitude positive. Is there a way to continue your game in some form as you get her into the tub?

4. **Your quality time tapped into some big feelings that need expression. When you first begin doing Special Time, your child is likely to feel a sense of great relief. Finally, he has you all to himself.** But now he's finally had your full attention and adoration, and he has to give you up all over again. He also feels safer after this closeness, so he's more likely to show you his grief from those times in the past when he wanted you and felt alone. So it's not surprising that when we start to disengage, he gets swamped with feelings. If your child has a hard time stopping your Special Time, make sure you allow an extra 10 minutes in case there's a meltdown after you've spent time connecting deeply. When he gets angry that you have to stop, stay compassionate and connected. If he cries, welcome his tears with understanding and be willing to sit with his pain. Be grateful that you've provided the safety to help him surface this pain. You're healing something much deeper than Special Time coming to an end. Acknowledge his feelings: "*You're upset that we have to stop playing. You just don't feel like it's enough right now. You can count on Special Time tomorrow, Noah. And right now we do have to stop... I'm sorry this is so hard for you.*"

What if he cries? Wonderful! That's an indication that the connection you've made is helping your child feel safe enough to go into scary emotional territory and show you some emotional baggage he's been dragging around. You'll be amazed at how cooperative and affectionate he'll be after a good cry in your safe presence. I know it's bath time and you want to move on with your family's schedule, but he won't cry forever and this won't happen every day.

Most parents in this situation get frustrated because we wonder if what we've just given our child made any difference at all. The answer is, *yes, yes, yes!* Every bit of love and patience you extend toward your child makes a huge difference. Your child is giving you an opportunity to help her heal. Don't take her reluctance to let you go as anything but a vote for more closeness and an SOS for your help.

## Practice: **Starting Special Time**

> The Special Time I had with my daughter really made a difference
> in the way she accepted her new sibling without jealousy.
>
> — Mari, mother of 4-year-old and 8-week-old

Before you announce to your child that your family is going to start having Special Time, you have a few decisions to make.

- How often can each parent manage Special Time? (Since Special Time strengthens the relationship, the child benefits from separate Special Time with each parent. But if one parent can only do it on weekends while the other does it during the week, that's still a net plus for the child.)
- How long will Special Time be?
- In addition to daily Special Time, can you also do a daily roughhousing session? (If not, you'll want to alternate as previously described.)

It's ideal if you can aim for half an hour daily with each child. But many families start with 10 minutes, because they're concerned about keeping siblings busy or about fitting the time for more than one child into an already busy schedule. Some parents worry that they won't be able to stay present and attentive for long, in which case 10 minutes is a good starting point.

If you're only doing 10 minutes one on one with each child, be aware that the transition at the end of Special Time may be a bit rougher, since your child may feel that he's just gotten started. But if 10 minutes daily is more than you're spending with each child one on one now, it's long enough to make a visible improvement in your relationship.

I recommend that you find an additional 10 minutes daily for roughhousing, which can usually be done with more than one child at once. (See the section Play and Laughter, starting on page 109.)

If you can't do Special Time daily, then prioritize a longer session on the weekend where the child chooses the activity, and make sure there's 15 minutes for a physical game with all the kids every day before or after dinner, plus at least five minutes of snuggling with each child (in addition to reading) at bedtime daily.

I know it's hard to find this time. But if it means the kids wear clothes still wrinkled out of the laundry basket, who cares? You're giving them the emotional foundation they need to thrive—now and for the rest of their lives.

Here's how to get started.

1. **Sit down with your children and tell them that you plan to have Special Time with each child.** Your goal is 10 minutes, and you'll do this as many days in the week as you can. (Why commit to this up front? Because your children benefit from looking forward to it and they feel like they're important to you. In addition, you're more likely to treat it as a priority if you make a commitment.) Call it by the most special name there is—your child's name. So in your house it might be Talia Time and Benjamin Time.

2. **If you have more than one child, set up a schedule on paper** (with photos of you with each child) so all siblings can look forward to their Special Time coming soon. One good strategy to keep siblings occupied when you have time with another child is to invite them to listen to audiobooks, which should absorb their attention enough to keep them from noticing you laughing with their sibling in the next room. (Headphones are essential for noise canceling, and if they need something to do with their hands, give them drawing materials to illustrate as they listen. Listening and drawing are great for brain development!) If they're too young for audiobooks, try making up a bunch of sensory bags or boxes and alternating them. Of course, if there's another adult to look after the other children, that's even better.

3. **Say, "*We'll alternate deciding what to do with our Talia and Mommy/Daddy Time. *** *Today it's your turn. I am all yours for 15 minutes. What would you like to do?*" If your child often has a hard time deciding what to do, work with them to brainstorm a list that you write down for them and post, so they don't spend the whole 10 minutes deciding what to do.

**4. Use a timer and schedule some open time at the end of Special Time.** Your child is almost certain to resist the end of Special Time, especially when you first start doing it. Using a timer helps her avoid feeling personally rejected by you when it's time to stop. Tell her that you know it's hard to stop Special Time, that you loved spending this time together, and you can't wait until next time. (For more ideas, see the section on The Transition from Special Time on page 119.)

## Reflection After Practice: Making the Most of Special Time

How did your child react when you announced that you'd be doing Special Time with him or her?

_____

_____

_____

Were you able to turn off all phones and screens?

_____

_____

_____

What did you actually do during Special Time?

_____

_____

_____

Were you able to let your child take the lead?

_____

_____

_____

How did it feel to do Special Time?

_____

_____

_____

Did you get bored?

_____

_____

_____

How did your child seem to react during Special Time?

_____

_____

_____

How long did you do Special Time for?

_____

_____

_____

How did your child react when you ended Special Time?

_____

_____

_____

What was your child like for the rest of the day?

_____

_____

_____

Is there anything you would do differently next time?

_____

_____

_____

# FINDING EASY CONNECTION OPPORTUNITIES IN THE DAILY ROUTINE

> "
>
> I've been trying to implement more connection (hugs, snuggles)
> right before a transition, and it has been transformative.
>
> — Vicky, mother of a two-year-old

A predictable routine helps children know what to expect, so they feel safe. Routines also help kids internalize constructive habits and develop a sense of mastery in handling their lives. For instance, in homes where there is no set time or space to do homework, kids may never learn how to sit themselves down to accomplish an unpleasant task. Kids who don't develop basic self-care routines, for everything from grooming to food, may find it hard to take care of themselves as young adults.

Routines can also help us as parents build regular habits of connection into our family lives. Parents are by definition overwhelmed; we don't need one more thing on our lists. But when we look at each part of our family routine as an opportunity to build closeness, we find that connection actually makes the routine easier by smoothing the transitions that are so hard for most children. For instance, if getting your child to stop playing and get dressed is a challenge every morning, add a meaningful connection time during that transition. Maybe you and your child can have a warm chat about what you're each looking forward to while he dresses every morning.

Why not create a few daily habits that deepen and sweeten your relationship with your child? After 30 days, any action becomes a habit, so you don't have to think about it. Here are some ideas to choose from, to work into your daily schedule:

- Snuggle with each child for five minutes when they first wake up. (Aim for 12 hugs or physical connections every day.)

- Take an extra minute to sit down with your kids at breakfast, asking what each one is looking forward to today.

- Instead of yelling at your child to keep him moving through the morning routine, empower him with a chart with photos of him doing each task, and let him be "in charge" of himself while you just smile and point to the chart, asking what he needs to do next. The connection part might include you giving him a hug after he completes each task.

- Write a love note to slip into her lunch box.

- Skip together as you walk to the school bus, or sing happy songs in the car.

- Hug when you say goodbye, when you're reunited, and as often possible all day long. Tousle hair, pat backs, and rub shoulders.

- As you hug him goodbye, tell him you can't wait to see him this afternoon and hear all about his day. Remember to say "*Have fun!*" instead of "*Be good!*"

- Take a few minutes to get organized before you leave the office, so you can really leave your work behind and turn off your phone. In the evening, you'll be able to give your family the best of you, not what's left of you.

- Turn off your phone and music when your child gets in the car with you at the end of the day, and listen to her most and least favorite parts of the day. Keep your phone turned off until your children are in bed.

- Spend 15 minutes of Special Time with each child, just following their lead and pouring your love into them. This habit alone can transform your relationship with your child.

- At dinner, ask an interesting question and give each child time to answer while everyone listens.

- Have a pillow fight or other roughhousing before bath time.

- Enjoy reading a bedtime story. Savor the smell of your child's hair and the warmth of her body.

- At bedtime, say goodnight to each part of your child's body, touching each part in turn gently, with a little massage. "*Goodnight shoulder, goodnight arm, goodnight elbow, goodnight forearm, goodnight wrist, goodnight hand, goodnight fingers.*" Take your time so your child relaxes each part of his body as you "recognize" it. The more you can simply relax and connect with your child, the more you help your child to feel fully present in his own body.

- Lie with each child for a few minutes in the dark, just snuggling companionably and telling her that you feel so lucky to be her parent.

## Practice: **Daily Habits to Strengthen Your Bond with Your Child**

On the next page, write three daily habits that you want to begin, to help you build a better relationship with your child.

### Example

Here's one mom's example:

1. I will spend at least 10 minutes every evening snuggling with each child at bedtime after lights out, just to connect and listen. This is in addition to any time spent reading and is not the time for me to bring up issues that may be bothering me. When my child brings up issues, I will listen and reflect ("That really bothers you") and assure him that we will address the issue tomorrow. The next day, I will follow through.

2. We will have dinner at the table where we can talk with each other rather than in front of the TV, and we won't answer the phone. I will make a list in advance of dinner-table questions to ask my kids to start interesting discussions. (For ideas, see the list of conversation starters at Aha! Parenting.)

3. I will get a notebook to share with my ten-year-old as a conversation journal[77] where we write back and forth to each other.

### Your Turn

(1) _____
_____
_____

(2) _____
_____
_____

(3) _____
_____
_____

## YOUR CHILD'S EMOTIONAL BANK ACCOUNT

Research on couples and on workplace relationships[98] consistently finds that we need at least five positive interactions to each negative interaction to maintain a healthy, happy relationship that can weather the normal conflicts and upsets of daily life. While I haven't seen research on the parent–child relationship, let's assume there's a similar ratio. When we're short on positive interactions, our relationship balance dips into the red. As with any bank account, we're overdrawn.

Every parent sometimes has negative interactions with their child. It's part of our job description as parents to guide our kids and keep them moving through the daily routine. All too often, that means setting limits, denying requests, and correcting behavior. Sometimes we're able to be emotionally generous, so our child doesn't perceive our guidance as "negative." More often, kids give us the benefit of the doubt because all the other loving, affirming interactions create a positive balance in our relationship account.

## Practice: **Fill Your Relationship Bank Account**

How would you rate your emotional bank account with your child at this time?

**1       2       3       4       5       6       7       8       9       10**

We need at least five positive interactions to balance out every negative interaction with our child. What can you do to build up a positive balance? Below, list as many things as you can think of, big and small. Post this list on your refrigerator so you always have "go-to" ideas. (I've started you off with some of my favorites.)

**(1)** Tell your child how lucky you are to be his parent.

**(2)** Have a cuddle.

**(3)** Smile and pat your child's back as you walk by.

**(4)** Ask your child to share her favorite music or song with you.

**(5)** Snuggle up on the couch and read a book together. (Even once children can read, they love to be read to.)

**(6)** Tell your child a story about what she was like when she was little, that highlights her determination or some other strength.

**(7)** Make your child's favorite food together.

**(8)** Put on music and dance together.

**(9)** Look at the stars together.

**(10)** Watch your child play, with full loving attention.

**(11)** Sit with your child as he practices his music, without making any corrections or suggestions, but simply appreciating and empathizing about the challenges.

**(12)** Give a foot massage.

**(13)** Play your child's favorite game with enthusiasm.

**(14)** Spend an afternoon on an outing that your child chooses, just the two of you.

**(15)** Special Time.

**(16)** Roughhousing.

**(17)** _____

**(18)** _____

(19) _____

(20) _____

(21) _____

(22) _____

(23) _____

(24) _____

(25) _____

## Practice: Connecting More Deeply with Your Child

Today, find at least three different times when you can connect with your child by doing some of the things in the list you made above. Pick one of your connections with your child to reflect on.

(1) What did you do to connect with your child?

_____

_____

_____

(2) Did you do anything to prepare yourself (for example, turn off your phone, use a mantra to focus your intention, meditate to center yourself)? If so, what? If not, what might have been helpful?

_____

_____

_____

(3) How did you feel throughout this interaction?

_____

_____

_____

(4) How did your child respond to you?

_____

_____

_____

**5** How did your child handle the end of the connection when you separated? If he or she had a hard time, is there a way you could make separation smoother in the future?

_____

_____

_____

**6** How did your child act later? Was there a change in mood, cooperation, or connection?

_____

_____

_____

**7** What did you feel good about in this interaction?

_____

_____

_____

**8** Is there anything you would do differently in the future?

_____

_____

_____

# MAKING REPAIRS

Every relationship has conflict. The question is how we handle those conflicts—so they build walls between us, or so they bring us closer? Our goal with our children is to model how to repair those inevitable relationship ruptures in ways that strengthen our bond with them.

What is a relationship rupture? When things get tense in your house and you snap at your child, or when your child gets very angry, that's a relationship rupture. Saying "no" to your child is a tiny relationship rupture, most of the time. Sometimes it's a big rupture if it comes on the heels of other disappointments for your child, or if they have a big backpack full of emotions that are ready to spill out, so your "no" becomes the straw that breaks the emotional backpack.

All parents sometimes find themselves saying exactly the wrong things, or they simply get so angry that they lose it and then later feel terrible, and they want to reconnect with their child. In those times when you feel bad about how you've acted, how do you reconnect? Start by apologizing.

## *How (And When) To Apologize To Your Child*

Most parents find themselves insisting that their child apologize to a sibling, friend, or adult on a regular basis. And yet it can feel awkward to apologize to our children, and many of us avoid it.

We sometimes justify this by saying that an apology will lessen the child's respect for us. But just the opposite is true. Don't you have more respect for others when they own up to their mistakes and try to make things better?

I think the sad truth is that most of us feel uncomfortable apologizing. Not just because we have to admit we made a mistake, but because it brings up feelings of shame for us, since we remember being forced to apologize as children.

But what does a child learn when a parent avoids apologies?

- Apologizing means you've done something bad, or you *are* bad. There's a feeling of shame attached.
- It's okay to damage a relationship and not acknowledge it or try to repair it.
- When you apologize, you lose status.

No wonder kids won't apologize to their siblings unless we force them! Wouldn't it be better to teach these lessons, which your child learns when you model apologies?

- We all sometimes make mistakes and we can try to make things better.
- We all sometimes hurt others. It's important to acknowledge when we do that and make amends.
- When you apologize, the other person feels better about you.

Apologizing still may not feel easy for your child. But if you "normalize" apologizing and let your child decide when she's ready to do it, you'll find she's much less resistant and even begins to take the initiative because she enjoys the feeling of redemption.

So when should you apologize to your child, and what should you say?

1. **Apologize easily and often**, including for small "oops" moments that are not a big deal but just part of life. "*Oops! Sorry I interrupted you.*" Any time you act in a way that you wouldn't want your child to act is a time to consider apologizing. Obviously, don't apologize for setting appropriate limits. But it's our job to manage our own emotions, no matter what our child does, so apologizing when we "lose it" is essential, unless we want our child to copy our "tantrums."

2. **Describe what happened and express your regret.** "*We were all so upset, right? You were yelling. Then I started yelling. I'm so sorry. No one ever deserves to be yelled at, no matter what. In our house, we try to find respectful ways to express what we need, and I didn't do a very good job of it then. So I'd like to try a do-over. But first, I want you to know that I'm really sorry, and I'm working hard to be respectful, even when I'm angry. We all get angry. It's okay to be angry. It's not okay to yell at other people.*"

3. **Be sure your apology acknowledges the effect of your action on your child.** You might say something like, "*You started crying. It must have been pretty scary when I yelled, huh?*" If your child just shrugs, that's an acknowledgement that, yes, it's scary, but they don't want to admit it. Sometimes your child might angrily say, "*I hate it when you act like that, Mommy,*" and you can again empathize. "*I know you do, Tess. It must be scary.*" Older children will sometimes act like it doesn't bother them when you yell, but it always does, so acknowledging that it must have been hard for them when you yelled is an important part of your apology.

4. **Resist the urge to blame.** Many of us start to apologize and then veer into excusing ourselves because the child was in the wrong. Sure, I yelled—but you deserved it! We all know, though, that two wrongs don't make a right. Besides, we're the adult. It's our job to be the role model.

5. **It's okay to explain, but don't ruin a good apology by making excuses for your behavior.** "*I had such a hard day, and I couldn't deal with one more thing going wrong. So I yelled at you. But that's no excuse. It's my job to manage my own emotions. Yelling is no way to work something out with someone you love.*"

6. **If your child thinks it's a big deal, acknowledge that, even if you don't think it is.** "*I told you I would get you a new notebook when I went to the store, and then I completely forgot. I'm so sorry. I know you were counting on me to come home with the notebook.*"

7. **Model accountability by taking responsibility for whatever you can in a given situation.** "*I'm so sorry I wasn't here to help you two work this out.*" You're not blaming yourself. You *are* sorry you weren't there. And your taking even a small share of the responsibility will help them step up and take responsibility themselves.

8. **Give yourself a do-over if appropriate.** *"Sorry, Amelia, I didn't mean to snap at you. Let me try that again. Here's what I meant to say…"*

9. **Make a plan for repair.** *"Tell you what. We'll stop by the store on the way to school in the morning to get your notebook."* This is an essential part of any apology: *"What can I do to make this right?"*

10. **Make a plan for next time.** Your child will learn a lot if you ask her what you could do differently next time and discuss it without getting defensive. Then, make a commitment. *"Next time I will Stop, Drop, and Breathe to calm down."* Then just do it. If someone you loved hurt you repeatedly and apologized every time, you'd stop believing the apologies sooner or later. Apologies are only meaningful if you know the person will act in good faith to avoid repeating the behavior.

11. **Ask your child if they're ready to reconcile.** This can be as simple as *"I hope you'll forgive me."* It helps the child make the emotional leap to let go of resentment and reconnect emotionally. Don't force this; children should not feel pressured to "forgive" before they feel ready. Some parents resist this step because they feel they're handing their power to the child, who might withhold forgiveness. But if the child isn't ready to forgive, you want to know that so you can help them resolve whatever upset they're still holding onto from the interaction.

12. **Notice there's no shame, no blame.** Instead, focus on making things better with your child. It takes courage to admit you were wrong and to ask for forgiveness. But it makes you a better parent, and it raises healthier children who value relationships and can take responsibility. Isn't it time we dropped the legacy of shame that gets attached to apologies?

# Apologizing to a Toddler

Since toddlers are not known for their conceptual thinking, the best way to make a repair with a toddler is to tell them the story of what happened. This helps them visualize the hurtful incident, understand better what happened, and see that things are different now—you are offering them warm physical interaction and showing that you don't approve of your previous actions.

*"You had applesauce in your bowl, right? And then you poured it down the stairs! See, right here? Oh, no! What a mess! And what happened then? That's right, Mama screamed. I was very upset. You were scared, right? I'm so sorry I scared you."* (Give a warm hug, and then continue.) *"I was very mad. But no more yelling. Yelling is scary. Right? No more yelling, Mama!"*

At this point, your child might express some feelings about the incident, or might echo you: *"No more yelling, Mama!"*

Agree with her. *"No more yelling, Mama!"* Finish with a big hug.

(Yes, you can then cheerfully enroll her to clean up the applesauce with you. But don't make it sound like a trade-off; make it sound like an adventure.)

# Practice: **Apologizing**

When was the last time you felt bad about an interaction with your child? Describe the interaction.

_____

_____

_____

If you could "do over" the interaction, what would you like to have said or done?

_____

_____

_____

Next time, what could you do to make it more likely that you will end up proud of how you acted?

_____

_____

_____

What can you say now to your child to make things better between you? (Example: If the interaction was a few days or more ago, you can bring it up by saying, "*I was thinking about last weekend, when you and I were talking about X and I said Y. I wish I had not said that. I think it hurt your feelings, and it isn't even what I meant to say. I'm really sorry if I hurt you; I never want to do that. As I always say to you, we can express our needs without attacking each other. Here's what I wish I had said at the time…*")

_____

_____

_____

## Part 3

# Coaching Instead of Controlling

**What is coaching, as opposed to controlling? Coaching is offering support to help the other person do and become their best. Controlling is using threat or coercion to force the other person to do what we want.** Decades of research clearly demonstrate that controlling parenting has negative results, raising children more prone to anxiety and depression, who do worse in school, work, and relationships.[99] But even when we're aware of this, most of us have the impulse to resort to control techniques in those tough moments when we can't get our children to do what we want. Why? Not just because we need her to cooperate in that moment. That wouldn't be worth such a high price to her long-term emotional health. I think it's because we're afraid. Afraid that unless we control our child, she won't get over her upset, or act appropriately, or learn the right lesson. Afraid that we're not good enough as parents. Afraid that our child will be acting like this forever. The stakes, after all, are high.

But what if we had faith in our child's goodness and in the power of Mother Nature to help our child grow and mature? What if we saw him as a struggling youngster just trying to meet his needs? What if we believed in the power of our relationship with our child to give him a bridge to become the best he can be? What if, instead of listening to the voice of fear that tells us to crack down and control, we listen to the voice of love?

Every choice we make, at its core, is a move toward either love or fear. In this part of the book, we'll look at why controlling—acting from fear—doesn't work to raise an emotionally-healthy child. We'll give you coaching and support tools to use instead. Think of them as love in action. Love never fails.

## WHY COACHING SUPPORTS KIDS TO BE THEIR BEST SELVES

There's an old adage that says that if you don't know where you're going, you'll end up somewhere else. So let's begin with our goal in raising children. We're really raising adults, right? And I think you'll agree that we want our children to grow up to be happy, caring, responsible people who contribute their unique gifts to make a positive contribution to the world.

Of course, we also need to get from here to there. So we want life with our children to be happy now, both for them and for us. We want to be able to enjoy them and find parenting a rewarding experience. We want them to learn as they grow, mastering the challenges of each developmental age. We want them to get along well with others and fit into society, but we also want them to follow their own inner compass. We want them to do what we ask, but to be able to think for themselves.

So you can see that we're going for short-term cooperation, but also for long-term individuation. The only way to get both is to use our daily interactions with our child to accomplish both our immediate goal (for example, to get our child into the bathtub) and our long-term goal (to raise a child who wants to take care of himself and has the capability to do so). While controlling the child can sometimes accomplish the first goal, only coaching does both. And on those all-too-frequent nights when we're willing to settle for simply getting the kid into the bathtub, it's useful to remember that doing the extra work to coach makes it more likely that tomorrow's bath will be easier. Coaching becomes more effective over time, because it strengthens your relationship with your child and gives your child the resources to manage himself.

Coaches don't play the game for the kids on their team. Instead, they support the team members to develop their skills so they can play their best game. Coaches figure out what skills each player needs to work on, teach those skills through demonstration and practice, and help the children develop those skills over time. Effective coaches don't try to "control" their charges with punishment. Even rewards don't work, if the child doesn't have the skills to play a winning game. Coaches also have to be amateur psychologists, helping children through their fears and insecurities and cheering them on. They understand that coaching self-management skills is as important as coaching specific sports skills. They support kids through their bad days, encourage kids to rise to the occasion, and believe in kids' potential. In short, coaches help children to be their best selves.

Coaching as a parent isn't much different, except that parents ask much more of children and thus rely more on their close emotional bond. Parents who coach help their child *want* to be his or her best self, instead of trying to control the child with punishment and rewards. They believe their child is doing the best he can and will do better with better support. They offer that support with:

- **Connection** or prioritizing the parent–child relationship so the child trusts that he has at least one adult who understands and believes in him. Research repeatedly confirms that parental responsiveness, including warmth, respect, empathy, and meeting the child's emotional and physical needs, is one of the most important factors in children's attachment security and emotional well-being.

- **Structure to meet basic needs**, which means managing the home environment to make sure the child's needs are met so she can thrive. Basic needs include physical needs (such as safety, sleep, healthy food, and physical affection) as well as psychological needs (such as attention, love, autonomy, and power). (There's nothing wrong with feeling powerful, able to navigate the world, and have an impact. It's when people use their power "over" others that it's a problem. And guess where people learn to do that? From the way they're treated as children.) We can think of structure as environmental management and preventive maintenance to keep children's inner resources replenished, so they can flourish and rise to the challenges of daily life.

- **Emotion coaching** to help the child through tough emotions, rather than trying to control or dismiss the child's emotions. Emotion coaching is the foundation of emotional intelligence, or EQ (now considered to be more important to a child's success than IQ). Parents who work on their own emotional intelligence are more comfortable emotion coaching and raise more emotionally-intelligent children.

- **Loving guidance** that fosters autonomy[100] via encouragement, empathic limit setting, and teaching the skills of repair, problem solving, and win–win solutions.

These four parental factors—connection, structure to meet basic needs, emotion coaching, and loving guidance—help children develop emotional intelligence, self-discipline, resilience, life skills, autonomy, and relationship skills including empathy, which are all essential components of a successful life. They determine the child's ability to cooperate with her parents, but also the child's ability to thrive for the rest of her life.

Any time a child is not "behaving," the most effective intervention will be in one or more of these four areas. That's true even when children are unusually challenging. In those cases, the child may have more intense needs, which can be harder for the parent to meet. But the most effective intervention is still to meet those needs rather than to cause pain—physical or emotional—to try to force the child to "behave."

Notice that coaches—whether team coaches or parents—always take an active role in guiding and influencing a child's behavior. But coaches don't force or coerce the child, they don't try to control the child's feelings, and they don't make the child feel bad about who he is. In fact, one of the hallmarks of successful parents (and successful coaches of children) is a warm appreciation of each unique child, and another is the use of connection and inspiration to motivate the child. That doesn't mean you don't provide loving guidance and clear limits. But you can do that with respect and empathy, which are more effective than force over time.

In fact, unless children have a secure attachment to a parent, have their basic needs met, and have the opportunity to develop some emotional intelligence, no amount of force can make them "behave." They simply don't have a brain and nervous system that's developed enough for them to manage their emotions and impulses.

Even if force does make a child behave temporarily, there are hidden costs. Autonomy is a universal human need, and virtually all children will rebel against control, either openly or passively.[101] Of course, there are some children who respond to force by trying very, very hard to be very good, deadening their connection to the "unacceptable" parts of themselves. But, if you think that kind of obedience is a good outcome, have a conversation sometime with an adult who did this in childhood about their own tendencies toward anxiety and depression.

Luckily, there are better ways to help children cooperate. Let's take a closer look at the pitfalls of controlling parenting. Then we'll spend the rest of the book giving you coaching tools and skills that *do* work.

## WHAT IS CONTROLLING PARENTING?

> Honey, when you grow up, I want you to be assertive, independent and strong willed.
> But while you're a kid, I want you to be passive, pliable, and obedient.
> — Anonymous

Controlling parenting is usually defined as being coercive, intrusive, or domineering, and includes enforcement of parental control with punishment and rewards, including threats, shaming, guilt, and love-withdrawal,[102] all of which make children feel bad about their emotional reactions and who they are as people. Numerous studies have linked "controlling parenting" to negative child outcomes such as depression,[103] anxiety,[104] perfectionism,[105] lack of empathy,[106] and difficulties in self-regulation.[107]

That doesn't mean you shouldn't guide and limit behavior, which is required of all parents. The key is limiting behavior while accepting emotion. For instance, a parent might ask their child to help bring in the groceries and not hit his brother. But a controlling parent takes this a step further, insisting that the child *should want* to help his mother or he must not love her, and *should love* his brother and never feel like hitting him—if not, the child is a bad person. So the child ends up feeling bad about who he is, since he knows that sometimes he doesn't feel like helping his mother and sometimes he does feel like hitting his brother.

Take a look at these examples—and what a parent using the coaching method might do instead.

| Child Behavior or Desire | Controlling Parent's Response | Coaching Parent's Response |
|---|---|---|
| Inappropriate behavior | Parent threatens or punishes. Fear works short term when kids are young as long as parent is present. | Parent uses empathy and connection in setting clear limits. Child chooses better behavior to follow parent and develops self-discipline. |
| Anger | Anger is punished, so kids repress it, which creates anger-management issues or anxiety. | Parent validates anger so child can verbalize rather than acting out. |
| Emotions | Parent ignores, dismisses, or punishes emotion. Child represses emotion, causing self-regulation issues. | Parent helps child work through emotions, developing self-regulation and resilience. |
| Developing values | Child is motivated to avoid punishment, rather than by concern for others. | Child respects parent so is open to the parent's teaching; child develops inner compass. |
| Developing life skills, from brushing teeth to doing homework | Parent rewards or punishes child, creating power struggles and incentives to "game" the system. | Parent provides child with support to enjoy becoming responsible for himself. |
| Making decisions | Parent makes decisions for child. | Child is encouraged to make choices and decisions. |
| Privacy | Parent invades child's personal space. | Parent allows child to have increasing personal privacy. |
| Autonomy and sense of self | Parent cannot tolerate child having different opinions, interests, or identifications. | Child is respected as a unique individual and is never asked to compromise her own integrity. |
| Developing self-motivation | Child is rebellious, but not self-motivated. | Child feels empowered and motivated. |

If you're feeling a bit nervous right now, let me reassure you. I don't think there is a parent in the world who has not at times exerted control to get a specific behavior from their child. And even when our intention is to accept our child's emotions, virtually all of us have times when we feel the urge to shut down our child's feelings, whether because those feelings trigger us or because they're just plain inconvenient!

So part of parenting is that we feel the urge to control. Our goal in parenting peacefully is to become more aware of our own emotional reactions to our child's behavior and expressions of feeling. Then, when we notice that we're headed into a power struggle, we can consciously let go of our urge to control our child's feelings and opinions, even while we limit her behavior. It's when we aren't consciously aware of our need to control that we inadvertently end up wounding our children. For example, one family I knew struggled with the common problem of getting their three-year-old to take a nap. The father—who I knew well and who was a good and loving father in so many ways—spanked the child until she complied. But it wasn't enough for him that she settled, sobbing, into her bed. He felt the need to teach her obedience, so he forced her to say that she *wanted* to nap.

Most of us know better than to get drawn into such an extreme power struggle. But any time we go beyond behavioral compliance to insist on controlling the child's feelings or sense of self, we're infringing on the child's autonomy. In fact, any time we coerce a child with punishment, we're relying on controlling instead of coaching.

## *Punishment Is The Ultimate Control*

Punishment is the root of violence on our planet.

— Marshall Rosenberg, originator
of nonviolent communication[108]

Most parents assume that children who know that they'll be punished for transgressions are better behaved than children who don't. However, research studies on discipline consistently show that punishment produces unhappy kids who feel bad about themselves and behave worse than other kids—and therefore get punished more![109] That's because punishment is the enforcement arm of controlling parenting. Here's what children learn from punishment.

1.  **"Might makes right."** Kids learn what they live and what you model. If kids do what you want because they fear you, it teaches them to bully. Physical force teaches kids to behave with violence toward themselves and toward others.

2.  **"I don't care what my parents want. They aren't on my side."** Because your relationship with your child is less close, your child loses interest in pleasing you and misbehaves more.

3.  **"I'm just supposed to do what I'm told."** Kids take less responsibility and are more willing to follow the peer group.

4.  **"I just have to make sure I don't get caught."** Research shows that kids who are punished are delayed in their moral development, because they're more concerned about avoiding punishment than about the cost of their behavior to others. They begin lying early in life and perfect it by the time they're teenagers.

5.  **"I'm secretly bad inside, because I have these feelings that make me want to do bad things."** Not surprisingly, children raised with authoritarian discipline are more likely to struggle with issues of self-worth.

6.  **"They can't make me."** Because the discipline comes from outside, kids resist it. Since they don't get a lot of practice giving up something they want for something they want more (that warm relationship with the parent), they don't develop the neural pathways for self-discipline. If you're surprised by this, consider that

virtually all adults today were raised with some degree of harshness, and we chafe at control to that degree—even when we're the ones imposing it! That means we end up with problems regulating ourselves. Sometimes this shows in resentfulness at any perceived limit or criticism, or by overreacting when we think someone is trying to tell us what to do. Sometimes it shows up in rebellion against the limits we impose on ourselves. For instance, we may harshly starve ourselves with a new diet and then rebel by binging. (Studies show that kids raised with strict parenting are more likely to become overweight, which is an issue of self-medicating as well as lack of self-discipline.[110])

I know parents who say that they punish their child from love. But punishment is effective only to the degree that the child experiences it as painful. So while parents may think they're using "loving discipline" to teach their child, the child will never experience pain that is purposely caused by the parent as "loving." In fact, the child will experience pain and shame. Punishment intensifies the shame response to toxic levels and sends the clear message that the child is so bad that the people who are supposed to nurture and protect her are intentionally hurting her, either physically or emotionally. That shame is so painful that, as a result, most of us carry the sense of being somehow defective throughout our lives.

So if punishment doesn't create better-behaved kids, why do we do it? Because we're frustrated and don't know what else to do! And because, most likely, we were punished, so it seems natural to us.

## The Research On Physical Punishment

Were you spanked as a child? If so, you may think it's a good way to guide your child. Or maybe you don't want to spank, but you find yourself doing it because you don't know how else to get through to your child. Interestingly, adults who were not spanked as children don't spank their kids. It just feels wrong to them. And you know what? They find other ways to get through to their kids. And their children turn out fine! In fact, research shows that it's the kids who are spanked who have a harder time regulating their emotions and who therefore get into more trouble. The past five decades of large, peer-reviewed studies consistently show that the more children are spanked, the worse they behave.[111,112]

Toddlers who are physically disciplined show drops in IQ and more aggression a year later.[113] In fact, studies consistently show that children who are spanked have lower IQs than children who are not spanked,[114] and are more aggressive throughout childhood and into adulthood.[115] As five-year-olds, children who have been spanked are more likely than non-spanked children to be defiant, to demand immediate satisfaction of their wants and needs, to become frustrated easily, to have temper tantrums, and to lash out physically against other people or animals.[116] Children who are physically disciplined are more rebellious as teenagers[117] and more prone to depression, anxiety, substance abuse, and domestic and other violence as adults.[118] These lifelong effects occur even when the adult says that the spanking they received as a child was deserved and did not hurt them.

> Recent studies show that regular spanking,
> like all repeated experiences, changes the brain.

Some studies show a more active amygdala,[119] which causes more reactivity. Others show that children who are spanked regularly have less gray matter and a less developed prefrontal cortex, and therefore are less able to evaluate the consequences of their actions and control their impulses.[120]

So, if you were spanked and think you came out fine, it wasn't because of the spanking. And, while you are (hopefully) fine, you would be healthier emotionally if you hadn't been spanked.

# Spanking Is on the Decline

We often think of spanking as controversial, but among scientists, spanking is not controversial at all. It's clearly destructive. The large body of research that's accumulating on the negative effects of spanking is slowly changing our approach to disciplining children all over the world. In all, 52 countries have now banned spanking. There's even been a 50 percent decline in spanking over the past 25 years in the United States[121] (which often lags behind in measures of child health[122]). In 2011, about 20 percent of median-income families spanked their children, while about 12 percent of wealthier families and 50 percent of lower-income families did so. Whether the class-based tendency to spank is based on education, cultural upbringing, or stress isn't clear, but most experts presume an interaction of all three factors.

Most parents who spank justify it as being good for their child, but don't admit a secret reason: spanking makes us feel better! When we feel angry and powerless, we lash out. Anger is a defensive reaction to keep ourselves from feeling the deeper fear and pain we have about our child's behavior. So the truth is that we spank to avoid our own pain.

(Parents sometimes ask if spanking at least empties the parent's emotional backpack. The answer is that no, expressing anger does not empty anyone's backpack. Anger is not in the backpack; it's a defense against feeling the more vulnerable feelings in the backpack. If you want to empty your backpack, you have to be willing to feel your own tears and fears.)

Hitting a child for any reason undermines the trust relationship every child needs with her parents. Discipline means "to teach." If we're serious about raising good kids, we need to use methods that teach kids to manage themselves. Spanking does not do that. Instead, it teaches children to be afraid of us, which is no basis for love.

If you've been using physical punishment, it might be hard to imagine life without it. But there are many families who never hit their children, and research shows those children are actually *better* behaved.[123] So the next time you get so angry you want to hit someone, tell your kids you're taking a time-out and you'll deal with them later. Then go into the bathroom, put your hands under the running water, and calm yourself down. Use the time to get calm, not to justify your anger. When you come out, tell your kids you need to think hard about what they did, but right now you need to fix dinner (or do the laundry, or whatever). Tell them you need them to be angels and you will talk when you are all calm later. Then follow through. Your discipline and teaching will be so much more effective. They'll learn a lot better from your guidance when neither of you is flushed with "fight or flight" neurotransmitters. And you'll be one step closer to becoming the kind of parent every child deserves.

## Practice: Getting Clear About Your Discipline Approach

What punishments were used on you as a child? How did you feel about them?

_____

_____

_____

What are your long-term goals for your child?

_____

_____

_____

Will authoritarian discipline accomplish those goals as well as positive parenting?

_____

_____

_____

Do you feel confident that you can never touch your child in anger? If not, what can you do next time you feel yourself losing control?

_____

_____

_____

## Time-Outs

Your pediatrician most likely recommends that you use time-outs, which are the most common disciplinary strategy for young children in the United States. That's because they're a lot better than spanking. But are they an ideal way to guide your child? No. They're a form of love-withdrawal, designed to remind the child that you could easily ban him from your presence unless he does what you want.

Banishing an upset child is pushing him away just when he needs you the most. Since your child's biggest fear is abandonment, which would threaten his survival, this can be an effective threat. But it doesn't solve the problem that led the child to misbehave to begin with, so the child will still act out. Because the child now feels shamed, blamed, and "bad," he's more likely to act "bad" in the future.

Parents often say they use time-outs to help their child "calm down." But the child isn't actually working through her emotions, she's stuffing them. Time-outs don't help the child learn to regulate her emotions so she can choose appropriate behavior. They give her the message that only her "pleasant" feelings are okay, that her authentic, messy, difficult feelings—part of who we all are—are unacceptable and unlovable. She feels like a bad person, so she stuffs those emotions. And remember what happens to stuffed emotions? They bubble up to get healed later, so the child acts out again. That's why time-outs don't create better-behaved children.

With a strong-willed child, you end up using threats and force to get them to time-out, so you're setting up power struggles, or worse. And with a more compliant child, you didn't need a time-out to teach the lesson to begin with, so you're just breaking their spirit.

Time-outs are a terrific calming technique for parents to use for themselves. When you find yourself losing it, take five. This keeps you from doing anything you'll be sorry about later. It models wonderful self-management for your kids. But notice this isn't really a time-out. It's a time-in! You aren't castigating yourself about what you did wrong. You're choosing to connect to your love instead of your fear, to support yourself through your upset. You're connecting with your deeper wisdom so you can self-regulate.

So, if you've been using time-outs and you're wondering what to do in those moments when you need to interrupt your child's off-track behavior and help him re-regulate, try using a time-in. We'll talk more about time-ins in the section on emotion coaching.

## Consequences

A consequence is a result. A child does (or doesn't do) something, and learns from the consequence of their action. Sometimes those consequences are imposed by parents, but often they're imposed by life. If the parents are *not* involved in the consequences—for instance, if the child doesn't study so they flunk their test, or they're mean to a friend so the friendship ends, kids can learn a lot from suffering the consequences of their actions.

Of course, you don't want the same bad result to happen frequently, or your child's self-image will become that of a person who flunks tests and can't keep friends, and they'll have learned an unintended lesson. It works better, if possible, for kids to skip such lessons and instead learn from you the necessary self-management habits that prevent failed tests and friendships. As a last-ditch strategy, though, we all learn from letting things go wrong—as anyone who's ever been stopped for speeding knows. Particularly with teenagers, letting them learn from their own choices can be an effective teaching strategy.

But of course there are some behaviors that most parents aren't willing to let our children "try out" and learn from the consequences, like not wearing bike helmets or being defiant to their teachers or breaking things when they get angry. So it's common to enforce those limits with threats of "consequences" that we ourselves will impose on our child if she doesn't observe our limits.

**This is where things get complicated, though, because when you, the parent, threaten your child with "consequences," something changes.** A parent-imposed consequence does not seem to the child like the natural result of their action. It seems like a hostile act from you. You're threatening punishment: either taking away something they like or imposing something they don't like. So, when a parent creates a consequence, a child will *always* see it as a punishment and will experience all the negative effects that come with such a punishment. This means that any time you come up with a consequence for your child, it will undermine your relationship.

You may be wondering, then, how will children learn? First of all, remember: if your child is "misbehaving" because he doesn't know the appropriate behavior, then it isn't actually misbehavior at all, and simply teaching him is sufficient.

What we're really asking is, how will the child do the right thing if he doesn't suffer from doing the wrong thing? But children *want* to be good people and live up to our expectations; they do the best they can just like we do. So if he knows the right behavior and is still "misbehaving," then it means he's struggling with big feelings or unmet needs that are overriding his desire to do the right thing. "Teaching a lesson with a consequence"—meaning imposing emotional or physical pain—won't help. What he needs is help to self-regulate.

**Does he still need to repair what he's messed up? Of course!** Maybe he needs to write a letter to his teacher acknowledging what he did and promising to make a better choice next time. Maybe you keep the key to his bike, which stays locked until he has a bike helmet on. Maybe she needs to buy you a new bowl, out of her birthday money. But these aren't punishments, they're repairs. They're the choice the child makes, with your guidance, to clean up a mess he made. This is more complicated than punishment, and a lot more effective in teaching the lessons you want to teach. (We'll talk more about helping kids make repairs and learn lessons without punishment in the section on loving guidance.)

In short, no control tactics—yelling, shaming, threats, time-outs, consequences, spanking—are as effective as peaceful parenting in encouraging cooperative behavior. (We talked about why and how to stop yelling in the first section of this book.) Why, then, do most of us use them? Because we're desperate! We don't know what else to do. So when we start to threaten, that's a signal that we need to come up with another strategy.

If you're feeling a bit worried about how to get your child to do what you want without time-outs and consequences, it's because, like many people, you've gotten into the habit of using threats to make your child obey you. But what if we reframe the whole picture? Let's assume children *want* to cooperate and consider how to give them the support they need to do that. Support instead of punishment may seem like a stretch, but it's what this entire book is about. When we connect warmly with children, meet their needs and help them with the emotions that drive them to "act out," they're much more likely to cooperate. They're humans, after all. Wouldn't you be more likely to cooperate with a boss who respected you and tried to problem-solve to meet your needs so you could perform well, as opposed to one who threatened you?

## Example: **Natural Consequences**

> I want to use natural consequences to help my son learn. But it doesn't always work. For example, my son doesn't want to wear shoes so I suggest we bring them with us, and he can put them on later. He steps on a rock and gets hurt, leading to the natural consequence—pain! But what if that's not enough to make him want to put shoes on, or he chooses instead to just be carried the whole time so he doesn't put the shoes on either?
>
> — Heather, mother of two-year-old and five-month-old

First, this is a terrific opportunity to let your child learn from the natural consequences of his choice, as long as you feel he's safe walking without shoes. When he steps on a rock and gets hurt, you comfort him. Then you pull out the shoes you've brought and ask if he'd like to wear them. As long as you don't make him feel that he's lost a power struggle by wearing the shoes, he'll put them on when he's ready. You've already decided that it's okay with you for him to go barefoot, so you don't care one way or the other, right? Of course, if he wants to be carried, that's a different issue. You don't have to agree. You can simply empathize with how much he wishes he could be carried, but say that it doesn't work for you to carry him right now.

## Aren't You Going to Punish My Sister?

When you stop punishing, your children will be relieved. But soon they'll realize that when one of their siblings does something that upsets them, they can no longer count on you as the instrument of revenge. You'll probably find yourself having conversations like this:

**Mom:** *"I hear how upset you are at your sister, Santiago, and I can certainly understand why you would be. I'll help you talk with her about this as soon as you're ready."*

**Santiago:** *"But aren't you going to punish her?"*

**Mom:** *"Do you think punishing YOU makes you want to be a better person?"*

**Santiago:** *"Not really. It makes me mad. But she deserves it!"*

**Mom:** *"Well, I think it would make your sister mad, too. And I don't think anyone deserves to be hurt on purpose. But I do think your sister needs to stop taking your things without asking. And I think you're the one to tell her that! I will be happy to go with you to help you. What do you think would make that conversation with her go as well as possible?"*

**Santiago:** *"If I take some deep breaths first?"*

**Mom:** *"What a great idea! If you can tell her what you need without attacking her, she's much more likely to listen!"*

## WHAT IS YOUR PARENTING STYLE?

Humans don't fit easily into boxes, but researchers beginning with Diana Baumrind[124] more than four decades ago have noticed that parents tend to act according to one of four basic parenting styles:

- controlling/authoritarian
- permissive
- uninvolved
- coaching, setting empathic limits

We'll explore these four styles further in this section. See whether you recognize yourself in one of them. (Or maybe more than one. For instance, many parents start off permissive, but get frustrated and end up veering toward controlling/ authoritarian.)

Imagine that strictness and permissiveness are on a continuum, a horizontal line. Most of us don't want to be too strict, which would mean setting our expectations high and enforcing them with punishment. But we also don't want to be too permissive, because we're afraid that then our child won't meet our expectations, learn essential life lessons, and grow up to be a responsible, considerate person. We're looking for the sweet spot, in which we set our expectations at a level our child can achieve. So in the chart below this continuum is called "Expectations" (though many researchers call it "Demandingness").

That still leaves the question of how we get our child to meet our expectations, if we aren't going to punish. Happily, a number of decades ago, researchers[125] observing parents interacting with their children realized that there's another way to help children cooperate: support! So they added a vertical line, which is the continuum of "Responsiveness," meaning support, empathy, and connection. In the chart below, I call this dimension "Support."

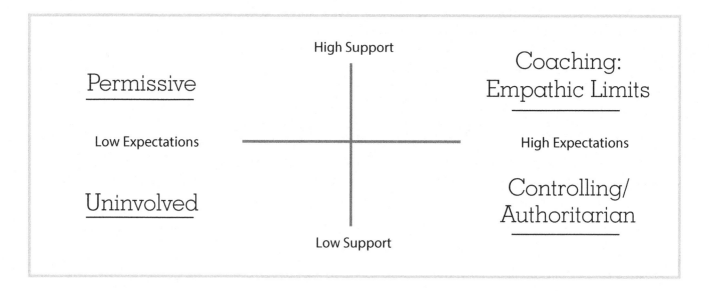

So we end up with four parenting styles, each indicated in the chart. (The original researchers called the top-right quadrant "authoritative," but I don't use that term since it is so easily confused with "authoritarian." Instead, I simply describe what these parents do, which is "coaching and setting empathic limits.") Here's what the research shows about how parents in each of these quadrants act (see page 145 for an equivalent list of how these parenting styles affect children).

- **Controlling/authoritarian** = high expectations and low support:
  o high expectations;
  o clear rules;
  o obedience is valued;
  o believe that emotions should be controlled rather than indulged;
  o enforces limits with punishment;
  o takes seriously the responsibility of "shaping" a "good" child, and may see shame and/or force as necessary to help "goodness" win out over "selfishness."
- **Permissive** = low expectations and high support:
  o rules and routine are inconsistent;

- ○ finds it difficult to set and enforce limit;
- ○ connection and nurturing are valued;
- ○ anxious when the child is emotional, so distracts child or "gives in" against their better judgment;
- ○ may have poor boundaries;
- ○ may use guilt to get child to meet expectations.
- **Uninvolved** = low expectations and low support:
  - ○ rules and routine are inconsistent or nonexistent;
  - ○ preoccupied and does whatever is easiest, with few expectations;
  - ○ erratic in setting and enforcing limits;
  - ○ expects child to take care of themselves;
  - ○ ignores emotions or promotes "self-medicating" with food and screens.
- **Coaching, setting empathic limits** = high expectations and high support:
  - ○ clear rules and expectations;
  - ○ connection, warmth, empathy, and nurturing are valued;
  - ○ emotion coaching is used to accept child's emotions and meet child's needs;
  - ○ sees child as a unique individual to be nurtured to become her best self, rather than shaped, and helps child develop inner compass with win–win solutions rather than insisting on blind obedience;
  - ○ sets clear limits and enforces with empathy;
  - ○ gives child support to meet expectations.

To understand how parents using these styles might respond to their child, consider a common scenario. A young child has a new toy that he loves. But it stops working. He gets frustrated. He shakes the toy. He screeches. Finally, he hurls it at the wall. The toy breaks and the child wails in dismay. What does each kind of parent say, and what does the child learn?

- **Controlling/authoritarian** = high expectations and low support. "*It's your own fault! You don't deserve nice things. Onto the naughty step with you! And stop crying or I'll give you something to cry about!*" The child learns that when he gets upset or emotional, he gets punished. He responds by trying to repress his feelings, stuffing them in his emotional backpack. But since they're now out of his conscious control, he finds it increasingly difficult to manage his anger.
- **Permissive** = low expectations and high support. "*Don't cry, don't cry! We'll get you another one.*" The child learns that emotions are scary and that he can use tantrums to get what he wants in life. He doesn't develop much self-discipline because he isn't asked to do so.
- **Uninvolved** = low expectations and low support. "*You have plenty of toys. You would have been tired of that in an hour anyway. Stop bothering me and go watch TV.*" Emotions are dismissed. This child learns that the parent does not understand him or care about what matters to him.
- **Coaching, setting empathic limits** = high expectations and high support. "*You're so sad. You loved that toy. But then it wasn't working… you didn't know what to do, right? So you threw it. It broke. No wonder you're so sad. No, sweetheart. We aren't getting another one. I see how sad that makes you. I'm here with a hug when you're ready.*" This parent is emotion coaching. The child gets help to form a coherent understanding of what he experienced. He sees—without shame or blame—how he created this situation and how he can manage himself to avoid repeating it in the future. He learns that he won't always get what he wants, but he gets something better: a parent who cares about him and understands, no matter what.

There are more examples of each parenting style in my book *Peaceful Parent, Happy Kids,*[126] but you can see the basic premise here. The parent who sets "empathic limits" respects the child, accepts the child's emotions, but still sets limits and guides the child. The authoritarian parent doesn't make room for emotions or support. The permissive parent doesn't hold to reasonable expectations. And the uninvolved parent doesn't hold expectations or give support.

## Why Peaceful Parenting Is Not Permissive

You can see that the permissive parent is being responsive to the child's expressed desire. But why are they really buying the new toy? Because they can't handle their child's unhappiness. And what message are they giving the child? Two possible messages are *"Money grows on trees"* and *"You don't have to value what you have because you can always get a replacement."* But there's another message that may be even worse: *"Your feelings are dangerous. I can't handle them. Do whatever you can to make them go away."* This can lead to a child becoming anxious, manipulating others with her emotional outbursts, or self-medicating to manage her feelings.

When parents don't set limits:

- **Parents grant desires that have harmful consequences**, such as regularly staying up too late, which results in a cranky and exhausted child who is not able to manage normal age-appropriate developmental tasks.
- **The child's desires are met at the expense of someone else**: a sibling, the parent, the restaurant where the family has gone to dinner, and so on. Beyond the impact on the sibling or the restaurant or the parent, the child learns to value his needs over those of other people.
- **The child learns that disappointment and sadness are intolerable**, when she realizes on some level that her parents will do almost anything not to let her experience disappointment. She then spends the rest of her life doing whatever is necessary to avoid feeling what she fears will be unbearable, possibly including avoiding all risks, insisting that she must have her way, or cheating to win.
- **The child never learns that happiness can be maintained in the face of disappointment**, but rather becomes conditioned to gauge his happiness from wish fulfillment and having one desire after another met. He is likely to spend his life pursuing one thing after another that he thinks will make him happy.
- **The child becomes anxious because she thinks her parents aren't in charge and she has to keep herself safe**. When people say, *"Kids will keep pushing till they find the limits,"* this is what they mean. It's pretty terrifying to a child to think that no one is in charge, protecting them from what can be a frightening world. These kids become demanding and bossy.
- **The child never learns to lovingly impose limits on himself**, tolerate frustration, or manage himself with self-discipline to meet his own goals.

Naturally, children won't always be happy about parental limits and expectations, but it's still our job to be the grown-ups and enforce appropriate limits. They shouldn't be unreasonable limits, and they should definitely be empathic limits in the context of a strong parent–child connection. But children's brains are not yet mature, and their wants are often in direct opposition to their long-term developmental needs and safety. Limits keep our children safe and healthy and support them in learning social norms so that they can function happily in society.

## What Kind Of Children Does Each Parenting Style Raise?

Researchers[127] have tracked how kids grow up with each kind of parenting. Given what you've learned so far about controlling and permissive parenting, these findings won't surprise you.

- **Controlling/authoritarian** = high expectations and low support:
  - often more obedient as young children because afraid of parents;
  - often rebellious or "sneak around" as teens;
  - uncomfortable with emotions;
  - because they repress emotions, they are less emotionally regulated and resilient;
  - prone to anger-management problems and/or depression;
  - often have issues with shame and self-esteem;
  - develop less self-discipline because discipline comes from outside;
  - compromised academic achievement;
  - challenging peer relationships.
- **Permissive** = low expectations and high support:
  - uncomfortable with emotions, managing them by being controlling or manipulative with others or with emotional outbursts and aggression;
  - because they repress emotions, they are less emotionally regulated and resilient;
  - can be impulsive, aggressive, domineering;
  - often seen by others as self-centered or "spoiled";
  - often have issues with guilt, anxiety, and/or a tendency to self-medicate;
  - don't develop self-discipline because they are never asked to.
- **Uninvolved** = low expectations and low support:
  - self-esteem and anxiety issues;
  - often have self-discipline issues;
  - often self-medicate.
- **Coaching, setting empathic limits** = high expectations and high support:
  - responsible, capable, higher achieving;
  - emotionally intelligent, empathic, self-regulated;
  - think for themselves;
  - because they respect their parents, they internalize their parents' limits and develop self-discipline;
  - because they accept their emotions, they can manage them and are more resilient and cheerful;
  - peer relationships are more positive.

## *Peaceful Parenting Raises Children With More Self-Discipline*

> Together with intelligence, self-control turns out to be the
> best predictor of a successful and satisfying life.
> — cognitive scientist Steven Pinker[128]

Self-discipline is an essential life skill, because it allows us to overcome obstacles to manifest our dreams. I've referred several times to the fact that when discipline comes from the outside, the child doesn't get the chance to develop *self-discipline*. Let's look now at what *does* help children learn self-discipline.

**We can define "self-discipline" as managing our impulses so that we're able to meet our own goals.** Specifically, when we exercise self-discipline, we usually give up something we want in pursuit of something we want more.

So every time your child chooses to shift gears from what she wants to do, to follow your lead, she's practicing regulating her impulses. She's building self-discipline muscle, or, more precisely, neural pathways. But, like muscle, neural pathways get stronger with use, so you can think of this as building a brain that's capable of more self-discipline.

As you've seen, permissive parenting doesn't help kids develop self-discipline because it doesn't ask them to exercise self-control in pursuit of their larger goal, and it doesn't help them learn to tolerate discomfort. But punitive limits—including "consequences"—also don't help kids learn to self-regulate, because the motivation comes from the outside. The child isn't *choosing* to rein in his own impulses. So, even if he does what you want, he's not actually "practicing" self-discipline and building that mental muscle.

Think about your son practicing his jump shot over and over. He may want to sit down and rest, but there's something he wants more—a basket! Being motivated toward a goal of their own (*not a goal we set for them!*) is one of the primary ways that kids develop self-discipline.

But kids also learn self-discipline from the daily limits you set, as long as you set them with empathy. Why is empathy essential to this process? Because your child is less likely to struggle against the limit. She may not like your limit, but she feels your understanding and compassion. She knows you're on her side. So she chooses to stop fighting for what she wants so she can have something she wants more—to stay lovingly connected to you. She *chooses* to regulate her own impulses. She accepts your limit and even, over time, adopts it as her own.

That's how your child internalizes your rules and values. It begins with the connection—he *wants* to please you, as long as he doesn't have to give up his own integrity to do it. Over time, as he follows your lead, he enjoys the benefits of his positive choices, and he begins to think of himself as the kind of person who brushes his teeth, does his homework, tells the truth, and lends a helping hand. The kind of person who can apply himself with discipline to achieve his goals. That makes for a confident, happy, cooperative child.

Since your warm connection with your child is the reason he eventually accepts and internalizes your limits, it's critical to stay connected while you set limits. You already know how to do that—empathy! Using empathy while you set limits keeps you connected even while you say "no." (We'll talk more about empathic limits in the section on loving guidance.)

# "I Don't Want My Child to Be a Pleaser!"

*"Dr. Laura, you always talk about how the child chooses the warm relationship with the parent over what they want, such as climbing on the TV cabinet or hitting their sibling. Sure, I want my child to do what I say. And of course I would rather have her choose to do what I say, so I don't have to force her. But I don't want her to grow up to be a pleaser!"*

— Boni, mother of a ten-year-old and a six-year-old

Many parents worry that if children are motivated by their love for us, they'll end up as pleasers, doing what other people want. But in fact, it's just the opposite. When children know that we accept all their emotions and love them unconditionally, they don't have to sacrifice their integrity to choose to follow our lead. Their inner voice has been listened to, so they learn to listen to it too—they develop their own inner compass. By contrast, when we control children with anger, guilt, and shame, they will usually try to do what we ask, because otherwise the pain is unbearable to them. But they won't necessarily be able to sustain that desired behavior in our absence. They aren't choosing it out of integrity but out of fear, so they aren't developing the inner compass they need to keep them on track.

### *Preventive Maintenance*

Just as with your car, a routine that allows your child's needs to be met as they arise helps her to maintain a state of optimal well-being. This enables her to handle what life (and you) ask of her, so she doesn't end up in the breakdown lane so often. In addition to physical maintenance (such as sleep, food, and physical activity), your child needs daily emotional preventive maintenance, including:

- Empathy 24/7, to meet the child's emotional needs to be seen and heard (see page 98);
- Daily roughhousing, to work through pent-up emotions (see page 110);
- Connection, including daily Special Time (see page 118);
- Routines, which help children know what to expect and feel safe (see page 123);
- Welcoming emotions (we'll talk more about these in the section on emotion coaching).

So, if you're having an issue with your child, always start with the basics: connection and meeting needs, including preventive maintenance. For instance, is your child getting enough sleep? Are you reconnecting daily, so that your child trusts you to meet her needs and wants to follow your lead? Is your child getting a good laughter session in every day? Then you can build on that foundation to help your child with feelings (emotion coaching) and/or guide behavior (loving guidance).

Just remember that if you aren't doing regular preventive maintenance, the tools in the rest of this book (emotion coaching and loving guidance) can't make up for that. Just as your car will end up in the breakdown lane if you don't give it fuel and regular tune-ups, you can count on misbehavior if you don't do daily preventive maintenance with your child.

## HELPING YOUR CHILD WITH EMOTIONS

> One afternoon when my daughter came home from school, I could see that something was bothering her. She was playing with play dough while her dad helped her cousin with math problems. He asked for some scrap paper to do calculations on and I took a few from the pile of papers my daughter used to play school with. My daughter burst into tears about the three scrap papers I took. I realized that she was crying because she desperately needed to let go of all her pent-up emotions. I took her in my arms and sat down on the carpet of her room with her on my lap and told her that she could cry as much as she needed to. I asked her if she wanted me to go ask Daddy if she could have the papers back, but she shook her head. She squished the ball of play dough as she screeched and cried on my lap. Then she started to yawn (I had to hide my smile), and 15 minutes later she skipped and sang happily while helping me with the laundry. I was truly amazed!
>
> — Mari, mother of 4-year-old and 8-week-old

Emotion coaching is the process of teaching children about emotions, both their own and those of other people. Most parents are highly invested in their child's intellectual development and spend a lot of time teaching: colors, names of objects, endless answers to the question *"Why?"* But we may not even notice the equally constant lessons we're teaching our child about emotions. What do we do when he cries? When she expresses anger, what is the implicit message in our response? What do we model when we ourselves get frustrated? How do we talk with our child when they see an interaction that upsets them—for instance, when another child is crying at the playground?

How we respond to our child's emotions, and how we handle our own, shapes our child's emotional development and creates the foundation of his emotional intelligence, or "EQ," which, as I have already mentioned, is now thought by most child development experts to be more important than IQ to a child's eventual life success. Any parent who is willing to do the work to increase their own emotional intelligence becomes a more adept emotion coach, which in turn boosts their child's emotional intelligence.

Emotion coaching helps children learn to self-regulate, but not because we're teaching children to "control" their emotions. In fact, most people, including most children, automatically try to control emotions by dismissing or stuffing them, which sabotages self-regulation. The magic of emotion coaching is that it helps children become more *aware* of their emotions. That conscious awareness allows us to notice what we're feeling, accept it, integrate it with other needs and feelings, and make a wise choice about how to respond.

For instance, if a child gets increasingly irritated at his sibling for singing loudly, but knows that he's supposed to be "nice" to his sibling and isn't sure how to solve the problem, he will probably explode sooner or later. If, on the other hand, he's able to notice his growing irritation, he has the choice about how to express his needs without attacking his sibling, which makes it more likely they'll work out an amicable solution. So emotion coaching helps the child "befriend" his emotions so he can manage them. Then, loving guidance teaches the child problem-solving skills to express his needs without attacking the other person, and to find win–win solutions.

# The Research on Emotion Coaching

Thousands of peer-reviewed studies have found that emotion coaching is one of your most important skills as a parent. Here are just a few of those studies:

- Emotion-coached children perform better academically, can focus their attention and motivate themselves, have fewer behavioral problems, have fewer infectious illnesses, are more emotionally stable, and are more resilient.[129]

- Research on the vagal nerve has repeatedly found that children who are emotion-coached are better able to self-regulate and calm themselves when they get upset than children who are not emotion-coached.[130,131]

- Emotion coaching helps children build more neural pathways between the prefrontal cortex and the limbic system, which allows them to regulate their emotions—and therefore their behavior—earlier than other children.[132]

- When parents emotion-coach children through negative emotions, children develop more social competence.[133]

- When parents of kindergartners are trained to emotion-coach instead of dismiss emotions, their children's behavior improves dramatically. In one study of children with extremely challenging behavior, more than half were no longer challenging after the program.[134] (The children with more usual levels of behavior problems also improved dramatically.)

- Maternal responsiveness to child sadness, anger, fear, and neutrality predicts children's social-emotional competence.[135]

- When parents accept children's full range of emotions, children are better able to tolerate emotions without lashing out in anger. When parents don't accept the full range of children's emotions, children have less ability to regulate their emotions, which, in turn, makes children more likely to be aggressive.[136]

- How responsive (acknowledging, accepting, warmly understanding) a parent is to a baby's expressed emotions is thought to be a critical factor in attachment security, and the child's attachment security in turn is a critical factor in the child's ability to self-regulate.[137]

When we add to this the numerous studies showing that punishment worsens behavior,[138] it becomes clear that emotion coaching is much more effective than punishment in improving child behavior.

## Emotion Coaching Develops Your Childs Brain

The human brain is born immature and develops in response to its environment, which enhances our chances of survival in different environments. This means that your child's brain is still developing until she's in her mid-twenties. (And even beyond, given that throughout life the brain adapts to any repeated experience, as we discussed in Part 1 of this book.) In practical terms, that means two things:

- **Your child's brain does not work the way yours does.** Children have a completely different sense of time than we do until they are about seven years old, so they live in the moment. Until puberty, children think more concretely, with less conceptual and reasoning power. Even into their early twenties, they have less ability to "forecast" the future and to imagine the results of their actions. Stable internal happiness, or the resilient ability to restore one's equilibrium regardless of external circumstances, solidifies in the teen years or later. Both because the prefrontal cortex is still developing and because of their lack of life context, kids' emotions are more powerful and their impulse control is weaker. Add to this that your child has less information about the world than you do, and you can begin to understand that she sees things very differently than you do and responds more emotionally and impulsively. So, if you have a child under the age of 25, you can expect "childish" behavior.

- **Because you are the most significant factor in your child's environment, you have tremendous power to influence the way his brain takes shape.** Your role-modeling and emotion coaching not only *teach* appropriate behavior intellectually, but also give your child's brain the *experience* of safe connection and emotional regulation. You can even affect the way your child's genes manifest. For instance, if your child was born with a tendency toward an overactive alarm system (which can manifest as anxiety, defiance, or aggression), you can help him settle his fear circuits with your soothing, connection, routines, and daily laughter.

The takeaway? Your emotion coaching helps your child handle her emotions in the moment and teaches her essential emotional skills—but it also shapes her brain for the rest of her life.

## How Do You Respond To Emotions?

John Gottman, the researcher who coined the term "emotion coaching," observed that an emotion-coaching parent does five things:[139]

1.  The parent is aware of the child's emotions.

2.  The parent sees the child's emotions as opportunities for intimacy or teaching.

3.  The parent describes the emotions the child is having. This might mean verbally labeling the feelings, or it might mean simply describing the child's experience: *"It sounds like you think the teacher was unfair."*

4.  The parent empathizes with or validates the child's emotions. This will look different for a toddler than for a teenager.

5.  The parent supports the child to problem-solve.

Notice that to do these five things, we need to be comfortable with our child's emotions. So often, we as parents miss opportunities to help our children with their emotions, because our automatic impulse is to try to make them go away. When children get upset, most adults get anxious. Not only do we want to prevent our child from feeling pain but our child's big emotions also trigger any unhealed emotions from our own childhoods. So, before we even know what we're doing, we're jumping in to stop the danger—the emotions—by fixing, threatening, cajoling, and dismissing. Gottman and his team noticed that the majority of parents find their child's emotions upsetting, so they respond by distracting, dismissing, or even punishing.[140] Gottman described four ways that parents respond to their child's emotions, which are reminiscent of, although not an exact match to, the four parenting styles developed by Baumrind that we have already discussed. Different researchers, different decades, even somewhat different terminology—but emotions are still at the core of how we relate to our children. Do you recognize yourself in any of the following four types of parent?

1. **Disapproving.** These parents believe that expressing emotions is a sign of weakness and loss of control. They often think that the child is attempting to manipulate them with emotions. These parents may punish emotions by ridiculing them or by sending the child away to "calm down." The child learns that her feelings are shameful and that, to be acceptable, she needs to repress them. So she pushes her emotions out of awareness, where they're no longer under conscious control, leading to anger-management issues or depression. (Do you notice how similar this is to the controlling/authoritarian approach? ) Common strategies—all of which make the child feel like a bad person for having the emotion—include:

   - **Punishing:** "*I'll give you something to cry about.*"
   - **Shaming:** "*A little scratch like that doesn't hurt!*" … "*Look at your brother; he doesn't have this problem.*"
   - **Ridiculing:** "*Don't be a drama queen.*" … "*Big boys don't cry.*"
   - **Blaming:** "*You must have done something to make her so mad at you!*" … "*This is all your fault so there's no point in crying to me about it.*"
   - **Isolating:** "*Calm down or go to your room!*"

2. **Dismissing.** These parents are uncomfortable with their own and their child's emotions, and try to make the emotions go away as quickly as possible. Often they perceive the child's upset as a demand that they (the parent) fix the situation. Note that the parent may be fine with some emotions, but not with others—for example, the parent may be nurturing if the child has a physical injury, but impatient with emotional neediness. Invalidating emotions this way teaches the child not to trust his own inner compass. It also erodes the trust between parent and child, because the child doesn't feel seen, heard, or understood. (Permissive and uninvolved parents both use this approach, as do authoritarian parents on a good day.) Common strategies—all of which shut down emotion—include:

   - **Fixing:** "*Don't get upset, I can do it for you.*"
   - **Distracting:** "*Do you want to watch your show? That will help you feel better.*"
   - **Minimizing:** "*You're overreacting. There's no reason to be upset.*"
   - **Asking questions:** "*Why are you so upset?*"
   - **Lecturing:** "*Here's what you need to do.*"
   - **Ignoring:** "*Don't bring it up. That will just remind her and make her sad.*"

3. **Laissez-faire.** These parents accept the expression of emotions. They even comfort the child and let the child know she's loved. So far so good, right? But laissez-faire parents are themselves overwhelmed by emotions, so they get anxious when their child is upset and don't know how to help their child manage her emotions. In fact, they may join their child in whatever emotion she's expressing. Instead of seeing the child's emotions as an opportunity for coaching or as a useful prompt to action, they see emotions as an unavoidable, negative part of life that must be suffered through. They tend to communicate their own worry to their child even while trying to reassure the child.[141] These parents don't want to dig deeper to find out why their child is feeling bad; they just hope the feeling will go away soon. If the child is angry, they leave the child alone to "cool off" rather than listening to the child's upset. The child learns that that she's all alone to manage her emotions, which leads to anxiety. Common responses to an upset child include:

- **Philosophizing:** *"You can't win them all."* (Notice that in the heat of the moment, this shuts down feelings. There's nothing wrong with sharing your wisdom about life, but wait until later. Right now your child just needs empathy so she can feel fully.)
- **Hunkering down:** *"The best thing to do when you feel bad is just ride it out."* (This enforces a feeling of powerlessness in the face of emotion.)
- **Distancing:** *"Let him be. He'll feel better once he calms down if you just leave him alone."* (This gives the message that the child is all alone to deal with big emotions.)

4. **Emotion coaching.** These parents accept their child's emotions and allow him to express them. But, unlike laissez-faire parents, these parents see emotions as a gift, part of the inner compass that needs to be listened to for us to be whole and healthy. Because they're comfortable with their own emotions, they see their child's unhappy feelings as an opportunity to teach him about emotions and to become more intimate by supporting him through the emotion. They aren't upset by their child's emotions, so they communicate a more matter-of-fact attitude and are able to take an active role in helping the child think about his emotions and reflect on the situation, leading eventually to problem solving about the situation. These parents want their child to feel safe coming to them when he's upset. Common responses to an upset child include:

- **Noticing:** *"You look sad."*
- **Listening:** *"Hmmm…"*
- **Empathizing:** *"Hearing your friend say that could really hurt your feelings."*
- **Validating:** *"No wonder you're upset!"*
- **Setting limits on behavior as necessary, even while allowing emotion:** *"I see how angry you are at your brother. Tell him in words! No hitting."*
- **Teaching self-soothing while honoring emotions:** *"It's okay to feel sad. What could you do to take care of yourself while you feel this way?"*
- **Problem-solving:** After the child has calmed down, the parent may coach her to repair or solve her problem: *"You and your brother have opposite opinions about this. I wonder how you can work this out?"* *"It sounds like you're sorry about what you said. I wonder if there's anything you can do now to make things better with her?"*

Remember that the same parent may treat the expression of different emotions in different ways. For instance, some parents are terrific at comforting a frightened or worried child, but punish when their child gets angry. Virtually all parents sometimes feel overwhelmed or anxious in response to their child's emotions and want to "fix" the feelings or the situation. So, if you see your own reactions in these lists, don't worry. That's your starting place. Our goal is for you to notice when you want to respond to your child's emotions in a way that shuts them down, and give you the opportunity to choose a healthier response. It takes time, but it is completely possible for you to shift your responses. It starts with your own awareness.

## Practice: Tracking Your Reactions to Your Child's Emotions

This week, notice when your child has a big emotion that you usually think of as negative: anger, fear, sadness, disappointment, annoyance, or frustration. Pay attention to how you feel inside, what you say, and what you do. Answer the questions below about your own reactions.

**(1)** What kinds of things did your child get upset about?

**( 2 )** What did you notice about your automatic tendency in responding to your child's emotions?

_____

**( 3 )** When your child gets emotional, how do you feel inside?

_____

**( 4 )** Can you just acknowledge your child's emotions?

_____

**( 5 )** Are there some emotions that are easier for you to empathize with than others?

_____

**( 6 )** Are you able to empathize even while you limit behavior?

_____

**( 7 )** Are you able to let yourself feel a little of what your child is feeling?

_____

**( 8 )** When you react differently than usual to your child's emotions, how does your child respond?

_____

## Your Child's Inner Compass

Since emotions give us messages about what we want and need, one of the goals of emotion coaching is to help children develop their own inner compass to navigate both their internal and external landscapes. If we want children to notice the small signals of danger from a predator, they need an inner compass they trust. If we want children to do what's right, even when it's hard, they need an inner compass that tracks how far a given action takes them from their integrity. If we want them to be happy in life, they need to turn toward things that give them joy, regardless of what others are doing. You can think of this as your child's homing device, or integrity barometer, an emotional GPS. It alerts them to move toward what resonates for them and to move away from situations that don't feel safe or actions that take them out of integrity.

**How do children develop this inner compass? From the way we respect and honor their experience.** Haim Ginott, the grandfather of positive parenting, said that when we tell children what they *ought* to feel, it makes them distrust what they *do* feel.[142]

| Undermining Development of Inner Compass | Supporting Development of Inner Compass |
|---|---|
| "You don't hate the baby. You love her!" | "You're so mad at the baby right now!" |
| "Of course the other kids like you." | "It sounds like you're worried the other kids won't want to play with you." |
| "Hug your uncle!" | "It's your decision who touches your body, and you need to say hello. How about a hearty handshake?" |
| "Of course you like softball. All three of your brothers play, and I played!" | "It sounds like you really don't like softball." |
| "You don't really want to go to another country to study. That would give me a heart attack." | "It sounds like you really want to go on the high school summer program to learn Spanish. I have to admit that the idea of you going so far away makes me nervous, but I love that you're so adventurous. Let's talk about it." |

## Talking With Kids About Emotions In Daily Life

Anthropologists say that the Inuit, whose world is full of snow, have at least 50 words for variations of snow. Inuit children learn those words and attach them accurately to the many varieties of snow simply by hearing them used. Similarly, children whose parents emotion-coach learn by listening to their parents to identify a wide range of emotions, what those emotions look like in others, what they feel like, and what the message of each emotion is.

So simply observing what your child and other people are feeling, and commenting on it in a non-judgmental, accepting way, teaches children to identify emotions in themselves and others. As you go through your day, look for opportunities to acknowledge your child's feelings:

- *"You want to do it yourself."*
- *"I hear you! You really don't like spinach and you wish you could never see it again!"*
- *"You look frustrated."*
- *"You're jumping up and down! You must be excited!"*
- *"I understand. You feel safer when you know exactly what's going to happen."*

If you and your child observe a child crying, you might ask questions like:

- *"That child looks so unhappy. I wonder why he's upset?"*
- *"What do you think he wants/needs?"*
- *"Is there anything we can do to help?"*

Talking with children about emotions also helps develop empathy. For instance, when parents talk (not lecture, but wonder and explore) with young children about what their baby sibling thinks, feels, and wants, the child develops more empathy for his sibling and the relationship between the two siblings is more positive.[143] When adults read books and talk to toddlers and preschoolers about how other children feel, their prosocial actions increase and their aggression toward their peers decreases.[155]

Teaching children about emotions includes teaching them the basic lessons we discussed in the first section of this book:

- All emotions are acceptable. While thoughts can cause emotions, we can't choose what we feel.
- We are responsible for the actions we take. We can always choose our actions.
- Emotions arise in response to what we perceive. They have valuable messages for us about what's important to us. But it can be hard to understand those messages while we're feeling the emotion. It's a good idea to wait until we're calm before taking action on our emotions.
- While we're feeling an emotion, it often feels like it will go on forever, and it's hard to imagine ever feeling anything else.
- We might say "*I'm angry*" but we are never that transient emotion—we are always much more. It's more accurate to say "*I feel angry.*"
- Once we let ourselves feel an emotion, it begins to dissipate.

Of course, children won't learn these ideas from a lecture, but from the comments you make as you go through life with them.

Helping children feel confident that they can handle emotions includes teaching them that every feeling has a different message for us. For instance:

- **When a child feels pain**, the message is to move away from whatever is hurting her body and to soothe and protect herself.
- **When a child is afraid**, the message is to find safety with a trusted adult and also for the child to reassure himself.
- **When a child is sad**, the message is to share her sadness with someone who cares and will comfort her, which is how she learns to comfort herself.
- **When a child is angry**, it's a message that something needs to change. Your child is likely to think that the situation, or the other person, is what needs to change. But of course your child can only control himself, not the other person or the external events. So the best questions to ask after your child calms down are, "*What can you change here? If you take that action, what would happen then?*"

When you talk with your child about emotions, ask questions to help him learn through reflection. For instance, you might ask questions like:

- "*If you felt angry at a friend, what could you do?*"
- "*If you felt angry at me, what could you do?*"
- "*If you felt angry that it was raining, what could you do?*"
- "*If you felt angry that your block tower fell down, what could you do?*"
- "*Do you make a better decision when you feel angry or when you feel calm?*"
- "*What helps you calm down when you're angry?*"

## *Teaching Children To Self-Regulate*

Entire books have been written about teaching children mindfulness strategies, and many of them are wonderful. These strategies are often fun for children to learn when they're calm, and if they become a regular part of your family life, your children may even remember to use them when they're angry. The challenge is that when a human is angry, suggesting they calm down is like throwing gasoline on a fire. (Do you recall the last time you were really outraged about something that mattered to you? What if your partner or friend, instead of listening to you, had suggested that you take a few deep breaths to calm down?)

**So, if you approach mindfulness practices with the attitude that you're "fixing" your child's inappropriate tendency to get emotional, your child will naturally resist.** If, instead, you make a family project out of what you might call "learning to be aware of our emotions so we can communicate in a kind way and choose our actions," your child will probably be open to the idea. If you play mindfulness games *with* your child and talk about how much you're enjoying and learning, your child will also enjoy and learn.

And of course, you'll still have to make sure that your child *wants* to calm down before you suggest any mindfulness strategies in that moment of upset. That means *first* making sure that your child feels you've heard what he's upset about, that you understand, and that you're committed to helping him solve his problem.

### Help Your Child Become Aware Of Her "Warning Signs"

Once kids are in the full flush of adrenaline and the other "fight or flight" neurotransmitters, they think it's an emergency and they're fighting for their lives. At that point, managing the angry impulses is almost impossible, and all we can offer kids is a safe haven while the storm sweeps through them. But if you can help your child notice when she's getting annoyed and learn to calm herself before she goes over the edge, she'll have many fewer tantrums.

When she's little, you'll have to know her cues and take preventive action—offering some snuggle time, or getting her out of the grocery store. Be sure to acknowledge how she feels verbally, and let her know she's safe and has you for backup: "*You don't like that. I'm right here. We can handle this.*"

As she gets older, you can notice when she's getting frustrated and let her know in a non-judgmental tone that you're there to help: "*Sweetie, I see you're getting upset about this. We can make this better. Let's take a deep breath together and figure this out. How can I help?*"

### Give Your Child Ways To Manage His Angry Impulses In The Moment

Once your child feels heard, he won't need to escalate. So, when he's angry, he needs to know that you understand how upset he is and why.

This means that your first response to your child's anger needs to be empathy to acknowledge why he's angry. Many parents punish their children for expressing anger verbally. But that forces children to act out physically. If you can take a deep breath and remind yourself that anger is normal and can be dealt with in healthy ways, your calm attitude will communicate itself to your child. So begin by listening.

Because anger is so physically powerful, kids sometimes need to express their anger physically to work through it. But the essential ingredient here is not "venting" the anger; it's that you "witness" the depths of his upset. Obviously, you aren't going to let him beat up his brother, no matter how badly his brother behaved toward him. But you can help him redirect his physical rage to punch a punching bag, dance it out, or draw an angry picture and tear it up. Remember, though, that what's healing here isn't acting out the aggression. In fact, acts of violence, even on inanimate objects, can make us more angry, because they signal the body that there's a threat.[156] What's helpful for your child is that he gets to show you exactly how upset he is, so that he feels understood.

## Practice: Working with Your Child on a List of Self-Calming Strategies

When your child is calm, brainstorm with her to come up with a list of constructive ways for people in your family to handle anger and upsets, and post it on the refrigerator. Here's a list to get you started. **The items with an asterisk have been proven effective in research studies, but anecdotal reports from parents say that all of these ideas are effective.** Sit down with your child, consider each idea in turn, and try them out. Add your child's own ideas to the list. Let her do the writing or add pictures so she feels some ownership of the list.

Then, practice each item on the list so that it will feel familiar and reassuring in a moment of upset. Model using it yourself when you're mad: *"I'm getting annoyed, so I'm checking our Mad List. Oh, I think I'll put on some music and dance out my frustration!"*

- Take five deep breaths and blow them out.*

- If you feel like hitting, clap your arms around your body and give yourself a hug. Yell *"Stop!"* or call for a parent at the same time.

- Watch fish swimming in a tank.*

- Shake a clear plastic bubble jar and watch the bubbles and glitter settle.

- Blow bubbles.*

- Listen to calming music.

- Put on music and do an "angry dance."

- Ask for a hug.

- Snuggle your favorite stuffed animal.

- Hit a punching bag or bobo doll. (Most kids resist punching the pillows on the couch, which feels artificial to them, but many love having a kids' punching bag to knock over.)

- Stomp your feet. (Young children often find it helpful to stomp their feet when they're mad. Don't worry, it's better than kicking their sister or the wall, and over time they will start using words.)

- Draw or write on paper what you're angry about, then fiercely rip it into tiny pieces.

- Use your Pause Button: breathe in for four counts through your nose and then out for eight through your mouth.

- Work out your annoyance on a squeezy ball.

## Practice: Empathizing When Emotions Get Charged

Read the situations below. Under each scenario, write what you could say and do that would help your child with their emotions—without necessarily doing what your child is asking.

**1** **Your child begs for a toy at the store.**

What you say:

_____

_____

_____

What you do:

_____

_____

_____

**( 2 ) Your child shouts at you in anger.**

What you say:

_____

_____

_____

What you do:

_____

_____

_____

**( 3 ) Your child doesn't want to go to school in the morning.**

What you say:

_____

_____

_____

What you do:

_____

_____

_____

**( 4 ) Your child is jealous of his brother staying up late.**

What you say:

_____

_____

_____

What you do:

_____

_____

_____

**( 5 )  Your child doesn't like the dinner you've fixed.**

What you say:

_____

_____

_____

What you do:

_____

_____

_____

## Practice: **Modeling Constructive Ways to Manage Emotions**

Can you stay calm during emotionally-charged discussions? Do you empathize when feelings are expressed? So will your child, eventually. Do you start snapping at people when you're under stress? Swear at other drivers? Have minor tantrums when things go wrong? So will your child.

Don't worry. You can have small tantrums once in a while and still raise an emotionally-intelligent child. But the more often you have them, the more of an impediment they are to your child's emotional growth, and even your child's brain development. So, after an upset, it's especially important to describe to your child what happened, to reconnect, and to share your plans to regulate better next time.

Babies and toddlers tune in to their parents' limbic (emotional) systems, using them as a model for their own. Older children pick up on their parents' emotions and respond to them, even when they aren't aware of doing so. We may not know we're teaching and they may not know they're learning, but our emotional modeling is one of the most important ways our children learn about emotion.

You can help your children integrate this learning by making a practice of sharing your own emotional state with your child in a matter-of-fact way that makes it clear that you're responsible for your own emotions and can regulate them: _"I'm frustrated looking for a parking space. Oh, well. We just have to be patient. We can handle this."_

What do you think you model for your children about handling these emotions?

- Fear and anxiety:

_____

_____

_____

- Sadness and grief:

_____

_____

_____

- Anger and frustration:

  _____
  _____
  _____

- Is there anything you'd like to change?

  _____
  _____
  _____

## Practice: **Positive Emotions**

Because this book is about emotional regulation for parents and children, we're focusing on the emotions that humans find it hard to accept and regulate, which are the ones we usually think of as negative or challenging: anger, sadness, fear, shame, and all their variations. The emotions we usually think of as positive aren't generally a problem for self-regulation because we accept them. Therefore, this book doesn't reference them very much.

It's worth noting, though, that parents give children constant messages about "positive" emotions, just as we do about challenging emotions. Those messages shape the child's experience of those emotions. So, for instance, many parents get exasperated with their child's silliness, which children may hear as a criticism of their whole-hearted delight and excitement. If a mother struggling with postpartum depression is unable to respond to her child's expressions of joy by acknowledging that joy, the child may receive the message that joy is off limits. If an introverted or noise-sensitive parent responds to his child's exuberant screeching by shushing the child, the child may get the message that happiness and celebration must be tamped down. And a busy parent might well ignore a child's excitement about life to rush her through the schedule, giving her an unintended but clear message about what's of value.

Given the pressures on parents, it's understandable that most of us cut off some of our aliveness at times by not fully experiencing the joy, happiness, and other positive emotions that are constantly available to us. But it's worth considering the impact of that choice on our children.

What messages do you think you received about joy, happiness, silliness, and excitement when you were a child?

_____
_____
_____

What messages do you give your child about joy, happiness, silliness, and excitement?

_____
_____
_____

Is there anything you would like to change about your messages to your child? How could you begin?

_____
_____
_____

## The Six-Step Process For Emotion Coaching When Your Child Is Upset

When your child is upset, you can support him to work through his emotions constructively by using these six steps:

**1.** Calm yourself.

**2.** Connect and create safety.

**3.** Empathize.

**4.** Double-check to be sure your child feels understood.

**5.** Deepen the conversation by offering support or validation.

**6.** Support your child to problem-solve.

Below, we'll explore each step in detail so you can learn how to use them. With practice, you'll find that the six steps will become automatic for you.

**1. Calm yourself first.**

- Use your Pause Button: Stop, Drop your agenda (just for now), and take a deep Breath before you engage with your child.
- Remind yourself that your goal is to calm the storm for your child, not escalate it.
- Don't take your child's emotions personally. This isn't about you, even if she's screaming *"I hate you!"* This is about her: her tangled-up feelings and still-developing brain.
- Calm yourself with a mantra: "*It's not an emergency*" or "*This is an opportunity to be there for my child when he's upset.*"
- Notice the sensations in your body.
- Notice if you feel annoyance, or the urge to make your child's feelings go away. Decide that your goal is to use this opportunity to build a closer relationship with your child and teach her helpful lessons about accepting and responding to emotions.

**2. Connect and create safety.**

- Reach out to connect emotionally and, if you can, physically.
- If you breathe slowly and deeply, your child will usually begin to breathe more slowly.
- Create safety with your touch, your warmth, your tone, and your attitude.
- Give your child the verbal and/or non-verbal message that "*I will help you... You're safe... You can handle this.*"

**3. Empathize.**

- Match your child's tone. When kids feel that you really get how upset they are, they don't need to escalate.
- Welcome the emotions and reflect them, mirroring your child's tone: "*You look so mad!*" or "*You seem a little worried about this sleepover.*"
- If your child is describing a problem to you, repeat back to him what you've heard: "*I hear you loud and clear. You're fed up with your brother going into your room and taking your gum.*"

- If your child is expressing anger at you, resist the urge to tell her to be "appropriate." Instead, acknowledge the feelings and invite her to tell you what she's upset about: "*You must be so upset to talk to me that way, Kayla. What's happening?*"

- If you don't know what your child is feeling or your child gets angry when you "name" her emotions, "upset" is a good all-purpose word: "*I hear how upset you are about this.*"

- Describing what your child is physically expressing helps him feel seen and heard, and can either help you name emotions or intentionally avoid doing so: "*I see you're biting your lip—you look worried*" or "*Your arms are crossed over your chest like this, and your brows are tight like this. I wonder what's going on?*"

- Acknowledge your child's perspective: "*You wish that…*" or "*This isn't what you wanted….*" or "*Nothing is going right for you today, is it?*"

- If your child is crying, words can be a distraction. Use words sparingly, just to create safety and welcome the emotion: "*Everybody needs to cry sometimes. It's good to feel those tears and let them go. I'm right here. You're safe.*"

4. **Double-check** to be sure your child feels understood by what you've said. This way, you don't have to worry about whether you were able to accurately reflect your child's feelings. Just ask:

- "*Is that right?*" or "*Is that what you're telling me?*" or "*Am I getting that?*"

- Your child may agree—"*Of course I'm mad!*"—and elaborate.

- Your child may correct you: "*I'm not disappointed! I'm mad!*" In that case, try again. If possible, use your child's exact words so they know you're listening: "*I'm sorry, Caleb. I see now how mad you are. Tell me more about why.*"

- Or your child may correct you—"*I'm NOT MAD!*"—even though it's clear that you were accurate in your perception. That's a signal that your child is feeling judged or analyzed rather than understood. Acknowledge the correction and start over, connecting more as you describe your child's perspective: "*I hear you, Lucas. You're not mad. Let me see if I understand. You wanted X. Is that right?*"

- Don't fight about what your child is actually feeling. What's important is that she feels understood. Her awareness of what she's feeling will shift as she moves through the emotions.

5. **Deepen the conversation.** You can do this by offering support, validating your child's emotion, or simply inviting your child to tell you more. Validation doesn't necessarily mean you agree, only that you understand why your child would feel this way. Let yourself feel some of what your child is feeling while you stay centered. If you really feel the emotion with your child, then you may get tears in your eyes at how heartbreaking this must be for them.

- "*Ouch, that must have hurt! Want to show me what happened?*"

- "*Oh, Sofia, no wonder you're upset.*"

- "*It could be really embarrassing to have your teacher say that.*"

- "*You're saying that I love your sister more… Ethan, it must feel so awful to feel that.*"

- "*I didn't understand how important this was to you. Tell me more about this.*"

- "*I hear how angry you are about this. What can I do to help make this better?*"

- "*So I hear you're upset because of X and also Y! Is there anything else?*" Asking if there's anything else often opens the floodgates and allows you to get to the heart of why your child is upset. She may start with what a lousy parent you are for making oatmeal again and end up telling you that she thinks you love her brother more, or that she's being bullied at school.

- *"Thank you for telling me this. I'm sorry that what I did upset you so much. Please tell me more."* When your child is angry at you, let him know you're listening. You may find out something that will transform your relationship for the better. Or you may find that his anger has nothing to do with you after all.

- Describe the incident without judging, so your child feels understood. *"Lena wanted to play with your doll and you were worried. You said 'No!' and hit Lena and you both cried. Right?"* Telling the story helps the child to calm down, reflect, and integrate the emotions, as the emotional experience of the right frontal lobe is articulated by the verbal, more rational understanding of the left frontal lobe.[146]

6. **Problem-solve.** Most of the time, when kids (and adults) feel their emotions are understood and accepted, the feelings lose their charge and begin to dissipate. This leaves an opening for problem solving. If your child still seems upset and negative and isn't open to problem solving, it's a sign that she hasn't worked through the emotions yet and you need to go back to the earlier steps. When your child is ready to problem-solve, resist the urge to solve the problem for her unless she asks you to. When you suggest solutions, you give her the message that you don't have confidence in her ability to handle the situation. If she feels stuck, help her brainstorm and explore options: *"Hmmm… So you think you might do X. I wonder what would happen then?"*

## *Emotion Coaching With A Younger Child*

Children under the age of five get more overwhelmed by emotions than older children because their brains are still developing, so their "thinking brains" have a harder time integrating all the incoming information and calming their "feeling brains." For that reason, they're more likely to cry if they're upset, particularly if they feel safe. That's a good thing, because it helps them empty their emotional backpack and regain their equilibrium, instead of spending weeks sulking with a chip on their shoulder as older kids can. But younger children are also more likely to feel frightened by their big emotions, which makes them more likely to lash out, especially given their lack of impulse control. Your four-year-old may be able to argue like a budding lawyer when he's calm, but his brain isn't developed enough for him to access words and logic while he's feeling emotional.

Given all this, emotion coaching young children needs to begin with providing a calm sense of safety. Then, young children often need help to know what they're feeling. I love the approach popularized by Becky Bailey, who has written many wonderful books on conscious discipline and specializes in emotion coaching in the classroom. Bailey suggests that the adult begin by making eye contact with the child and taking slow, deep breaths. The child automatically responds by taking slower, deeper breaths herself, which helps her begin to calm down.[147]

Then, Bailey suggests the adult try mirroring the child's facial expression and gestures while describing them. For instance, the adult might say, *"Your face is going like this."* (Demonstrate.) *"You seem angry."* This helps the child become aware of what he's feeling, from the signals his body is giving him. The awareness that he's having a feeling helps the child make the shift from "I am" to "I feel" in experiencing the emotion. (See "You Are Not Your Emotions" in Part 1 for more discussion of how transformative this shift can be.) If the adult sees that the child is still anxious, she might say, *"Breathe with me"* and reassure the child: *"You can handle this."* Fear, after all, is ultimately the worry that we can't handle something.

Bailey brilliantly points out that mirroring also helps the adult attune to the child. That might seem secondary while you're reading about it—of course we're attuned to our child!—but one of the most common issues I hear from parents about using empathy is that the child did not feel understood and therefore did not respond with cooperation. Mirroring gets you in the habit of really connecting with your child while you emotion-coach, which makes it more effective.

## Do You Need To Name It To Tame It?

> When I say 'You must be so mad, ' he yells 'I am NOT MAD!'
> When I say 'You must be so sad, ' he yells 'Stop talking!'
>
> — David, father of six-year-old and four-year-old

Parents are often urged to "name it to tame it," which means to name their child's emotions so the child will understand what he's feeling and can learn to self-regulate. Indeed, research shows that when adults "name" an emotion that is troubling them, their distress decreases.[148] And when children are young enough that they don't yet feel defensive, they often appreciate having their emotions named. "*Mad!*" thinks the toddler. "*That's what I am. And Daddy understands!*"

But many parents say that their child reacts badly when they name the emotion. That's because when we "name" our child's emotions, it often seems removed and analytical, rather than empathic. Consider the difference between these two comments:

- *"Oh, Mariana, I can't believe your best friend is moving. I'm so sorry!"*
- *"It must make you sad that your friend is moving."*

The first comment is empathic, "feeling with" the other person, even though no emotion is named. The second comment names the emotion we think the child is feeling and is well-intentioned, but it's a step removed, so she might even feel put on the spot and analyzed. We aren't "feeling with her." We might even be making an unwarranted assumption or implying a "should."

So when someone else names what they think you're feeling, it can trigger resistance. To help your child feel understood, you could say something like this instead:

- *"Oh, Nate... I hear how much you want it. You really wished we could do this, didn't you?"*
- *"Grrrr! That is so frustrating!"*

Notice that you're describing the child's desires, labeling what anyone might feel in the situation, or even acknowledging how the situation would make you feel. But you aren't putting the child on the defensive by stating what you assume he is feeling.

As a general rule of thumb, in the heat of the moment, *empathy*—feeling *with* the other person—is what matters; naming the emotion is only helpful if it can be done with empathy.

Later, when your child has calmed down, it's a great idea to "label" the emotion while you tell him the story of what happened, to help him integrate it into his experience: *"I said 'No'. You were so mad and sad! You were yelling and crying. You told me how much you wanted... We hugged and you cried more. Then you felt better. We can always talk about it when we get upset, and then we feel better."* (For more examples of "telling your child the story of what happened" see pages 99, 130, 162 and 204.) And of course during moments when your child is less upset, labeling emotions will help her learn to use this skill for herself, even when she's upset. (See "Talking With Kids About Emotions In Daily Life" on page 153.)

Finally, if you feel you are being empathic and your child is still getting angry when you express empathy, then maybe what's going on is that your child doesn't want to feel those emotions. When we empathize with someone in distress, they feel their emotions more acutely. (Think of how you would feel if you were trying to hold it together after a disaster and then someone you trusted walked into the room and hugged you. You would probably burst into tears.) So, when you acknowledge with empathy how sad your child must be, your child feels even more sad. That doesn't feel good—and it feels even worse if your child is worried about whether you'll be able to help him with his sadness. But that doesn't mean your empathy isn't helping your child, by helping him feel and work through those emotions. Just use your words sparingly and be sure you're creating safety with your hugs and empathy.

---

# Writing to Tame Emotions

One way to "name and tame" emotions that children often find helpful is to write them down. For instance, if your child is missing Papa, who's out of town, suggest that you write a letter together about how she feels. Let her dictate while you write, and then sign it and tape it where Papa will see it.

You can even use this method to help your child deal with frustration when, for example, you're rushing out the door and he can't find the toy car he wanted to bring to school. Write down a promise to yourselves: *"As soon as we get home, Riley and Mom will find his green car!"* Then sign it and tape it to the wall so you'll see it when you walk back in the door. You'll be amazed at how this written promise helps your child manage his upset. Even for children who can't read, writing has magic.

---

## But What About...?

We've been focusing on how to respond to your child's emotions rather than his behavior. We'll get to behavior in the next section on loving guidance—but you probably have some questions that begin with *"But what about...?"* Let's answer those questions.

**"But what if my child's a drama queen?!"** Perhaps you can emotion-coach if your child gets legitimately hurt, but you get frustrated when it feels like she's overreacting to every little thing. Remember, all pain is legitimate. Children feel emotions deeply, and disappointments that seem small to us can feel like the end of the world to them. The definition of getting triggered is that current events trigger old upsets, which spill out of the emotional backpack. The current problem might be small, but the old upset causes lots of tears. So, if you think your child is overreacting, it just means she's emptying her emotional backpack.

**"But what about 'fake crying'?"** If your child is "fake crying," it's because she needs comfort from you but isn't sure it's safe to really let go and show you the depth of those tears. If you can respond with tenderness and compassion, you'll see the real tears. And if you're worried that maybe your child is "manipulating" you with her tears, remember that you aren't changing your limit. You're simply acknowledging her upset with as much compassion as you can.

**"But what about bad behavior? I'm not going to let him get away with breaking the rules because he's upset!"** Of course not! But I assume you don't have rules against emotions. Accepting emotions does not mean that you don't stop off-track behavior. And accepting your child's upset about bedtime doesn't mean he gets to play longer, no matter how much he cries. Behavior may need to be limited; all feelings are allowed.

**"What if my child gets inappropriately emotional about something when he should be able to control himself? Last week when I said 'No cookie before dinner' he was fine, but today he exploded."** Your child is not choosing to misbehave; he's dysregulated. Most children don't have the skills and ability to *consistently* stay regulated so they can behave appropriately. Even with our much more developed brains, most adults get dysregulated from time to time and behave in "negative" ways we can avoid when we're less stressed.

**"But aren't we rewarding bad behavior by coddling a tantrum?"** Emotions are not bad. They're part of our inner compass, alerting us to what we need and want. You aren't "giving in" or "letting your child win" by accepting her emotions. You're helping her become aware of them so she can learn to self-regulate.

**"If children don't experience the consequence of their bad behavior, how will they learn?"** You're right that the goal here is for your child to learn, but what he's learning is new skills, such as managing his emotions, working out conflict, or remembering his chores. If we think through how to help our child develop those skills, we realize that learning comes from reflection, discussion, and practice, not punishment. After all, punishment provokes anger, not motivation. And the learning centers of the brain shut down when humans are upset.

**"But surely children need to be punished for unacceptable behavior, when they really cross the line?"** It's tempting to think that hurting a child physically or emotionally will teach her not to hurt her brother, steal, lie, or engage in other "inexcusable" behavior. But when a child crosses the line, it's a cry for help. If we can help the child reconnect and re-regulate, she'll be ready to learn and repair. With unconditional love, there is no line. There's only love.

## Example: Emotion Coaching When Your Child Is Angry

Let's take an example of how you might emotion-coach when your child is angry. Say you're making dinner when you hear loud voices from the yard, where your kids are playing. Suddenly your eight-year-old bursts into the kitchen, slamming the door hard behind him. You make a decision to Stop, Drop, and Breathe. So you turn the burner low, take a few deep breaths, and glance at the clock, giving yourself permission to take 10 minutes to deepen your relationship with your son by supporting him.

First, you connect with your child by meeting his eyes and putting your hand gently on his arm, then you **empathize**. *"Wow! You seem really mad."* In this case, you think your child can handle an immediate **limit**, as you empathize again. *"No slamming the door, Mateo; it will break… I see you're furious."*

*"Of course I'm furious!"* He rants about how mean his brother is, and all the terrible things his brother said to him. As he speaks, you resist looking at the stove or the clock. Your face and little murmured noises communicate your concern.

When your son finally pauses and looks at you for a response, you deepen the conversation by **validating**: *"That must really have hurt to have your brother say that. No wonder you're so mad."* You give him a hug and his eyes tear up. Then he pulls himself together to again rant about how his brother doesn't even know the rules. When he looks at you expectantly, you offer non-judgmental observations: *"So you thought you should play the game the way you always do, but your brother had a different idea about the rules? Hmmm… How frustrating for both of you!"*

Because you're coaching anger, you help him notice that under his anger, there's hurt: *"So you tried to tell your brother X? And then your brother was so mad, he said things that really hurt your feelings, huh?"*

Finally, he seems calmer. Aware of the need to get back to cooking dinner, you feel out whether he's ready to move on: *"I wonder what you could do now to work this out? Do you want me to come with you while you tell your brother how you feel?"*

He responds defiantly: *"I'm not telling him anything! I hate playing with him! I'm never playing with him again!"*

You realize there's still some hurt to express before he can move on, so you back up and empathize. *"Wow! You are THAT mad and hurt!"*

He tears up again. Then he says, less defiantly and more vulnerably, *"I WON'T. I won't EVER play with him again."*

You hug him. He blows his nose. Notice he hasn't said much, but he's felt a lot. You sense the energy shifting and see that now he can't resist looking out the window to see whether the game is going on without him. You see that he's starting to feel more regulated and is considering going back outside. You help him evaluate his options: *"If you feel ready to talk with your brother, I'd be happy to go with you. And I hear you might still be way too mad. It sounds like you're so mad, you think maybe you'll avoid problems like this if you never play with your brother ever again. I wonder what might happen then?"*

*"He'll miss me, that's what. He'll beg me to come play with him!"* your son says defiantly.

You smile warmly. *"You want him to notice how much he likes playing with you, and miss you so much that he would beg you to play with him again!"*

Your son enjoys the idea so much he smiles. *"Well… he might not beg. But he WOULD miss me."* Now that he feels better, he's thinking more clearly and feels more empowered. *"I know, I'll tell him 'Our family rule is be kind! If you aren't kind to me, I don't want to play with you!'"*

You smile back at him and ruffle his hair. *"It sounds like you know just what you want to say. And you want people to treat you right, or you don't want to play. Good for you. I wonder what might happen if you say that?"*

*"It doesn't matter. If he's kind, I'll play. If he's not, then I won't play with him. I'll figure something else out to do until dinner. He'll be jealous if I get to help cook!"*

Is it always this easy? Of course not. Sometimes you'll need to accompany your child and coach him as he expresses his upset to his sibling. (For examples of scripts like this, see my book *Peaceful Parent, Happy Siblings.*[150]) But empathizing in this way is always where you begin. If you can resist denying your child's feelings and trying to solve the problem for him, you'll see that your emotion coaching increasingly helps him move through the emotions and shift into problem solving. And the more you practice, the easier this gets—for both of you!

## Practice: Emotion Coaching

Sometime in the next few days, your child will get upset about something. Instead of getting annoyed or upset yourself, seize the opportunity to practice your emotion coaching. After your child calms down, answer these questions.

What was your child upset about?

_____

_____

_____

Were you able to stay calm yourself? What helped and what didn't help?

_____

_____

_____

Did you feel you were able to "create safety"? What helped and what didn't help?

_____

_____

_____

Were you able to find the words to acknowledge your child's perspective and empathize?

_____

_____

_____

What did you say?

_____

_____

_____

How did your child react?

_____

_____

_____

How did you feel throughout this interaction?

_____

_____

_____

What did you feel good about in this interaction?

_____

_____

_____

What would you like to change in your next emotion-coaching interaction with your child?

_____

_____

_____

## *Your Child's Emotional Backpack*

Kids who get very upset over a minor disappointment or injury are discharging pain from past experiences. They don't know it, but they're emptying their emotional backpack. How does that work?

Imagine your child coming home from school. Even ordinary days are filled with experiences that are difficult to deal with on her own, without Mom or Dad to support her. Maybe another child pushed her or took her toy. Maybe when you dropped her off, she had to work hard not to cry. Maybe the other kids were mean to her at lunch or she was embarrassed when the teacher called on her. All day long, uncomfortable feelings that she didn't feel safe to work through during the day went into her emotional backpack.

When you pick her up at the end of the day, that full backpack makes her tense and ornery. Now that she's safe with you again, her body says, "*Let's process these feelings and heal them, so we can get on with other things.*" But she stuffed those emotions to begin with because they didn't feel good. Now, as they come up to get healed, she feels overwhelmed and frightened. What does she do? What we all do when we feel threatened: fight, flight, or freeze. Maybe she asks for screen time to escape (flight). Or a treat to numb her feelings (freeze). Or maybe she lashes out, either at you or her sibling (fight). Remember the discussion of the emotional backpack in Part 1 of this book? **Anger isn't in the emotional backpack. Anger is the "fight" defense, a response to perceived threats from both outside and inside.** The threats from inside are the more vulnerable emotions that got stuffed—variations on fear and grief. Anger actually feels much safer to us than fear or grief.

So something minor happens that triggers those stuffed feelings. Sometimes kids burst into tears. More often, they respond with anger. But if you can stay calm, create safety, and empathize, the child can often relax the anger and show you the pain beneath. Is she overreacting to the situation? Absolutely. But emotions are always legitimate. She needs to cry or to express her upset. Your loving attention gives her a safe place to heal this old hurt, so she can move on. Time for time-in!

## *Transform Your Time-Outs To Time-Ins*

> William wouldn't move to his side of the car and put his seatbelt on.
> There was a lot of screaming, crying, and throwing shoes in response to our impatient demands.
> A few days later, after reading your book, we got a chance for a real-life 'do-over.' I get anxious
> about what my husband will do, so I just reassured him that we had time for this. Then I moved
> close to William and was very empathic, acknowledging how he wanted to be closer to his brother
> and how disappointed he was that he had to sit on the other side of the car. Eventually he moved
> himself over and put his seatbelt on. William and I reflected later on how much better it was when
> I kept my cool and how much closer we felt when we worked on the problem together.
>
> — Margaret, mother of an eight-year-old and a six-year-old

Sometimes, despite your best efforts to express understanding, your child gets emotionally dysregulated. When you realize that your child is getting to that dangerous over-wrought place, suggest that the two of you take some "cozy time"—snuggle up and read a book. Often the connection and the shift to his "thinking brain" will help your child re-regulate.

But sometimes your child is too far gone for a book. He lashes out and hits someone, or throws himself on the floor and howls. This is the time for "time-in." Every home (and classroom) needs a "cozy corner" where children can take themselves to calm down. But instead of sending your child there—which would feel like banishment—you go with your child.

**Once a meltdown starts and your child is swept up with emotion, your goal isn't really to help him calm down; it's to be his witness for all these feelings so he can express them.** He needs you to be his safe place, his anchor. Your job is to communicate with your calm demeanor that his out-of-control feelings aren't dangerous and will pass.

You can hold your child, or simply stay close. Your calm, loving presence helps your child re-regulate. If your child won't let you touch him, just stay nearby so you don't trigger his abandonment panic. Don't give in to whatever caused the meltdown; instead, offer your total empathy and be ready to reassure him of your love once he calms down.

Keep your words minimal and soothing. Remember that your child can't listen or learn or even manage his behavior when he's in this state. (Think back to your last parental tantrum and then magnify the overwhelm by a factor of 1,000 because of his immature brain.) Later, you'll be able to talk about the upset and what each of you could have done differently to better meet both of your needs. But, while your child is calming down, your focus is only on restoring a sense of safety. Notice that you can't do this unless you use the practices from Part 1 of this book to calm yourself.

If she runs away, stay near. If she yells at you to leave, say, "*I hear you... I will step back to here... I won't leave you alone with these big feelings.*" (Later, kids usually say they don't want us to leave, even when they've just screamed that they hate us. If your child is older and insists that you leave, I would respect that but stay as close as possible and keep working to increase the level of trust.) If your child tries to distract herself (asks to nurse, or find Daddy, or watch TV), just say, "*We can do that soon, but not right now. Right now, we will sit here for a few minutes... I'm sorry it's hard... It will feel better soon, I promise. You're safe... I'm here.*"

It's important that you wait to teach. After kids have a meltdown, they're ready to reconnect with you. But while your child is vulnerable after the meltdown is not the time to have a discussion about his transgression, or even about his emotional outburst. He probably doesn't know why he was so upset, and feeling analyzed will make him feel less likely to trust you with his inner life. Just scoop him up, hug him, tell him he did some hard work, and reassure him that everyone needs to cry sometimes and that you love him no matter what.

If you feel you must teach, wait until after your child is calm to remind her about appropriate behavior, preferably with a light touch that acknowledges that she already knows the rule: "*Let's think of three things that are good to throw... You think baseballs, stuffed animals, snowballs? Great list! I notice that iPads aren't on this list. Not to throw? Right!*

*Give me five!*" If he's actually broken the iPad or hurt his sibling, you'll need to have a more serious conversation that includes the expectation of repair, but you'll still need to wait until he's calm before he feels the desire to make a repair.

## Setting-Up Your Cozy Corner

Every home (and classroom) needs a soothing space or calming corner. This is simply a comforting place where people in your home go to calm down. It can have a big easy chair, a stuffed beanbag chair, or simply a fluffy rug. I recommend stuffed animals, books about emotions, calm colors, and a small jar of bubbles (because blowing shifts us into deeper, slower breathing). It's also helpful for children to be able to play audios that take them through a guided meditation. Watching fish swimming in a tank has been proven to be calming, but you can certainly go the simple route with a clear plastic jar full of bubbles and glitter. There's more information online at AhaParenting.com.

Just remember that you need to go to the cozy corner with your child, at least for the first 10 or so times they use it. No child wants to be sent away to calm down. But once your child gets used to going to the cozy corner with you and savoring the comfort of it, you'll find them heading there on their own when they're upset.

Can you take two children at once to the cozy corner? Sure. Just be sure there are two separate beanbag chairs or other cozy places, so they don't fight over who sits where. Then, insist that the rule in the cozy corner is only soft voices.

## BEYOND DISCIPLINE: LOVING GUIDANCE

Discipline comes down to one simple phrase: Connect and Redirect. Our first response should always be to offer soothing connection, then we can redirect behaviors. Even when we say no to children's behavior, we always want to say yes to their emotions, and to the way they experience things.

— Daniel J. Siegel and Tina Payne Bryson[151]

What kind of discipline is best for children? I'm hoping you'd suggest guidance to help the child develop their own inner compass so they can navigate the problems of life with integrity, compassion, and responsibility. But it's a bit of a trick question, because the word "discipline"—while it originally meant "to teach"—has become synonymous with "punishment," so you might have found yourself thinking about consequences, time-outs, or other punishments. That's why I suggest that we move beyond the word "discipline," which no longer serves us, and instead use loving guidance to teach our children. Loving guidance simply means coaching our child to be her best self, in a positive, respectful way that resists any temptation to be punitive. Loving guidance is setting appropriate limits while you stay connected to your child through empathy and emotion coaching.

When we use loving guidance instead of punishment or discipline:

- The child feels understood, so is less resistant to the correction and more likely to cooperate. It strengthens the parent–child relationship so the child *wants* to follow the parent's lead, at that moment and at other times.

- It helps to prevent children misbehaving when they feel bad about themselves, overwhelmed by emotion, or disconnected from us. Loving guidance addresses those needs and feelings so the child has the emotional ability to cooperate.
- It helps the child to develop a brain that is capable of self-regulation.
- It helps the child to develop an inner compass to navigate the challenges of life.

In other words, loving guidance fosters the motivation, emotional regulation, brain development, and inner compass that help us resolve problems constructively. And what is discipline, but the way we work things out with our child when our needs, desires and values conflict? How you solve those problems that inevitably arise with your child will be her model in every future relationship.

## Practice: Understanding Your Child's Behavior

Of course, your intention is always to guide your child respectfully, but there will probably be times when you find yourself starting to reach for bribes or threats. Let's give you loving guidance skills to use instead. We'll begin by taking a closer look at what might be driving your child's behavior.

Which of your child's behaviors would you most like to change?

_____

_____

_____

What have you tried to change this behavior, and did it work?

_____

_____

_____

Why do you think your child is engaging in this behavior? What unmet needs and upset emotions are driving it?

_____

_____

_____

# Can Ignoring Misbehavior Be a Good Strategy at Times?

There's a popular idea that if we ignore misbehavior, children will stop doing it. This probably works sometimes with some children. For instance, maybe your four-year-old is saying forbidden words to shock you. If you act like you don't even notice and point out the cool tow truck ahead, it's possible that your four-year-old will drop his effort to shock you and will allow himself to be drawn into a warm interaction with you about tow trucks. But notice that you haven't simply ignored him—you've redirected his effort to connect with you. And, if you've ever had a four-year-old, you know that he's entirely likely to try out his forbidden words again later, possibly on Grandma.

The problem with ignoring misbehavior is that children misbehave for a reason, and ignoring the behavior doesn't address the reason. If your 14-year-old slams the door and you ignore it, he's likely to start kicking the wall. That doesn't mean you punish him for slamming the door, any more than you punish your four-year-old for trying out swear words. But don't you want to know what's behind the behavior? If you ignore it, you won't find out. Meanwhile, your child will either escalate the behavior to make you pay attention or look for some other way to meet his needs. Either way, you'll almost certainly wish you had intervened earlier.

## Setting Empathic Limits

Parental limits are the boundaries where your child's desires smash up against what you're asking. Since he thinks those desires will make him happy, he's not going to give them up easily. That's why he tests every limit, just to be sure. But when humans come up against a limit that won't budge, we do eventually give up—the human race is still here because we don't keep on banging our heads against immovable walls. As we give up the fight, our body shifts from being governed by the sympathetic nervous system (fight or flight) to being governed by the parasympathetic nervous system (regroup and replenish). A signal is sent to the lacrimal glands of the eyes, which is where tears come from. So when we give up, we cry. We grieve what we're losing. Our tears offload stress chemicals, we feel better, and we can move on.

The developmental psychologist Gordon Neufeld calls those the "tears of futility."[152] His term illustrates why your limits need to be clear and firm. If they aren't, your child—particularly if she's strong willed—won't think the situation is futile at all. Maybe she can get you to reconsider? **So, if you want your child to accept your limits, you have to believe in the limits you're setting and communicate that resistance is futile!**

But here's the catch. Your child needs to know he's tried everything. If he doesn't feel you understand, he'll escalate his anger to "make" you see his perspective (just in case you somehow missed how outrageously unfair it is that he's not allowed to do whatever it is he wants to do). And, really, if your child doesn't think you're on his side, that you understand, why should he do what you want?

That's why empathy is an essential part of setting limits. It communicates that you understand your child's perspective and you *are* on your child's side, but your limit is firm. So your ability to match your child's emotional tone is crucial. As we discussed in the section on empathy, mechanically parroting your child's words will not help him feel understood. But, if you match his level of passion, he'll know you really get it:

- *"You LOVE running, don't you?! You can run all you want in the grass. Streets are not for running; streets are for cars. You may hold my hand while we cross the street or I can carry you. You can run by yourself again on the other side of the street."*

- *"Wow, Sara put up those photos from Saturday?! That's so exciting! And the rule in our house is still that homework comes first. You can go online once your homework is finished. I know, it's hard to wait! But it's always good to have something to look forward to, once you finish your homework. That's a good self-management trick."*

## • INVITING COOPERATION BY MEETING DEEPER NEEDS •

Remember our discussion about self-discipline? To accommodate your limits, your child has to switch gears, giving up what he wants for something he wants more. Ultimately, what he wants more than anything is that warm relationship with you. But as you set limits, you can also offer your child something else he wants and needs, and this will make it easier for him to switch gears. Here are some examples of what you can offer:

- **Autonomy:** *"You have a choice. You can take the medicine from the spoon or we can put it in a smoothie to disguise the taste. You're in charge of this decision."*

- **Partnership with you in solving problems:** *"You two are really loving this game! And we have a problem to solve. The baby's asleep and voices this loud will wake her. What should we do?"*

- **Mastery:** *"I love how you're in charge of getting your water yourself. The way to keep our precious water from slipping away down the drain is to twist the handle very tightly when you turn the water off. Do you think you can show me how to do that?"*

- **Contribution:** *"The baby is so much happier in his carseat when you make faces at him. See how much he loves that? Thank you so much for helping him feel better!"*

- **Playful connection with you:** (putting a sock on your ear and speaking in a funny voice), *"Is this Ben's foot? Where's Ben's foot? I'm his sock and I need his toes inside me, quickly!"*

- **Fantasy fulfillment:** *"It sounds like you would love some ice cream, right this minute! What if we had a huge bowl of ice cream the size of this car? What kinds of ice cream would you put in your huge car bowl?"*

These are all examples of meeting your child's deeper needs for autonomy, play, contribution, and so on. Start with a clear limit, add your understanding, and then sweeten the deal for your child by meeting a deeper need.

## Examples of Needs

Children who are hungry or tired, who haven't been able to run around all day, or who don't feel safe will simply not have the internal resources to manage themselves, no matter how brilliantly you emotion-coach or how empathic your limits. Notice that meeting emotional, mental and spiritual needs is as essential for healthy development as meeting physical needs.

**Physical needs**, such as safety, food, sleep, activity, touch, and physical nurturing.

**Emotional needs**, such as acceptance, intimacy, understanding, affection, respect, appreciation, trust, and belonging. All humans need to feel seen, heard, and valued for themselves.

**Mental needs**, such as autonomy, exploration, learning, self-expression, integrity, mastery, excitement, contribution, power, competence, significance, and unstructured time.

**Spiritual needs**, such as love, play, creativity, beauty, spaciousness, peace, order, celebration, and connection with our deeper selves and the divine.

Note: The separation of needs into physical, emotional, mental, and spiritual types is useful conceptually but somewhat artificial, since humans are really a holistic integration of these aspects.

## • SETTING EMPATHIC LIMITS WHEN YOUR CHILD ISN'T YET VERBAL •

Receptive language develops much faster than expressive language, so even a child who doesn't speak much yet will understand a lot of what you say. And, since so much of what we communicate comes from tone, even non-verbal children often understand what we're communicating.

It's amazing how acknowledging your child's anger can stop a brewing tantrum in its tracks.

- **Before you set a limit, acknowledge his perspective:** *"You wish you could have more juice; you love that juice, right?"* (Look, he's already nodding yes!)
- **Then set the limit:** *"You need to eat some eggs, too. We'll have more juice later."* (As you say this, move his cup out of sight.)
- **If he responds with anger, acknowledge it:** *"That makes you so mad. You really want more juice. Right?"*

Three things are key to making this work:

- **Keep your language simple:** *"Juice later. First, healthy food."*
- **Label emotion:** *"You're mad!"*
- **Match your child's level of emotion:** *"You LOVE juice!"*

Usually, just having her feelings acknowledged helps the child cooperate with your limit. If your child tantrums despite your empathy, remember that she may just need to cry. Or maybe your limit is really hard for her to accept. Either way, stay compassionate as she cries. Over time, she'll develop the impulse regulation to accept your limits. Your job now is to stay connected as you set those limits, so she *wants* to cooperate once she gains the ability.

## • SETTING EMPATHIC LIMITS WHEN YOU WANT TO STOP • YOUR CHILD FROM DOING SOMETHING

When you want your child to *stop* doing something, always begin by checking in with yourself. If you have an anxious edge to your voice, that's what your child will respond to, no matter what words you use. Next, make eye contact if possible. Then:

1. **Communicate understanding** by acknowledging the child's perspective: *"You love jumping on the couch, don't you?"*

2. **Set the limit:** *"Shoes get the couch dirty. You can jump once you take your shoes off."*

3. **Redirect** (tell the child what he can do instead to meet his needs): *"Jump into my arms and I'll help you with those shoes."*

That's your basic three-step process. If you do preventive maintenance with your child daily and you're able to stay emotionally regulated as you set limits, then this three-step process of setting limits will elicit cooperation much of the time. Does that sound like magic? It's the magic of your child feeling understood, seeing the firmness of your limit, and understanding what he can do instead to get what he wants.

But the magic won't always work. Some strong-willed experiential learners need to test *every* limit. Others will only test your limits when they're having a hard day. But, ultimately, it is your child's job to test your limits and your job to hold to them firmly but kindly.

Expect your child to test your limits. Remember, make it easier for her to switch gears by meeting her needs:

- **Empathize again:** *"You're having a hard time stopping jumping, aren't you?"*

- **Autonomy (give choices):** "*You have a choice. You can jump on the couch without shoes, or you can jump in the back yard on the trampoline. Up to you.*"

- **Describe the "problem" and invite partnership in solving it:** "*You love jumping! The problem is that shoes bring dirt from outside and get the couch dirty. How can we solve this?*"

- **Invite mastery:** "*Wow! Look at you jump! Do you think you can jump right off the couch and keep jumping all the way to the trampoline?*"

- **Connect with playfulness:** "*Time to pay the jumping toll! Kisses and shoes please!*" (As you grab her, kiss her belly and take off her shoes, in between jumps.)

- **Grant your child's wish in fantasy:** "*You say you're going to jump so high you'll fly?*" (Intercept her mid-jump to fly her around the room.) "*Wow! You ARE flying! Zoom!*"

- **Use an "I" statement to tell your child what you need**, so she can contribute to the well-being of the family (or in this case the couch): "*I see a couch that's in extreme danger! I need your help to save it, quick!*"

- **With young children, you may need to intervene physically:** "*I've got you, you jumping bean girl, you. Let's see how far you can jump in the back yard.*"

My two-year-old twins still sleep in adjoining cribs. Over the past couple of months, they have gotten in the habit of pulling up their mattresses, moving all of their stuffed animals underneath to prop them up, and then jumping on the crib frame. For safety reasons, that terrifies me, obviously. I used to go in, shout at them to stop, yank the mattresses back down, and so on—and it didn't work. I would be going back and forth into their room numerous times because they enjoyed the power struggle and thought it was a really fun game.

I've changed my approach now, as a result of peaceful parenting. When I see what they've done with the mattresses, I realize that my anger is exacerbated by my fear, so I verbalize what I'm feeling, calmly. I started to tell them, 'I can see that you want to play under the mattress. That's not safe. I won't let you do that. Please move your toys back on top of the mattresses and get back on them yourselves. We don't go *under* the mattress, we go on the mattress.' I would repeat that last line over and over, partly because it helped me to remain calm and partly because it was a short, declarative statement they could remember and repeat back to me. Now, when I go in and see them under the mattresses, they start moving their stuffed animals back on top on their own, and say to me, 'No under the mattress, need to go on the mattress. Help please, Mama.'

There's no argument, there's no yelling, and there's no drawn-out power struggle. They go under their mattresses because they're two and because they're testing the limits—I get that. But it never escalates and it's handled swiftly and calmly, and we can all hug afterwards and say 'thank you' to each other. I love it.

— Lea, single mom of two-year-old twins

### • *SETTING EMPATHIC LIMITS WHEN YOU WANT YOUR CHILD TO DO SOMETHING* •

When you want your child to do something, always begin by:

- **Checking in with yourself.** If you have an anxious edge to your voice, that's what your child will respond to, no matter what words you use.
- **Connecting with your child.** Make eye contact and "join" your child emotionally: "*Wow! Is that a spaceship you're building?*"

Then:

- **Acknowledge the child's perspective:** "*You're having such a great time with that!*"
- **State what you want your child to do:** "*It's almost time to get ready for bed.*"
- **Tell your child what he can do instead to meet his needs:** "*Do you want some help to move your project to a safe place so you can finish it tomorrow?*"

If you're not sure your child is listening, make physical contact with a gentle hand on his arm and make eye contact. Ask your child, "*What did I say? What do you need to do?*" Keep your tone light and respectful. Again, if your child feels connected and you're regulated, he may be able to cooperate easily. Expect your child to test your limit. Make it easier for him to switch gears by meeting his needs:

- **Autonomy (give choices):** "*It's almost time to get ready for bed. You can take your bath now or in five minutes. Your decision.*"
- **Describe the "problem" and invite partnership in solving it:** "*You wish you could keep working on this, I see. The problem is that lights out is at 8pm so you're rested for tomorrow, and you need a bath, plus we need to find out what happens in our chapter book! Remember how the car started flying? How can we work together to get everything done?*"
- **Invite mastery:** "*Can you show me the countdown procedure for how your spaceship takes off, so it can fly up to the bathroom?*"
- **Connect with playfulness:** (in a mechanical voice as you stalk your child and scoop him up) "*I am the bath alien and I always get my man!*"
- **Grant your child's wish in fantasy:** "*I bet when you grow up, you'll stay up and play, all night every night, and never go to bed, right?!*"
- **Use an "I" statement to describe the situation and invite cooperation:** "*I need your help! I see a boy who hasn't taken his bath and a clock that's ticking fast. I need a clean boy who's ready to start our chapter book by 7:30pm. Let's go!*"
- **With young children, you may need to intervene physically:** "*Grab your spaceship, Captain, because we're blasting off for the bath!*"

> Today when my daughter didn't want to pick up her toys, I started to get frustrated as usual. Luckily, I remembered to get down on her level and ask if she had any ideas on how we could pick up the toys together. She came up with an option that worked for her! And I was able to reframe my perceptions. It wasn't that she just wanted her way—she needed to feel she had a choice.
>
> — Devon, father of a three-year-old
> and a five-year-old

# Example: Enforcing Your Limit When Your Child Resists

Let's consider an example that every parent knows. The only thing harder than getting a young child into the bathtub is getting him out.

**Dad:** (in a calm voice to create safety since he knows his limit will be unwelcome) *"Liam, our extra five minutes is up. It's time to get out of the bathtub."*

**Liam:** (angrily pounding the water with a big splash) *"NO!"*

**Dad:** (wet, but not taking it personally, making an effort to connect) *"I see your face going like this"* (Dad makes an angry face that looks ready to cry) *"and your hands pounding the water like this"* (Dad brings his fists down in the air, in imitation of Liam). *"You look sad and mad. I guess you don't feel ready to get out of the tub."*

**Liam:** (tearing up in anguish but no longer aggressive because he feels understood) *"I'm playing with my new boat!"*

**Dad:** *"You really wish you could stay in the tub longer and play with your new boat."*

**Liam:** (feels understood; tests the limit) *"Yes! Please? Five more minutes?"*

**Dad:** (calm, affectionate, setting a firm limit) *"We already had our extra five minutes, Liam. It's time to get out now. I know that feels sad to you. You can play with your boat in the bath tomorrow."*

**Liam:** (one last try) *"I want to play now!"*

**Dad:** (calm, firm, affectionate) *"It's hard to stop playing and get out of the tub, Liam. AND you can handle this. I will help you. Let's go."*

**Liam:** (still sniffling but sees the limit is firm; begins to adapt and look for a win–win solution) *"Can we dry my boat so it can listen to my bedtime story with me?"*

**Dad:** (partnering) *"Sure! Drain the water out like this. Now out you go!"*

Crying is not testing the limit; it's a sign that your child sees your limit is firm and is grieving. But notice that even when your child feels understood, he tests the limit. That's his job. If the parent loses his temper at that point, everything spirals downhill. But if the parent can understand the child's point of view, he can remain calm and uphold his limit.

# Practice: What Could You Say to Set This Empathic Limit?

Read the situations below. Under each scenario, write what you could say and do that would help your child to feel understood and at the same time set the necessary limit. If you can use playfulness, that is always helpful, but if your child is too far gone or you're too tired, just stick to empathic limits and coaching. The first scenario has a suggested answer to get you started thinking.

**(1) Your child is standing up to look out the bus window.**

What you say:

- First, I would ignore everyone around me who might be watching. My only obligation is to my child.
- Then, in a warm voice, I'd acknowledge what my child is seeing and enjoying, matching my tone to his level of excitement: "You LOVE looking out the window! You can see everything! It's so exciting!"
- Then I'd set my limit, using empathy: "The rule on the bus is that everyone sits, so we're safe. The bus is bumpy. You could fall."

- Then I'd tell him what he can do: "You can sit here next to me, or you can sit on my lap and look out."

What you do:

- Move in close, put my hands on his waist to stabilize him as the bus moves, and hold him there as I connect and share the view with him. Then ease him back onto my lap.
- If he protests, I would empathize more: "You LOVE looking out the window!" I would look for a win-win solution: "Do you want to stand in my lap and I will hold you while you look out?"

**( 2 ) Your child wants a cookie just before dinner.**

What you say:

_____

_____

_____

What you do:

_____

_____

_____

**( 3 ) Your child ignores you when you ask her to start getting ready for school.**

What you say:

_____

_____

_____

What you do:

_____

_____

_____

**( 4 ) Your child forgets to do his chore.**

What you say:

_____

_____

_____

What you do:

_____

_____

_____

**( 5 ) Your child throws her cup in anger.**

What you say:

_____

_____

_____

What you do:

_____

_____

_____

**( 6 ) Your child teases his sibling.**

What you say:

_____

_____

_____

What you do:

_____

_____

_____

**( 7 ) Your child refuses to wear her coat as you're leaving the house.**

What you say:

_____

_____

_____

What you do:

_____

_____

**(8) After you put your child to bed, he keeps getting out of bed.**

What you say:

_____

_____

_____

What you do:

_____

_____

_____

**(9) Your child says that the dinner you've prepared is disgusting.**

What you say:

_____

_____

_____

What you do:

_____

_____

_____

**(10) Your child hits her sibling.**

What you say:

_____

_____

_____

What you do:

_____

_____

_____

There are no right answers to these situations. But there are some example answers at the Aha! Parenting website at this link: AhaParenting.com/ExampleLimits. You'll learn more if first you try to answer the questions on your own, before you look at the example answers.

# Practice: **Redirecting**

Your child isn't trying to create a problem for you. She's just trying to help herself feel better in the best way she can see how at this moment. Can you redirect her to meet whatever need she's expressing in a way that's constructive? Consider the examples below and then create your own.

| Instead of Telling Him What He Can't Do... | ... Tell Him What He *Can* Do |
|---|---|
| "No throwing toys!" | "You feel like throwing, don't you? No balls in the house. Stuffed animals are safe to throw inside. Or you can take your ball outside." |
| "Don't grab!" | "You can tell your sister, 'It's my turn now.'" |
| "Stop splashing!" | "Water stays in the tub. You can stir it to make it move." |
| "You're getting marker on the floor!" | "Markers stay on the paper. Here's your tray and more paper." |

| What You Usually Say When You Tell Your Child What He Can't Do... | What You Can Say Instead To Tell Your Child What He *Can* Do |
|---|---|
| | |
| | |
| | |
| | |
| | |

## • *SETTING EMPATHIC LIMITS WHEN YOUR CHILD TESTS AND PROVOKES* •

> My son was being unusually angry and defiant and I was at a loss for how to cope. Implementing this loving, accepting strategy has worked so well! The first time I did it (using your words—it's so great to have a script!) my little boy's rage melted within five minutes. I notice that my son has been extra loving and cuddly since I started doing this. I think he must feel accepted and loved and safe.
>
> — Rebecca, mother of a four-year-old

When your child looks right at you and breaks the rules, or shouts at you in defiance, you probably want to smack him. But this is a signal that he needs your help. He's got some big emotions bubbling up. Maybe something made him really angry and he needs to be heard. Or maybe he desperately needs to cry, but that feels like an emergency, so he's in fight, flight, or freeze mode. He might have begged for treats (to numb himself—that's freeze) or screen time (that's flight). But now he's in fight mode and you look like the enemy. What can you do?

If he's not too far gone, start by trying to turn the situation around with humor: "*What do you mean you're not going to take a bath? C'mere, you no bath-taker, you!*" If he smiles, you can initiate a little roughhousing to get him laughing. Remember, laughter helps your child with those pent-up emotions almost as well as tears would, so this might totally save your evening. (What if he's too far gone? See the upcoming scenario: "Setting Empathetic Limits When Your Child Gets Enraged.")

After you've laughed and reconnected, you can acknowledge his unhappiness about having to take a bath while you insist on your limit and emphasize the good parts: *"You didn't want to take a bath, did you? It's hard to stop playing and get ready for bed. Even though you know we're on chapter three of our new book and we need to find out what happens!"*

Later, as you settle down to read together, you might say, *"Remember when you yelled at me that you weren't going to take a bath? When you yell, I feel attacked. You never need to yell for me to hear you and pay attention. I won't always be able to give you what you want, but I will always listen. Okay?"*

It was two weeks before my son was to start kindergarten, and time for him to start wiping his own bottom. Luckily, I had just finished reading about setting empathic limits, and I decided this was a limit that needed to be set. I wouldn't have felt like a responsible parent sending my son to school without knowing how to take care of his own body. First, we had a problem-solving conversation about the wiping. We wrote down all of our ideas, from 'Mom and Dad will keep wiping' to 'I will wipe myself' to 'Call Grandma to come over and wipe each time!' We finally settled on having Mom and Dad visit and sing silly songs while my son took care of business.

The next morning, I was called in for a clean-up. When I started the new strategy (visit and sing silly songs), my son refused to clean himself. He went from power-struggle flat-out refusal to anger pretty quickly. I managed to stay calm and tried to reflect back to him what I was seeing: a boy who didn't want to wipe his bottom, a boy who was angry, and so on. I tried to elicit from him what it was about wiping that he didn't want to do: Was it icky? Was he worried about getting it on his hands? Was it too hard to do? At one point, he closed and locked the bathroom door, shouting at me.

Then something dawned on me. I said, 'Do you think that if I won't wipe your bottom that I don't love you?' The different wave of emotion came through. My son's voice choked up as he said, 'Yes,' and started to cry. He opened the door, half-crawled into my lap (not all the way, since we still had a poopy bottom going on), and proceeded to cry into my arms. I myself teared up. He was able to release all his worries of feeling unloved, and at the end was completely willing to wipe his own bottom.

— Carrie, mother of a five-year-old

## • SETTING EMPATHIC LIMITS WHEN YOUR CHILD GETS ENRAGED •

What if you tried humor or roughhousing to get your child to cooperate, but your child became more enraged?

First, consider the situation. This often happens when kids are told to turn off a screen. Since screens are addictive, especially for children, some kids simply can't handle them and blow up when you enforce your limit.

Or maybe your child has simply had a hard day or too little sleep or too much stimulation, and she just can't hold it together. For whatever reason, she responds to your limit with fury.

This is what I call the breakdown lane. If you had seen this coming, you could have intervened at many points along the way to prevent this moment. Maybe your child needs more connection or more sleep, or shouldn't be using screens so much. (If so, make a mental note to yourself to do some serious problem solving after the kids are in bed to avoid a similar problem in the future.)

But for now, you have a kicking, screaming child. What can you do? You can remember that behind anger is fear and/or hurt. Your child is using the anger as a defense against those feelings that are so upsetting to her. Most of the time, when we move into compassion and kids feel heard, they stop hitting us and start crying. Once the underlying feelings are expressed, they begin to evaporate. The defensive anger will no longer be needed, and it will melt away.

So your goal now is to create safety, so your child can show you the tears and fears under her anger.

- **Keep yourself from moving into "fight or flight" mode** by taking a few deep breaths and reminding yourself that there's no emergency. Your calm will help your child feel safer, so he begins to shift out of "fight or flight" himself.

- **Listen.** Carl Rogers, one of the founders of humanistic psychology, said, "*The truth about rage is that it only dissolves when it is really heard and understood, without reservation.*"[153] Often, when children don't feel heard, they escalate. By contrast, when your child feels understood, she'll begin to feel calmer—even when she doesn't get her way.

- **Try to see it from your child's point of view and acknowledge why he's upset.** The more compassionate you can be, the more likely your child will find his way to the tears and fears under the anger: "*Oh, Joseph, I'm sorry this is so hard… You're saying I never understand you…that must feel so terrible and lonely.*" You don't have to agree or disagree. Just acknowledge his truth in the moment.

- **Don't get hooked by rudeness or personal attacks.** Parents are often hurt when children yell at them. But your child doesn't actually hate you, or want a new mom or dad, or whatever she's yelling. She feels hurt and scared and powerless, so she's pulling out the most upsetting thing she can think of, so you'll know how upset she is. Just say, "*Ouch! You must be so upset to say that to me. Tell me why you're so upset at me. I'm listening.*"

- **Your child is not "behaving badly" or "whining."** He's showing you in the best way he can at the moment just how upset he is. As he realizes that he doesn't have to raise his voice or go on the attack to be heard, and that it's safe to show you his vulnerable emotions, he'll develop the capacity to express his feelings more appropriately.

- **Set whatever limits are necessary to keep everyone safe, while acknowledging the anger and staying compassionate.** "*You're so mad! You can be as mad as you want, AND hitting is still not okay, no matter how upset you are. You can stomp to show me how mad you are, but no hitting.*"

- **If your child is already in a full meltdown, don't talk except to empathize and reassure her that she's safe.** Don't try to teach, reason, or explain. When she's awash with adrenaline and other fight or flight reactions is not the time to explain why she can't have what she wants, or get her to admit that she actually loves her little sister. Just acknowledge how upset she is: "*You are so upset about this… I'm sorry it's so hard.*"

- **Remind yourself that tantrums are nature's way of helping immature brains let off steam.** Children don't yet have the frontal cortex neural pathways to control themselves as we do. (And please note that we don't always regulate our anger very well, even as adults!) The best way to help children develop those neural pathways is to offer empathy, both while they're angry and at other times. It's okay—good, actually—for your child to express those tangled, angry, hurt feelings. After we support kids through a tantrum, they feel closer to us and more trusting. They feel less wound-up inside, so they can be more emotionally generous. They aren't as rigid and demanding.

- **Remember that anger is a defense against threat.** It comes from our "fight, flight, or freeze" response. Sometimes the threat is outside us, but often it isn't. We see threats outside us because we're carrying around old stuffed emotions such as hurt, fear, or sadness. Whatever's happening in the moment triggers those old feelings, and we go into fight mode to try to stuff them down again. So, while your child may be upset about something in the moment, it may also be that he's lugging around a full emotional backpack and just needs to express those old tears and fears. A new disappointment can feel like the end of the world to a child, because all those old feelings come up. Kids will do anything to fend off these intolerable feelings, so they rage and lash out.

- **Make it safe for your child to move past anger.** It isn't the anger itself that's healing. Rather, the tears and fears beneath the anger wash out the hurt and sadness and make the anger unnecessary, so it vanishes. We make it safe for our child to express those hurts by meeting her anger with compassion.

- **Stay as close as you can.** Your child needs an accepting witness who loves him even when he's angry. If you need to move away to stay safe, tell him, "*I won't let you hurt me, so I'm moving back a bit, but I am nearby. Whenever you're ready for a hug, I'm here.*" If he yells at you to "*Go away!*" say "*I hear you and I am moving back.*"

- **Keep yourself safe.** Kids often benefit from pushing against us when they're upset, so if you can tolerate that and stay compassionate, terrific. But if your child is hitting you, move away. If she pursues you, hold her wrist and say, "*I don't think I want that angry fist so close to me. I see how angry you are. You can hit the pillow I'm holding, or push hard against my hands, but no hurting.*" Kids don't really want to hurt us—it scares them and makes them feel guilty. Most of the time, when we move into compassion and they feel heard, kids stop hitting us and start crying. (If that isn't happening with your child, please see the next section "Empathic Limits When Your Child Is Provocative or Angry But Doesn't Cry.")

- **Don't try to evaluate whether he's overreacting.** Of course he's overreacting! But remember that children experience daily hurts and fears that they can't verbalize and that we don't even notice. They store them up and then look for an opportunity to "discharge" them. So if your kid has a meltdown over the blue cup and you really can't go right now to get the blue cup out of the car, it's okay to just lovingly welcome his meltdown. Most of the time, it wasn't about the cup, or whatever he's demanding. When children become impossible to please, they usually just need to cry.

- **Soften yourself.** If you can really feel compassion for this struggling young person, she'll feel it and respond. Don't analyze, just empathize. "*You really wanted that; I'm so sorry, sweetheart.*" Once you recognize the feelings under the anger, she will probably pause and stop lashing out. You'll see some vulnerability or even tears. You can help her bring those feelings to the surface by reminding her of the original trigger: "*I'm so sorry you can't have the _____ you want. I'm sorry this is so hard.*"

- **Don't interrupt the tears.** When our loving compassion meets her wound, that's when she'll collapse into our arms for a good cry. And all those upset feelings will evaporate.

- *After* **he's calmed down, you can talk.** Resist the urge to lecture. Tell a story to help him put this big wave of emotion in context. "*Those were some big feelings… Everyone needs to cry sometimes… You wanted… I said no… You were very disappointed… You got so angry… You were sad and disappointed… Thank you for showing me how you felt.*" If he just wants to change the subject, let him. You can circle back to bring closure later in the day or at bedtime, while you're snuggling. But most young children *want* to hear the story of how they got mad and cried, as long as it's a story from their point of view, not a lecture about what they did wrong. It helps them understand themselves and makes them feel heard.

- **What about teaching?** You don't have to do as much as you think. Your child knows that lashing out hurts others and hurt your relationship. It was those big feelings that made her feel like it was an emergency and that it was necessary to break the rule about being kind. By helping her with the emotions, you're making a repeat infraction less likely. Wait until after the emotional closure, and then keep it simple. Recognize that part of her wants to make a better choice next time, and align with that part. Be sure to give her a chance to practice a better solution to her problem. "*When we get really angry, like you were angry at your sister, we forget how much we love the other person. They look like they're our enemy. Right? You were so very mad at her. We all get mad like that and when we are very mad, we feel like hitting. But if we do, later we're sorry that we hurt someone. We wish we could have used our words. I wonder what else you could you have said or done, instead of hitting?*"

Accepting your child's emotions in this way helps him develop resilience. Gradually, your child will internalize the ability to weather disappointment and learn that while he can't always get what he wants, he can always get something better—someone who loves and accepts all of him, including the yucky parts like disappointment and anger. He'll learn that emotions aren't dangerous—they can be tolerated without acting on them, and they pass. Gradually, he'll learn to verbalize his feelings and needs without attacking the other person, even when he's furious.

You'll have taught him how to manage his emotions. And you'll have strengthened, rather than eroded, your bond with him. All by taking a deep breath and staying compassionate in the face of rage. Sounds saintly, I know, and you won't always be able to pull it off. But every time you do, you'll be helping your child grow the neural pathways for a more emotionally-intelligent brain. And you'll be gifting yourself and your family a lot less drama—and a lot more love.

## • *SETTING EMPATHIC LIMITS WHEN YOUR CHILD* •
### *IS PROVOCATIVE OR ANGRY BUT DOESN'T CRY*

In the previous section ("Setting Empathetic Limits When Your Child Gets Enraged"), the parent creates safety and the angry child is able to break through to tears. But many parents tell me their child just gets stuck in anger and yells at them. What then?

We know what's happening here. Your child has a full backpack of tears and fears that she doesn't want to feel, and she's fending them off at all costs. She wants to heal, and her body even knows how. But she's terrified.

Luckily, we know how to solve this. Give your child three critical kinds of support:

- **Laughter.** Not in the moment that your child is raging, but as a form of preventive maintenance (which I recommend for every child). Spend the next two weeks reducing the pressure in your child's emotional backpack by siphoning off the top layer of anxiety or fear. What's your siphon? Laughter! When your child laughs, she's offloading some of that anxiety she's been lugging around, so she doesn't have to defend so hard to keep all those feelings down. She's softer. There's easier access to the deeper tears and fears. In biological terms, laughter changes the body chemistry so the person feels less tense. That makes it easier for her to cry.
- **A clear, kind limit,** in the moment when your child is pushing. Remember those tears of futility (see page 171)?
- **Even more safety.** That means daily preventive maintenance. Special Time is non-negotiable. Aim for 24/7 empathy. Then, in the moment, ratchet up your compassion. If you have tears in your eyes, your child will feel that you fully understand and you aren't a threat.

When your child is behaving provocatively, remember that he needs to cry and is hoping you'll help him. Many parents describe how their child keeps escalating until they lose their temper and yell. The child cries, but the trust between them is eroded, and they feel terrible afterwards.

Instead, set your limit with playfulness. "*You keep making those loud noises even though I've asked you to stop. The problem is that it will wake the baby.*" Next, speaking playfully, say, "*I think maybe you know that, and you WANT to wake the baby, is that right?*" Grab him and kiss him all over as you say, "*Come here you rascal, you! I think you must be out of hugs again!*"

Toss him around until he's laughing hysterically, then sink down on the couch with him in your lap, look him in the eye, and set a clear, empathic limit: "*You wish you could wake the baby because you get mad at her sometimes, right? It's okay to be mad at her. I want to hear about that. But it's not okay to wake her up with loud noises.*"

Either he'll feel happily connected with you and be able to comply with your limit, or he'll go right back to his provocative loud noises. If he does, repeat your warm, playful, physical connection again.

At some point, either you'll be too tired to continue or he'll be too frenzied and escalate his noises. At that point, take a deep breath and shift into feeling as much compassion as you can. Again, set your limit, at the same time acknowledging the tears and fears that are driving his behavior. "*Okay, my love, no more playing. I can't let you wake the baby. You must get so jealous of the baby, huh? You have to be quiet when she sleeps. She takes a lot of my time and you might even wonder sometimes if I love her more. Right?*"

At this point, you'll have built enough safety that your child will probably begin to talk about his resentment of the baby. He might even begin crying. If not? Go back to preventive maintenance. Soon, you'll find he's willing to trust you with his heart and show you those tears. And his behavior toward his sibling will finally change.

## Practice: How to Set an Empathic Limit with Your Child

Sometime in the next few days, your child will do something that you don't want her to (for example, grab a package of cookies off the shelf at the market) or will *not* do something that you *do* want her to do (for example, wash her hands before dinner). Instead of getting angry, can you seize the opportunity to practice setting limits with empathy? Here's your game plan—post it on your refrigerator so you see it often.

1. **Calm yourself.** Take a few deep breaths. Remind yourself to see the situation from your child's point of view. Use a mantra that you know calms you.

2. **Create safety** with your calm, warm attitude. If your child will let you, touch him reassuringly.

3. **Acknowledge her perspective and empathize.** "Join" with your child emotionally by letting your tone reflect some of what your child is feeling, such as excitement or sadness.

4. **Set the limit clearly and kindly.**

5. **If possible, redirect your child** so he hears another option for what he *can* do with his impulse, instead of just what he can't do.

6. **Expect your child to test the limit.** That's his job. How else will he know whether you mean it? Keep your sense of humor as you hold your limit. If necessary to prevent danger, intervene physically—calmly and gently—to enforce your limit.

7. **Allow feelings.** If your child resists, hold firm to your limit but allow your child to express her dismay. She has a right to want something different from what you want. If she needs to cry, that's fine. Be kind and understanding: "*I'm sorry it's so hard right now.*" If she's overreacting, then she's emptying her emotional backpack, which is a good thing. Once she's done, she'll either fall asleep or be affectionate and cooperative.

If you're worried that your child is "whining" by expressing dismay, then you're focusing on the wrong thing. You need to set limits on behavior, but not on emotions. As long as you're clear about your limit, your child has the right to his feelings about it.

# Reflection After Practice: **Learning to Set Effective Limits**

What happened when you set a limit with your child?

_____

_____

_____

What was your child doing or not doing that caused you to set a limit?

_____

_____

_____

Were you able to calm yourself first? What helped and what didn't help?

_____

_____

What did you say to set the limit empathically?

_____

_____

_____

What did you do, either to uphold your limit or to connect with your child?

_____

_____

_____

How did your child react?

_____

_____

_____

How did you feel throughout this interaction?

_____

_____

_____

What did you feel good about in this interaction?

_____

_____

_____

What would you like to change in your next limit-setting interaction with your child?

_____

_____

_____

## • SETTING EMPATHIC LIMITS WITH A STRONG-WILLED OR OPPOSITIONAL CHILD •

"Strong-willed" people are governed by their own inner compass and won't accept being "bullied" into submission. No human likes being told what to do, but these children simply can't stomach it because it violates their sense of integrity. Whatever they do, it has to be _their_ idea. Strong-willed kids are spirited and courageous, not easily swayed by others. They desperately want to be "in charge" of themselves, and will sometimes put their desire to "be right" above everything else. Strong-willed kids have big, passionate feelings and live at full throttle.

Because they're impervious to peer pressure or even parental pressure, the only way to influence a strong-willed person is through your connection with them. They like win–win solutions that meet both your needs and theirs, but they spit on attempts at bribery. They want to learn things for themselves rather than accepting what others say, so they don't take "no" for an answer and they don't think limits apply to them.

That doesn't mean your strong-willed child won't give up what they want in order to do what you're asking. But they must *choose* to do so, from their trust and love for you. If you try to force them, they'll fight with everything they have.

**You can see that with a strong-willed child, the "empathy" part of empathic limits is critical.** They need to feel you're on their side, even when you set a limit. If you aren't, you're inviting a fight.

**But the "limits" part of empathic limits is also essential with these children.** Remember those "tears of futility" (see page 171)? Strong-willed children need to know that your limit won't budge. They also need to save face. If they feel like they're losing by doing what you want, they won't do it.

Children who are extremely defiant are sometimes diagnosed as having "oppositional defiant disorder," or ODD. Parents often describe this as having their sweet child turn into a raging stranger who shouts abusive obscenities and lashes out physically, often in response to minor disappointments. Many oppositional children also have hyperactivity or attention issues, or struggle with anxiety. In the past, these kids were seen as having parents who were over-punitive, which indeed worsens defiance in children. But in recent years, clinicians have begun to realize that these children are born with issues that make it hard for them to take direction. If their parents use conventional parenting, the child will simply defy them. Because conventional parenting answers defiance by increasing the punishment, the parents are given advice to become more punitive. The child refuses to be forced and responds with aggression, so these families quickly get caught in an escalating cycle of anger and aggression.

> Kids with ODD do not bend to the will of others, so there is no bribing them or punishing them for transgressions. In fact, the more you try to coerce or punish, the harder kids with ODD fight. Instead, it requires a completely different type of parenting, one that involves working with your child to find a mutually-acceptable solution to whatever problem you're dealing with.
>
> — Laura Wright, ODD blogger and mother of two[154]

Some experts think that oppositional children have a delay in brain development that causes them to overreact to frustration. Others think they have an overactive alarm system—a form of anxiety—so that even minor disappointments and limits can feel like threats to their survival and send them into extreme "fight or flight" mode. My own opinion, both from working with families and from following the research, is that both of these issues are operating, but there's yet another factor. These children combine low frustration tolerance and anxiety with being "strong willed." Not all strong-willed children are anxious or have low frustration tolerance, of course. But I suspect that virtually all children diagnosed with oppositional defiant disorder are strong willed as well as anxious and challenged by frustration.

Since this is an issue of brain development, you can help your child's brain change by giving him the repeated experience of feeling safe, loved, and connected, especially when he's upset. Think of your child as a highly-sensitive barometer of connection. If he starts feeling even the slightest bit disconnected, he won't feel safe.

So what can you do to make cooperation more likely if you have a strong-willed or oppositional defiant child? Here are some ideas:

- **Focus on connection so that your child is more likely to follow your lead.** That means 24/7 empathy and daily Special Time are essential.
- **Resist all the advice you receive to punish your child.** It will only make your child's behavior worse.
- **You can, and should, expect your child to make amends when he calms down and feels better.** You will find that your child feels terrible about the things he has said and done, and wants to repair, as long as you aren't punishing or shaming him.
- **Assume that your child is doing her best.** When she isn't cooperating, consider what she needs to restore her equilibrium and feel safe. (It may just be expressing her upset and feeling heard.)

- **Your child feels safer when he's in control.** Give your child as much control as possible, within your parameters of what's acceptable to you.
- **Train yourself to see your child's challenging behavior as a message that she needs your help to find a win–win solution.** What can you do to help her save face and get some of what she needs in this moment?
- **If your child is easily frustrated, don't let that tension build up.** That means daily roughhousing and laughter sessions are essential.
- **If your child tends to be anxious, daily roughhousing and laughter sessions are again essential.** In those moments of defiance, remind yourself that he's afraid. What can you do in this moment to help him feel safer?
- **If your child is easily overwhelmed, don't expect to do what other families do.** Only accept invitations that you think your child can handle. Prepare your child for every new experience.

> After playing an imaginative game of a human-eating whale, it was time to leave the playground. When my son informed me that he 'wasn't going,' as if on cue, my chest tightened. Somehow, through my frustration, I remembered that he might need options for *how* he wanted to leave the park. After taking a moment to myself to gather up our things, I approached him and said, 'We need to leave now. How would you like to leave the park?' He thought for a moment, then decided we should finish our game of the human-eating whale by having the whale swallow a squid that would squirt black ink, making it too dark inside the whale, and the boy would have to come out. Less than a minute later, we were peacefully leaving the park, hand in hand.
>
> — Carrie, mother of a five-year-old

## Example: What's the Difference Between Punishment and Enforcing Your Limit?

Your son James is in the sandbox. He picks up a handful of sand and throws it. One of the other children yells, "*Hey, stop!*" The other parents are looking at you accusingly. What do you say?

- **Permissive:** "*James, would you please stop that?*"
- **Authoritarian:** "*All right, that's it! Out of the sandbox! Time-out for you!*"

But you know how to set an empathic limit! You say: "*James, did you hear him ask you to stop? Sand is not for throwing. It could hurt someone's eyes.*" But James hasn't read this book. He looks right at you, picks up more sand, and throws it. What now?

You hop into the sandbox, pick him up, and take him out of the sandbox. Of course, he begins to howl. You get him as far from prying eyes as possible, so you can parent without worrying what others will think. You say, "*James, the rule in the sandbox is no throwing sand. Sand hurts. Can you stop throwing sand?*"

James looks angrily at you. He doesn't say "yes," he doesn't say "no." So you set a firmer limit. "*James, if you want to go back in the sandbox, we need a deal that you can follow the rule. Can you follow the sandbox rule and not throw the sand? Can we shake on it?*"

If James shakes on it, he'll probably keep the agreement, because he's actually committing himself. If he can't shake on it, he can't go back in the sandbox, no matter how much he cries or begs, in which case you say, "*You know what? It's just too hard for you today. Let's go to the swings instead. We'll try again tomorrow in the sandbox.*" James might have a complete meltdown. That's okay. Until he can agree not to throw the sand, he can't go back in the sandbox. That's the rule under which all of us are allowed to be in the sandbox.

What if he says, "*Okay, I won't throw any more sand, I won't,*" and he gets into the sandbox and plays a little bit, and then he begins throwing sand again? This is a safety issue, so there are no further warnings. You take him out of the sandbox and you say, "*James, it was just too hard for you today. We'll try again tomorrow. Now we need to go home. The rule is no throwing sand.*" That's it. That's your limit.

**Is this a limit or a consequence?** It's true that the consequence, or result, of throwing sand is that you can't be in the sandbox. But "consequence" has come to mean a punitive, unpleasant thing that we impose on a child when they break a rule. Instead, what you're doing here is simply enforcing your limit. You're not being mean or punitive; you're being understanding, so it isn't a punishment. It's sort of like turning off the light. The consequence is that it's dark, but it's nothing punitive; it's just a result. So the result of not being able to follow the rules in the sandbox is that you can't be in the sandbox. No shame, no blame, and we'll try again tomorrow. Because you used a limit rather than a consequence, your child skips the baggage of the shame and blame and is motivated to choose to follow the sandbox rule. He doesn't get stuck in a power struggle.

## • SETTING EMPATHIC LIMITS WITHOUT SHAME •

Because shame was thought by prior generations to be a good teaching tool, many of the ways we habitually set limits are designed to provoke shame. That includes any ridicule or negative judgment about:

- **What the child needs:** "*What? Are you a baby?! Don't you see I have enough to do taking care of your sister?*"
- **What the child wants:** "*You just want more, more, more! You have a whole room full of toys; isn't that enough for you?*"
- **What the child feels:** "*You do NOT hate your brother; don't say such terrible things!*"
- **Who the child is:** "*You'd lose your head if it wasn't glued on!*"

Shame is that heavy, sinking sensation that tells us to rein in our impulses and switch direction. Mild shame seems to be a universal biological reaction that helps us learn to live with other humans, although what's socially acceptable, and therefore considered shameful, varies from culture to culture. It's how we learn social rules such as not peeing on the floor. If parents support children through it, the learning experience can override any negative conclusions about the self. Remember the child who interrupted the tribal chief and whose parent helped him recover, from the first section of this book (see page 53)?

By contrast, consider the parent in the supermarket from the same section (see page 53-54). They felt ashamed when their child misbehaved in public, so they passed that shame on to their child, who suddenly felt publicly mortified. When we shame children, we imply that there's something wrong with them. The child concludes that they can't even fix what's wrong by trying to behave differently, because it's who they *are* that's flawed.

The four examples above instill shame because they don't allow the child to distinguish her needs, feelings, and wants from who she *is*. Luckily, we can completely sidestep the shame by empathizing and setting a limit without judging or criticizing. Let's rephrase the examples from above:

- "*Everybody wants to be babied sometimes. You will always be my baby, no matter how big you get. I can't carry you right now, but come here and let me give you a big cuddle.*"
- "*That toy looks pretty cool. You really wish you could have it. We're not buying toys today, Malia. We can write it on your birthday list and maybe you can have it then, if it's still what you want most.*"
- "*Sounds like something happened that made you furious at your brother.*"
- "*You lost your jacket? Oh no! Let's think about where you could have left it. And let's figure out a way for you to check whether you have all your things before you leave someplace.*"

# Example: **Using Empathic Limits Instead of Shame**

Let's take the example of a safety issue with a toddler. Setting the limit with empathy completely bypasses any judgment about who the child is and what he needs, wants, or feels. You simply say, "*You love climbing! And the TV cabinet is not a safe place for climbing. Let's go outside where you can climb safely.*"

The child doesn't want to stop climbing, but his parents, who he trusts, are insisting. He's being asked to rein in his impulse to climb, which is like applying internal brakes to the activated inner accelerator of climbing. The inner brakes cause that heavy, sinking feeling that adults recognize as mild shame. But the child sees how reassuring the parent is. His parents don't think he's bad, or even that climbing is bad. They'll help him climb where it's safe. The child turns and takes refuge in the parent's arms. The parent will have to state and enforce this limit repeatedly with a toddler. But sooner or later, he'll hears their voice in his head as he begins climbing, and he'll stop. You might think of this as the beginning of conscience and self-discipline.

What if, instead, the parent said: "*You know better than to climb on that! You naughty boy! Can't you stop giving me trouble for one minute?*" When the child feels the mild shame that's the biological result of reining in his impulses, that feeling gets all mixed up with the idea that he's a bad boy who's trouble for his parents. He's just being himself, but there must be something wrong with him. He can't bear that feeling, so he climbs away from them, higher.

Does he *want* to switch gears, to "listen"? Not really. He's already given up on pleasing his parents. Sure, they can haul him off the TV cabinet, but he isn't *choosing* to follow their lead. So he isn't actually building the neural wiring he needs to switch gears. Now, his long-suffering parents give him a time-out, so he'll learn to "listen." As he sits in time-out, does he vow to obey them next time? Not likely. He's overwhelmed with shame. But the shame feels so unbearable that he'll do anything not to feel it. Instead of showing remorse, he lashes out in anger. He blames others. He rebels against that emerging voice of conscience in his head. He becomes defiant. But underneath, he's developing a sense that he's defective, which—if this experience is repeated often enough—may haunt him for years to come.

# Practice: **Re-scripting Your Usual Limit Setting**

List the limits that give you and your kids the most trouble. First write down what you are most likely to say when you set that limit. Then, consider how you might be able to set that same limit with more empathy so your child feels heard, but without wavering on your limit.

As you frame your limit try to recognize the feeling and/or the wish. Maybe you can even grant her desire in fantasy. For example, "*I hear you, Rebecca, you wish you didn't have to go to school. It would be so much fun if we could just stay home and play today, wouldn't it? We could just stay in our PJs and not even get dressed! And still, it's Monday, so I have to go to work and you have to go to school. What can we do to make this a good day?*"

( 1 ) How I say it now: _____

_____

How I can say it more empathically: _____

_____

_____

_____

**2** How I say it now: _____

_____

How I can say it more empathically: _____

_____

_____

_____

**3** How I say it now: _____

_____

How I can say it more empathically: _____

_____

_____

_____

**4** How I say it now: _____

_____

How I can say it more empathically: _____

_____

_____

_____

> ❝
>
> When my children get into a resistant mood, I bypass the power struggles and change the tone by offering two choices for everything: 'Would you like to wear the pants with pockets or without? Would you like your toast with peanut butter or cheese? Would you like to wear your sneakers or your sandals?' They get so excited about choosing that they forget to resist!
>
> — Carmen, mother of a three-year-old and a five-year-old

# Practice: Side-Stepping Power Struggles

No one wins a power struggle. If you often find yourself in power struggles with your child, remind yourself that power struggles take two people. You don't have to attend every power struggle you're invited to!

If you notice that you and your child get into frequent power struggles, make a concerted effort to give your child choices whenever you can. Of course, there are decisions your child isn't ready to make. But every time you give him the right to choose, he feels more autonomous, less pushed around. Because that need is being met, he doesn't need to resist so much on the decisions where he doesn't get a choice. You're also modeling win–win solutions where the needs of both people are considered. And there's another, huge benefit: every time your child makes a choice, she's developing her inner compass.

What are your recurring power struggles with your child? Each one represents an issue where something is important to you and something different is important to your child. Is there any part of the issue where you can give your child a choice and still get what you want?

## *Example*

| We Fight About: | What's Really Important to Me: | What I Can Let Her Choose: | I Can Live with This Because: |
|---|---|---|---|
| Her clothes every morning. | Stopping the fighting and getting her dressed so we can leave the house. | She can choose her own clothing each morning from what is in her drawers, even if the clothes don't match. | I will remove all unacceptable choices (such as out-of-season or fancy clothes) from the drawers she can access. |
| He doesn't come to the table when I call him for dinner. | I want to be able to sit down and start dinner before the food gets cold. I also want him to eat dinner, so he isn't hungry later. | He can come now, when I call him, or in five minutes (and I will always give a five-minute warning). He can bring a stuffed animal to sit in his chair with him. | It's no big deal for him to have a "friend" at the table and for me to give a five-minute warning, if that gets him to the table without a fight. |

## Your Turn

| We Fight About: | What's Really Important to Me: | What I Can Let Her Choose: | I Can Live with This Because: |
|---|---|---|---|
| | | | |
| | | | |
| | | | |
| | | | |
| | | | |

# Practice: **Using Routines to Avoid Power Struggles**

Which parts of your day present recurring problems? Using a routine at that time of day lets you sidestep power struggles. That way, you're not the bad guy—it's just the family routine at that time of day. Work with your child to make a chart of your morning and bedtime routines (with photos if your child can't read), with items such as brushing teeth, bath, and storytime listed with the time by each item. Post your new routine where your kids can see it, and make a big deal out of making it fun, with a special treat the first day to celebrate your new routine. Every day as you go through the routine, point to the chart and ask your child, "*What do we do next?*" In a month or less, the new routine will become habit for everyone, and you'll see many fewer power struggles.

**( 1 )** Time of day: _____

Suggested routine—Who does what, and when:

_____

_____

_____

**( 2 )** Time of day: _____

Suggested routine—Who does what, and when:

_____

_____

_____

**( 3 )** Time of day: _____

Suggested routine—Who does what, and when:

_____

_____

_____

### *Using Win–Win Solutions To Solve Recurring Problems*

> "
>
> I have trouble enforcing limits such as 'no disrespectful language.'
> My kids just keep insulting each other until I threaten, which I hate doing.
>
> — Makayla, mother of four and six-year-olds

There will be times when you feel completely stuck and setting an empathic limit doesn't solve a recurring problem. Remind yourself that the way you solve this problem will become a model for your child for how to solve interpersonal problems, so it's worth investing special effort.

First, be sure you're addressing any structural issues. In the previous example, the obvious presence of sibling rivalry suggests that these kids need more preventive maintenance: one-on-one time with parents, opportunities to express their feelings about their siblings, and specific interventions from parents during fights in order to teach peaceful conflict resolution. (You can find these strategies in my book *Peaceful Parent, Happy Siblings*.[144])

But in addition (not instead), invite your children to work with you to create a win–win solution.

1. **Start with an invitation** at a time when your children are *not* fighting: "*We have a problem that I need your help to solve.*" Have a pad of paper handy.

2. **Begin by acknowledging your kids' feelings.** That invites them into the process. "*I notice that sometimes you two get so angry at each other, you start insulting each other. That can't feel good to either one of you.*" Listen to their responses and empathize. If they start to fight, stay calm and acknowledge that all this fighting is leaving some unhappy feelings and that's what you want to solve.

3. **Then, express your concerns.** "*The number-one rule in our house is that we treat each other with kindness and respect. Right? When you two get so angry at each other, I end up threatening you. I know that isn't respectful either, but I get so frustrated and I don't know how to help.*"

4. **Invite your children to brainstorm with you.** "*I understand that there will be times when you get angry at each other. What ideas do you have to work things out when you get angry, without insults? And how can I help in these situations, instead of making things worse? I'm going to write down all your ideas. All ideas are welcome. After we brainstorm, we will cross off the ideas that don't work for all of us.*" Kids—even if they can't read yet—love it when you write down the possible solutions as they're suggested. Parents can keep things light and encourage a breadth of ideas by contributing funny suggestions that will end up getting crossed off.

**Your list might look like this:**

- Michelle could stop when Diego says "*stop,*" instead of continuing to say mean things.
- Diego could disappear.
- Mom could put on headphones whenever Michelle and Diego fight.
- Mom could win a free trip to Hawaii every time Michelle and Diego fight.
- When Mom doesn't like our tone, she can just say "*TONE*" and that is our signal to move to separate rooms until we can be calm while we talk and not use insults.
- Mom could get a magic wand that would make everything Michelle and Diego say to each other totally loving.
- Mom could NOT YELL and instead remind us to express our feelings without attacking each other.
- We could have a special code word and if anyone uses it, we all have to be silent and look at each other until we start laughing.
- Michelle and Diego—and Mom!—could each pick a special mantra to say when upset, to help them calm down.
- After anyone says the special code word during a fight, anyone who says anything mean has to do the dishes that night. If both kids keep insulting, they both do the dishes.
- We could stop fights before they get out of hand by using a special code.
- Michelle can always make Diego laugh.

Then go through the list and cross off the suggestions that anyone vetoes. This process clarifies what's truly important to each of you and where you feel okay about compromising. You might end up blending a few ideas. Then, type up an agreement, have everyone sign it at the bottom, and shake on it. When you shake, smile and affirm that "*We always keep our promises.*" (Of course, this applies to parents as well.) Then post your agreement. For example:

**We all agree that:**

- We will try to stop fights before we get too angry, by using our code word that makes us both laugh.
- Mom will NOT YELL and instead will remind us to express our feelings without attacking each other.
- If we don't calm down, Mom will just say "*TONE PLEASE*" and that is our signal to move to separate rooms until we can be calm while we talk and not use insults.
- If one or both of us doesn't go to separate rooms, then we have to do the dishes.
- If Mom yells, she will do as many push-ups as she can.
- Michelle, Diego, and Mom will each pick a special mantra to say to ourselves when we're upset, to help us calm down.

Note that the kids came up with the idea that they would do the dishes, and Mom came up with the push-ups. It's fine for agreements to include consequences of breaking the agreement, but be sure to ask all parties how they will feel if they end up having to do what they've agreed to. You don't want to set up a power struggle.

The next time your children begin to fight, take the signed agreement over to them and say, "*I know you're both angry right now. Let's all take a deep breath and solve this together. I agreed to not yell and instead remind you to express your feelings without attacking each other. I'm here to help you do that. If you're too angry right now, we can go to separate rooms and work this out once we calm down.*"

What if your children ignore you and keep yelling at each other? Do your best to soothe the storm using empathy, and help them listen to each other to work things out. Then, repeat the brainstorming process later. What worked? What didn't? What else would help? Create a revised agreement.

Of course, you could have come up with this "agreement" by yourself, but then your children wouldn't feel invested in it. When kids do this process often enough, they become convinced that their concerns will be addressed, and they're more likely to compromise to meet your needs as well.

Does this seem like a lot of work? It is! But over time, your children learn to do it for themselves. And it works, unlike yelling and punishment. That's because it helps your children solve the problem they're having. You're also giving your kids constructive problem-solving skills for life. Finally, this technique raises a teen for whom it's second nature to meet your concerns—before you even ask!

Discipline is helping a child solve a problem. Punishment is making a child suffer retribution for having a problem. To raise problem solvers, focus on solutions, not retributions.

— L. R. Knost[145]

# Practice: **Win–Win Solutions**

Think of the areas in your life where you and your child have the most conflict. List your concern, your child's concern, and possible win–win solutions. Discuss the issue with your child and come up with a mutually-agreeable solution together. Try the solution to be sure it's doable. If necessary, discuss the issue again and revise the agreement. (Remember, the solution has to be win–win. This isn't about either you or your child giving up what's really important to each of you.)

**Issue #1:**

_____

_____

_____

Parent's concern:

_____

_____

_____

Child's concern:

_____

_____

_____

Possible win–win solutions:

_____

_____

_____

Agreed-upon win–win solution:

_____

_____

_____

Revised solution (if necessary after experimenting):

_____

_____

_____

**Issue #2:**

_____

_____

_____

Parent's concern:

_____

_____

_____

Child's concern:

_____

_____

_____

Possible win–win solutions:

_____

_____

_____

Agreed-upon win–win solution:

_____

_____

_____

Revised solution (if necessary after experimenting):

_____

_____

_____

## Practice: **Alternatives to Threats and Punishment**

Post this on your refrigerator.

When you're upset at your child, what could you do besides punishing? Below, list as many things as you can think of. I've listed some we've talked about already, to get you started.

**(1)** Stop, Drop (your agenda, just temporarily), and Breathe!

**(2)** Empathize as you set the limit.

**(3)** Redirect.

**(4)** Tell the child what she *can* do instead of what she *can't* do.

**(5)** Give choices.

**(6)** Use "When... then..." (*"When we've cleaned up your room, we can go to the playground."*)

**(7)** Use "When you're ready..." (*"When you're ready, I know you will think of the perfect way to make things better with your brother."*)

**(8)** Express your feelings and ask for your child's help. (*"I'm worried that we need to go now or we'll be late... I need you to put on your shoes now."*)

**(9)** Meet your child's need to feel valued. (*"I love it when you help me like this... I couldn't have done it without you!"*)

**(10)** Meet the need that is driving the behavior.

**(11)** Find a win–win solution.

**(12)** Make it fun.

**(13)** Grab your child in a big hug and say, *"Are you out of hugs again? Let's see what we can do about that!"*

**(14)** Say, *"I wonder what each of us could do to make things better now."*

**(15)** _____

**(16)** _____

**(17)** _____

(18) _____

(19) _____

(20) _____

(21) _____

(22) _____

(23) _____

(24) _____

(25) _____

(26) _____

(27) _____

(28) _____

(29) _____

(30) _____

## Reflection After Practice: **Taking Stock**

Many parents worry that they're letting their child "get away with something" when they don't punish misbehavior. But punishing doesn't stop misbehavior. In fact, since it makes kids feel bad about themselves, doesn't help them with their emotions, and erodes the parent–child connection, punishment creates more misbehavior. When kids are acting out, they're dysregulated and the brain can't learn. If we can help kids to feel safe and connected, they can start regulating their emotions, which helps them choose better behavior.

( 1 ) What are the positive things you're noticing about your child now that you're finding ways to stop yelling, start connecting, and coach your child for emotional intelligence and better behavior?

_____

_____

_____

**2** Have you been able to move beyond discipline, to find alternatives when your child is acting out? What have you tried?

_____

_____

_____

**3** How are you calming yourself enough to try these alternatives?

_____

_____

_____

**4** How did your child react when you used an alternative to punishment?

_____

_____

_____

**5** Have you been able to suggest repair, without shaming or blaming your child? How did your child react?

_____

_____

_____

**6** Do you still find yourself in power struggles? What could you do instead?

_____

_____

_____

**7** What alternatives to punishment would you like to try more of?

_____

_____

_____

**8** Have you been strengthening your connection with your child? That is the single best way to prevent misbehavior.

_____

_____

_____

## *Teaching Lessons Without Punishment*

Parents often worry that without punishment (suffering), children won't "learn" the lessons parents want to teach. But let's look at what children learn from conventional "discipline" versus empathic limits.

### • SETTING LIMITS •

**Conventional discipline:** "*Stop that! You know better!*"

    **What your child learns:** You don't understand what they want and don't care about helping them get it, so they're on their own to try to meet their needs, even if it means breaking the rules.

**Empathic limit:** Take a deep breath, acknowledge your child's perspective, set your limit, and try to redirect your child's impulse into acceptable behavior:

- "*Ava, you love your sister, and she loves you, AND she needs to decide about being hugged. Can you ask before you hug her?*"
- "*The rule is no screaming in the car so I can drive safely. I hear you're really mad, and I want to hear about it—in a voice that I can listen to safely. Can you stop screaming, or do I need to stop the car?*"

**What your child learns:**

- "*When Mom and Dad tell me to stop doing something, they mean it. But they always understand why I was doing it, so I don't feel like a bad person.*"
- "*I don't have to yell. My parents always listen.*"

### • WHEN YOUR CHILD TESTS YOUR LIMIT •

**Conventional discipline:** "*I told you to clean this room! How many times do I have to tell you? Do you want a consequence?!*"

    **What your child learns:** You aren't serious until you raise your voice. It does *not* teach self-discipline, because your child isn't *choosing* to give up what he's doing (since he's being forced from outside) to do what you're asking.

**Empathic limit:** Acknowledge his perspective, and give him his wish in fantasy: "*I hear you, cleaning your room can be boring. Don't you wish we had a cleaning robot that would move through this room like lightning and put everything where it goes? Me too! Until we get one, you do need to put your toys back on the shelves, and your dirty clothes in the hamper. Do you want to start with the clothes or the toys?*"

**What your child learns:**

- "*I don't always get what I want, but I get something better—a parent who understands, no matter what.*"
- "*It's worth it to give up what I want (to play more) for what I want more—that warm relationship with my parent.*"

### • DEALING WITH EMOTIONS •

**Conventional discipline:** "*Go to your room until you can speak to me in a civil tone, young lady!*"

    **What your child learns:** She's all alone trying to manage those big emotions. You don't care how upset she is, so she'd better yell louder.

**Empathic limit:** "*Ouch! You know we speak to each other respectfully in this family. You must be so upset to speak to me like that. What's going on, sweetheart?*"

**What your child learns:**

- "*It's safe to show my parents when I'm upset. They understand and they help me.*"
- "*Feelings aren't dangerous, and we always have a choice about how we act on them.*"
- "*My words have the power to hurt, and I don't want to do that. I'm grateful to Mom for not flying off the handle when I was so upset. She helped me calm down.*"

## Making Amends: Reflection, Repair, And Responsibility

You may be wondering, though, how to help kids take responsibility for their mistakes and make amends without the use of conventional discipline. You make this more likely when you forgo lectures and punishment and instead teach your child the three Rs of reflection, repair, and responsibility.

**Reflect:**

- Ask open-ended questions to help her reflect and develop good judgment.
- Help her "narrate" what happened, so her rational brain gains understanding. This gives her more control over her emotions and behavior in the future: "*We had a hard time, didn't we? You were so disappointed when I said we didn't have time to go to the playground today… You were sad and mad… You yelled at me… Then you cried… I hugged you and told you I understood… Then you felt a little better… It's hard when you want something very much and then it doesn't happen… I feel that way too, sometimes… It helps to tell someone how you feel… Let's have another big hug, and later we can talk about what to do next time you feel so mad you want to yell at someone.*" (For more examples of "telling your child the story of what happened" see pages 101, 131, 165 and 166.)

**Repair:**

- Empower your child to repair what she's damaged, especially relationships. Can she get an ice pack for her brother? Rebuild his tower? Do his chore for him?
- Let your child choose the repair, so it doesn't feel like a punishment.
- If you model apologies your child will follow your lead. Don't force him. Just teach and model and expect repair: "*Your sister was hurt when you said that to her. What could you do to make her feel better? Great! Do you think she might also like a hug?*"

**Responsibility:**

- Teach that she can always make a choice of how to act in any given situation: this is "response-ability."
- Offer observations as he goes through his day to help him notice the choices he's making and the results: "*Lucas sure looked happy when you gave him a turn.*"

Unlike punishment or forced apologies, the three Rs of making amends give your child the foundation to manage both her emotions and her behavior. Let's continue tracking our comparison of what kids learn from conventional discipline compared to empathic limits.

### • EMPOWER TO REPAIR •

Children want to know how to make things better when they mess up. Not while they're mad, of course. No one does. But when they're no longer angry, they want a chance to redeem themselves, to restore their good feelings about themselves, to repair their relationships. Don't we all?

**Conventional discipline:** "*You go apologize to your brother this minute!*"

**What your child learns:** "*My parents prefer my sibling and humiliate me by making me apologize. I will never be nice to him!*"

**Empathic limit:** Help your child with the emotions that caused her to lash out. Then, once your child has regained her equilibrium, empower her to make things better:

- "*Your brother was pretty upset when you went in his room and broke his project. I wonder what you could do to make things better with him? Hmm… You think that would help him feel better? What a great idea!*"

- If she says, "*I never want to make things better with him! I hate him!*" then she's still too angry and needs your help with her emotions. Go back to acknowledging her feelings and helping her work through her upset: "*You're still pretty mad at your brother. Right now, it's hard to remember that sometimes you feel good about him and that you could get back to that good place. It sounds like maybe you have something you need to tell your brother about how hurt you felt…want some help to do that?*"

- Once she's on the road to feeling calmer, try again. If she still resists, leave the repair up to her: "*I know you're still feeling upset at your brother, and I understand why… I know when you feel better, you'll think of the perfect way to reconnect with him and make things better.*"

- You'll be amazed that your child will actually try to make reparations, once your family has a clear expectation that that's what everyone does—and once she doesn't feel pushed into it.

**What your child learns:**

- "*When we damage a relationship, there's a cost—and I can take responsibility to clean up my own messes.*"

- "*I don't mind apologizing, once I calm down.*"

### • HELP YOUR CHILD REFLECT •

Teaching your child the important lessons in life takes a whole lot of listening as well as a whole lot of teaching. But teachable moments are only teachable if the student is ready to learn.

**Conventional discipline:** "*You know better than this… Lecture… Lecture… Blah… Blah.*"
  **What your child learns:** "*My parents don't listen. They don't understand. I wish I could do better, but I don't even know why I always mess up.*"

**Empathic limit:** Share your observations without judgment and "wonder aloud" to help your child reflect on why he's acting as he is, and also on the results of his actions:

- "*I know you used that tone of voice because you were worried that we would be late to the birthday party, Amber. I get anxious when I hear shouting, and I can't drive safely. I wonder if there's another way to let me know when you get super-worried like that?*"

- "*I notice your brother doesn't want to wrestle with you these days… I wonder whether there's anything you can do to help him feel safe and have fun?*"

- "*It's disappointing to miss words on your spelling test, I know… The good news is that your brain is like a muscle, and if you exercise it, you can learn anything and get smarter. Want me to help you learn your words for next week?*"

**What your child learns:**

- "*It's possible to stay calm and come up with solutions.*"

- "*My parents help me to solve my problems.*"

- "*Even when I get upset, my parents understand that I'm good inside and I'm trying; I was just having a hard time. They're there to help.*"

- "*I trust my parents.*"

Look at everything your child has learned! Don't those sound like lessons you really want to teach?

## Giving Encouragement

Encouraging children is an essential part of lovingly guiding them. All humans, and certainly all children, need a steady flow of encouragement. But encouragement doesn't necessarily mean praise, and healthy praise doesn't necessarily mean what we think it does. Haim Ginott famously said, "*Praise only the child's efforts and accomplishments, never his character.*"

I would add that since children have no control over their looks and brains, those things don't count as accomplishments, and praising them doesn't help the child do better or feel better.

Here are some tips for healthy encouragement:

- Empathize instead of evaluating: *"You did it!"*
- Be enthusiastic and genuine.
- Be specific. *"Good job!"* doesn't tell the child what they did right.
- Instead of evaluating, let the child know you see him. So instead of *"Good job!"* you might say *"I see you way up there!"*
- Instead of evaluating (*"I'm proud of you"*), let the child evaluate (*"You must be so proud of yourself!"*).
- Instead of evaluating behavior (*"Good sharing!"*), describe the reason the behavior is of value (*"Brandon's face really lit up when you shared your truck with him!"*).

And here are some ideas of encouraging words you could use:

- *"I noticed that you…"*
- *"Thank you for…"*
- *"I really loved that you…"*
- *"I love to watch you…"*

## You Can Do This Hard Thing

Finally, make sure your child knows that when something is hard, it doesn't mean there is something wrong with him. Here are some encouraging words for those times when things feel hard for your child:

- *"You don't have to do this perfectly. Just give it your best shot."*
- *"You can do hard things."*
- *"Most things that are worth doing are hard."*
- *"You've done a lot of hard things. For instance, you did XYZ and also XYZ. You just decided and you kept trying and you did them."*
- *"Doing hard things is how we grow."*
- *"This is hard. Take your time."*
- *"I know it's hard. And I know that if you keep practicing, you can do it."*
- *"This is hard. It's okay to take a rest and come back later when you're fresh."*
- *"You can do this hard thing! I am right here to support you and cheer you on!"*

"

# Encouraging When Your Child Is Frightened

*My daughter and I went to an adventure park where she did a lot of climbing, with me cheering her from the ground. At one point the route she was on got difficult. She started crying and was obviously scared. To get down she would have had to go back a couple of stretches, which added to her distress, as she just wanted to get to the ground and into my arms. A park employee took notice of our situation and joined us, trying to talk her into continuing climbing, describing the technique, and telling her not to cry. Not helpful. I asked the lady to give us a minute, then turned my attention to my daughter, asked her to just take a couple of breaths and rest for a little bit, letting her know there was no immediate need to rush.*

*Then I talked her through our options: if she felt up to it after a short rest, she could continue her way to the end of the route, where she would get to the ground safely, or she could go back a couple of stretches, where there was a ladder and the park lady would help her climb down it. She chose to climb back through the portions she had already done and use the ladder. Everything worked out, and she was relieved to be on the ground again and feel safe. I was able to comfort her, acknowledging her great effort in the park.*

*This could have been the end of the story, but then I noticed that my daughter was insisting that she was done and that we leave immediately. I felt that if we left things like that, she would leave the park feeling like she'd failed, despite my efforts to be supportive. So I told her we would not leave just yet but would go for a short walk, to just breathe some fresh air and regain our calm. We stopped by a little creek and that helped a lot. When I felt Maria was calm enough, I told her what an amazing thing she accomplished today: she learned about her safety limits! She identified the riskiest thing she could handle in the adventure park, tackled it, and then decided to retreat, when her internal safety compass told her so. I told her that listening to her inner safety compass would help her greatly in life. That it is absolutely okay to stop when you feel you've reached a limit. That the smartest thing to do is go a little back and regroup, take a while to think and find another solution (such as train more or climb several simpler routes, to build up mastery), or even let a little time pass and knowledge accumulate until you tackle the issue again.*

*In about half an hour I carefully asked whether she wanted to try the difficult route again, with some extra training beforehand. She expressed some worry but was encouraged by the fact that she could once more get down safely, just as she had before, if she still felt it was not safe for her to finish the tricky portion. And that no matter the outcome, we would later celebrate today's great efforts with ice cream!*

*After completing a less difficult route and feeling confident in her abilities, my daughter tried the route she had not been able to finish the first time. When she got to the tricky part, she gave herself a short pep talk and she went on. Needless to say, she conquered it! The joy on her face spoke louder than any words. It brought tears to my eyes!*

— Corina, mother of seven-year-old

# Putting It All Together

**Take a moment now to think back to what your family life was like before you began this book. What is different now?**

Are your children more open about their emotions? They may be crying more, but are you noticing that, in between, they're happier and more cooperative? Are there more moments of warm affection and closeness? Is there more laughter, more playfulness?

Do you notice that you're more patient, more able to catch yourself before you explode? Are you more empathic, more able to see things from your child's perspective? Are you getting better at setting limits *before* you get angry, while you have a sense of humor and can stay kind or playful?

And what about your relationship with yourself? Are you more loving toward yourself, more forgiving? Are you checking in with yourself more on a daily basis to see what you need? Are you finding ways to meet your own needs and care for yourself, even in the busyness of family life?

You may even notice that your relationships with others—your partner, family members, or colleagues—have improved.

You may be thinking that you're still not perfect. I'm afraid that since you're human, perfection just isn't possible. Not for you, not for me, not for our children. But what *is* possible is taking one step toward more emotional intelligence and wholeness, and then taking another. Eventually, even with some backsliding, those steps will get you into a whole new landscape.

In these last four exercises, you have an opportunity to re-imagine your life.

## Practice: **Giving Yourself Credit**

How well have you been regulating your emotions recently, on a scale of 1 to 10?

| 1 | 2 | 3 | 4 | 5 | 6 | 7 | 8 | 9 | 10 |
|---|---|---|---|---|---|---|---|---|---|

Now, turn back to page 3, at the beginning of this book, where I asked you this same question. Has your rating improved?

If the answer is no, why not? What support can you give yourself now to improve your self-regulation?

_____

_____

_____

If the answer is yes, what do you think has made the difference? Give yourself huge credit!

_____

_____

_____

# Practice: **Rewriting Your Least-Proud Parenting Moments**

Below, list some of the past situations with your child of which you are least proud. Notice any feelings of shame that arise. Use what you learned in Part 1 of this book to forgive yourself and let those feelings go. You aren't beating yourself up here. You're supporting yourself for the future. You did the best you could with what you had at the time. Now, you know more, and you've given yourself more internal and external resources. Now, you can do better!

This is your opportunity to make a plan to show up the way you want to if a similar situation should ever present itself again. What could you do in that situation *before* you lose your cool to keep your connection and get your kids cooperating?

**( 1 )** There was the time when I:

_____

_____

_____

Next time, to prevent this, I could:

_____

_____

_____

**( 2 )** There was the time when I:

_____

_____

_____

Next time, to prevent this, I could:

_____

_____

_____

**( 3 )** There was the time when I:

_____

_____

_____

Next time, to prevent this, I could:

_____

_____

_____

# Practice: **Trouble-Shooting**

We're all works in progress, and all progress is two steps forward, one step back. So don't worry if you backslide. In fact, assume that will happen. Decide right now to forgive yourself and use it as an opportunity to strengthen the support you're giving yourself. Use this worksheet any time you need to get back on track. Remember, no blame. We're looking for solutions!

What's not working as well as you'd like?

_____

_____

_____

If you know why this is happening and what the solution is, describe the solution here. (If you don't know, that's fine. You don't need to know to get back on track. You just need to use the tools.)

_____

_____

_____

What additional support could you give yourself to stay centered? Include both self-care and external support. Flip through Part 1 of this book for inspiration, paying special attention to the sections on mindfulness, stress and self-care.

_____

_____

_____

Are you using the basic preventive maintenance tools daily to help your child with emotion and strengthen your relationship? Evaluate your progress on the chart below. (Be honest—this isn't a test. It's an opportunity for you to give yourself a transformative gift!)

| Tool | Yes, I Am Using This Tool | I Could Improve My Use of This Tool | No, I Am Not Yet Using This Tool |
|---|---|---|---|
| Empathy | | | |
| Routines | | | |
| Special Time | | | |
| Laughter and roughhousing | | | |
| Welcoming emotions | | | |

Please don't underestimate these tools. I often hear from parents that they're feeling stuck with their child. But once they begin to consistently use these tools, everything shifts. Challenging children will always be challenging, but these tools help even the most challenging children to be their best selves. In fact, I have never seen these tools fail to transform the parent-child relationship. Use the next exercise to make a plan for preventive maintenance.

# Practice: **Your Next Preventive Maintenance Steps**

Now, let's give you the tools to stay on track in the future. I consider the five basic preventive maintenance practices (listed in the chart at the end of the previous exercise) essential to maintaining a strong connection with your child and helping your child manage emotions. What next steps will help you increase these tools' effectiveness in your family life? Below is an example of a completed chart of next steps. After that you'll find a blank chart for you to use. (If you're feeling overwhelmed, keep these steps modest at first. Every step in the right direction helps.) Post your completed chart where you'll see it every day.

## *Example*

| Preventive Maintenance | What Is the Next Step for You to Do More of This Practice? |
|---|---|
| Empathy | When I get annoyed, remember to Stop, Drop, Breathe, and re-state what I heard her say. |
| Routines | Instead of getting mad when the toys are all over, I want to start working with the kids to clean up every night after dinner and before bath. Also, we need a better evening routine to settle them down. Try a short massage? |
| Special Time | Order an audiobook to keep the little one busy while I do Special Time with his sister. On weekends, alternate the kids so we each get an hour with each child |
| Laughter and Roughhousing | We're pretty good about this, but it would help to come up with a list of games to post for when I run out of ideas. Be sure to do this every day after school and snacks and before homework. |
| Welcoming Emotions | When she is acting up, get her laughing. If that doesn't work, then get the little guy busy with a sensory box. Then stop and get really calm and empathic with her, so she feels my connection. Then set a limit as kindly as I can and help her feel safe so she can cry. |

## *Your Turn*

| Preventive Maintenance | What Is the Next Step for You to Do More of This Practice? |
|---|---|
| Empathy | |

| Preventive Maintenance | What Is the Next Step for You to Do More of This Practice? |
|---|---|
| **Routines** | |
| **Special Time** | |
| **Laughter and Roughhousing** | |
| **Welcoming Emotions** | |

# Afterword

. . . . . . . . . . . . . . . . . . . . . . . . . .

You've reached the end of this workbook! Thank you for your very hard work. You have just accomplished a tremendous feat. I want you to know that you've done a lifetime of work, packed into one workbook. Of course, you never really finish this work. You just take it to the next level.

I hope you'll continue to use these tools and that you'll dip back into this book and go to the Aha! Parenting website over and over again, any time you need reminders or inspiration. Please remember that I also offer a 12-week self-paced online course (AhaParenting.com/peaceful-parenting-course) that enlarges on the work in this book and includes a private facebook discussion forum, if you want more support to work on these issues. And please don't hesitate to seek counseling or coaching if you feel you need more support to put these ideas into practice.

**As you've learned, being peaceful all the time isn't possible. But here's what *is* possible. You can commit to peaceful parenting:**

- Regulating your own emotions;
- Connecting with your child;
- Coaching your child.

That's it. You commit to this intention. You put one foot in front of the other. You choose love. You mess up. You hold yourself with compassion. You apologize. You start again. You show up and act like the grown-up. You love your child through the hard times. You love yourself through the hard times.

You choose love over and over. And you end up with a lot less drama and a lot more love in your life.

Hard work, I know. But you can do hard things. You've already done the hard work to get to here. You got this. Now all you have to do is keep going. I'll be here cheering you on, every step of the way.

# References

**1** Karen, R. (1998). *Becoming attached: First relationships and how they shape our capacity to love*. Oxford, UK: Oxford University Press.

**2** Schore, A. N. (1994/2012). *Affect regulation and the origin of the self*. New York, NY: Psychology Press.

**3** Neufeld, G. (2006). *Hold on to your kids*. New York, NY: Ballantine Books.

**4** Kohn, A. (2006). *Unconditional parenting*. New York, NY: Atria Books.

**5** Gottman, J. (1998). *Raising an emotionally intelligent child*. New York, NY: Simon & Schuster.

**6** Kohn, A. (2006). *Unconditional parenting*. New York, NY: Atria Books.

**7** Ibid.

**8** Markham, L. (2013). *Peaceful parent, happy kids: How to stop yelling and start connecting*. New York, NY: Perigee Books.

**9** See AhaParenting.com/audiotapes/how-to-partner-coparenting-team

**10** Ginott, H. (1975). *Teacher and child: A book for parents and teachers* (p. 7). New York, NY: Macmillan.

**11** Zelano, C., Jiang, H., Zhou, G., Arora, N., Schuele, S., Rosenow, J., & Gottfried, J. A. (2016). Nasal respiration entrains human limbic oscillations and modulates cognitive function. *Journal of Neuroscience, 36*(49), 12448–12467. doi:10.1523/JNEUROSCI.2586-16.2016

**12** Barrett, L. F. (2017). *How emotions are made* (pp. 2–3). New York, NY: Houghton Mifflin Harcourt.

**13** Ibid.

**14** Bushman, B. J. (2002). Does venting anger feed or extinguish the flame? Catharsis, rumination, distraction, anger, and aggressive responding. *Personality and Social Psychology Bulletin, 28*(6), 724-731.

**15** Dalai Lama. (Mar. 7, 2014). Speech on Capitol Hill, Washington, D.C.

**16** Ueshiba, M., & Stevens, J. (2013). *The essence of aikido: Spiritual teachings of Morihei Ueshiba* (p. 19). Tokyo: Kodansha International.

**17** Graham, L. (2013). *Bouncing back*. Novato, CA: New World Library.

**18** Ibid.

**19** Ibid.

**20** Doidge, N. (2007). *The brain that changes itself*. New York, NY: Penguin.

**21** Graham, L. (2013). *Bouncing back*. Novato, CA: New World Library.

**22** Siegel, D. (2010). *Mindsight*. New York, NY: Bantam Books.

**23** Wilson, A. (n.d.). Four ways to strengthen your stress resilience. *Kripalu*. Retrieved October 6, 2017, from https://kripalu.org/resources/four-ways-strengthen-your-stress-resilience

**24** Ecker, B., Ticic, R., & Hulley, L. (2012). *Unlocking the emotional brain: Eliminating symptoms at their roots using memory consolidation*. Abingdon, UK: Routledge.

**25** Hanson, R. (2009). *Buddha's brain*. Oakland, CA: New Harbinger.

**26** Walton, A. G. (2015, February 9). 7 ways meditation can actually change the brain. *Forbes*. Retrieved October 6, 2017, from https://www.forbes.com/sites/alicegwalton/2015/02/09/7-ways-meditation-can-actually-change-the-brain/#62dbbbc41465

**27** Lutz, A., Brefczynski-Lewis, J., Johnstone, T., Davidson, R. J. (2008). Regulation of the neural circuitry of emotion by compassion meditation: Effects of meditative expertise. *PLOS One, 3*(3), e1897. https://doi.org/10.1371/journal.pone.0001897

**28** Taren, A. A., Creswell, J. D., & Gianaros, P. J. (2013). Dispositional mindfulness co-varies with smaller amygdala and caudate volumes in community adults. *PLOS One, 8*(5), e64574. doi:10.1371/journal.pone.0064574

**29** Lazar, S. W., Holzel, B. K., Carmody, J., Vangel, M., Congleton, C., Yerramsetti, S. M., & Gard, T. (2011). Mindfulness practice leads to increases in regional brain gray matter density. *Psychiatry Research: Neuroimaging, 191*(1), 30, 36–43. doi:10.1016/j.pscychresns.2010.08.006

**30** Hanson, R. (2009). *Buddha's brain.* Oakland, CA: New Harbinger.

**31** Frankl, V. (2006). *Man's search for meaning.* Boston, MA: Beacon Press.

**32** Zelano, C., Jiang, H., Zhou, G., Arora, N., Schuele, S., Rosenow, J., & Gottfried, J. A. (2016). Nasal respiration entrains human limbic oscillations and modulates cognitive function. *Journal of Neuroscience, 36*(49), 12448–12467. doi:10.1523/JNEUROSCI.2586-16.2016

**33** Graham, L. (2013). *Bouncing back.* Novato, CA: New World Library.

**34** Markham, L. (2015). *Peaceful parent, happy siblings: How to stop the fighting and raise friends for life.* New York, NY: Penguin.

**35** Gershoff, E.T. (2002, July). Corporal punishment by parents and associated child behaviors and experiences: A meta-analytic and theoretical review. *Psychol Bull, 128*(4), 539-79.

**36** Brody, G. H. (1998). Sibling relationship quality: Its causes and consequences. *Annual Review of Psychology, 49*(2), 1-24.

**37** Holden, G. (2014). Eavesdropping on the family: A pilot investigation of corporal punishment in the home. *Journal of Family Psychology, 28*(3), 401– 406.

**38** Finley, G. (2008). *The essential laws of fearless living: Find the power to never feel powerless again.* Newburyport, MA: Red Wheel Weiser.

**39** Lyons, L. (2013). *Anxious children, anxious parents.* Deerfield Beach, FL: Health Communications Inc.

**40** Jeffers, S. (1987). *Feel the fear and do it anyway.* London, UK: Century.

**41** Brown, B. (2007). *I thought it was just me (but it isn't): Making the journey from "What will people think?" to "I am enough".* New York, NY: Avery-Penguin Random House.

**42** Siegel, D., & Hartzell, M. (2013). *Parenting from the inside out.* New York, NY: TarcherPerigee.

**43** Brown, B. (2007). *I thought it was just me (but it isn't): Making the journey from "What will people think?" to "I am enough".* New York, NY: Avery-Penguin Random House.

**44** Brown, B. (2007). *I thought it was just me (but it isn't): Making the journey from "What will people think?" to "I am enough".* New York, NY: Avery-Penguin Random House.

**45** Bradshaw, J. (1990). *Healing the shame that binds you* (p.18). Deerfield Beach, FL: Health Communications Inc.

**46** Saint-Exupéry, A. de. (1943). *The little prince* (chapter 21). Paris, France: Gallimard.

**47** Brown, B. (2015). *Daring greatly.* New York, NY: Avery.

**48** Siegel, D., & Hartzell, M. (2013). *Parenting from the inside out.* New York, NY: TarcherPerigee.

**49** Hardy, B. P. (c. 2017). Why keeping a daily journal could change your life. *Medium.com.* Retrieved November 20, 2017, from https://medium.com/the-mission/why-keeping-a-daily-journal-could-change-your-life-b9421a69912a

**50** Graham, L. (2013). *Bouncing back.* Novato, CA: New World Library.

**51** Helmstetter, S. (1991). *What you say when you talk to yourself.* New York, NY: Thorsons.

**52** Shapiro, F. (2012, March 16). Expert answers on EMDR. *The New York Times.* Retrieved October 6, 2017, from https://consults.blogs.nytimes.com/2012/03/16/expert-answers-on-e-m-d-r/?_r=0

**53** van der Kolk, B. (2015). *The body keeps the score.* New York, NY: Penguin.

**54** Emdria. (2017). EMDR related research. Retrieved October 6, 2017, from http://www.emdria.org/?page=EMDRResearch

**55** http://emdria.site-ym.com

**56** Ecker, B. (2012). *Unlocking the emotional brain: Eliminating symptoms at their roots using memory consolidation.* Florence, KY: Taylor & Francis.

**57** Graham, L. (2013). *Bouncing back.* Novato, CA: New World Library.

**58** Ibid., p .114.

**59** Siegel, D., & Hartzell, M. (2013). *Parenting from the inside out* (pp. 131-134). New York, NY: TarcherPerigee.

**60** Hanson, R. (2016). *Hardwiring happiness: The new brain science of contentment, calm, and confidence.* New York, NY: Harmony.

**61** Graham, L. (2013). *Bouncing back.* Novato, CA: New World Library.

**62** Dienstmann, G. (c. 2015). Scientific benefits of meditation: 76 things you might be missing out on. *Live and Dare.* Retrieved October 6, 2017, from http://liveanddare.com/benefits-of-meditation

**63** Walton, A. G. (2015, February 9). 7 ways meditation can actually change the brain. *Forbes.* Retrieved October 6, 2017, from https://www.forbes.com/sites/alicegwalton/2015/02/09/7-ways-meditation-can-actually-change-the-brain/#757f3a9d1465

**64** Taren, A. A., Creswell, J. D., & Gianaros, P. J. (2013). Dispositional mindfulness co-varies with smaller amygdala and caudate volumes in community adults. *PLOS One, 8*(5), e64574. doi:10.1371/journal.pone.0064574

**65** Ireland, T. (2014, June 12). What does mindfulness meditation do to your brain? *Scientific American.* Retrieved October 6, 2017, from https://blogs.scientificamerican.com/guest-blog/what-does-mindfulness-meditation-do-to-your-brain

**66** Fredrickson, B. L., Cohn, M. A., Coffey, K. A., Pek, J., & Finkel, S. M. (2008). Open hearts build lives: Positive emotions, induced through Loving-Kindness meditation, build consequential personal resources. *Journal of Personality and Social Psychology, 95*(5), 1045–1062. http://doi.org/10.1037/a0013262

**67** Shook, V. (1986). *Ho'oponopono: Contemporary uses of a Hawaiian problem-solving process.* Honolulu, HI: University of Hawaii Press.

**68** Zeng, X., Chiu, C. P. K., Wang, R., Oei, T. P. S., & Leung, F. Y. K. (2015). The effect of Loving-Kindness meditation on positive emotions: A meta-analytic review. *Frontiers in Psychology, 6,* 1693. http://doi.org/10.3389/fpsyg.2015.01693

**69** Greater Good Science Center. (2017). Expanding the science and practice of gratitude. Retrieved October 6, 2017, from https://ggsc.berkeley.edu/what_we_do/major_initiatives/expanding_gratitude

**70** Childre, D. (2000). *The HeartMath solution.* San Francisco, CA: Harper Collins.

**71** Emmons, R. A., & McCullough, M. E. (2003). Counting blessings versus burdens: An experimental investigation of gratitude and subjective well-being in daily life. *Journal of Personality and Social Psychology, 84*(2), 377–389. doi:10.1037//0022-3514.84.2.377

**72** Froh, J. J., & Bono, G. (2014). *Making grateful kids: A scientific approach to help youth thrive.* West Conshohocken, PA: Templeton Press.

**73** Keller, A., Litzelman, K., Wisk, L. E., Maddox, T., Cheng, E. R., Creswell, P. D., & Witt, W. P. (2012). Does the perception that stress affects health matter? The association with health and mortality. *Health Psychology, 31*(5), 677–684. doi:10.1037/a0026743

**74** White, C. P., Bradley, S. L., Neverve, L., Stirewalt, L., & Summers, X. (2015). Does maternal fatigue influence maternal verbal control in a stressful parenting task with toddlers? *Journal of Child and Family Studies, 24*(2), 351–362. doi:10.1007/s10826-013-9843-x

**75** Stifflelman, S. (2015). *Parenting with presence.* Novato, CA: New World Library.

**76** Gottman, J. (2002). *The relationship cure.* New York, NY: Harmony-Crown.

**77** Kohn, A. (2006). *Unconditional parenting.* New York, NY: Atria Books.

**78** Markham, L. (1998). Mothers' mental representations of their relationships with their toddlers. Dissertation Thesis. New York, NY: Columbia University.

**79** Siegel, D., & Hartzell, M. (2013). *Parenting from the inside out.* New York, NY: TarcherPerigee.

**80** Ciaramicoli, A. P. (2016). *The stress solution*. Novato, CA: New World Library.

**81** Gordon, M. (2009). *Roots of empathy*. New York, NY: Experiment Publishing.

**82** Higgins, H. M. (1990). Empathy training and stress: Their role in medical students' responses to emotional patients. PhD diss., University of British Columbia. Retrieved October 6, 2017, from https://open.library. ubc.ca/cIRcle/collections/ubctheses/831/items/1.0076869

**83** Pert, C. (1999). *Molecules of emotion*. London, UK: Pocket Books.

**84** Blakeslee, S. (2007, February 6). A small part of the brain, and its profound effects. *The New York Times*. Retrieved October 6, 2017, from http://www.nytimes.com/2007/02/06/health/psychology/06brain.html

**85** Bergland, C. (2013, October 10). The neuroscience of empathy. *Psychology Today*. Retrieved October 6, 2017, from https://www.psychologytoday.com/blog/the-athletes-way/201310/the-neuroscience-empathy

**86** Richardson, C. (2006). *The unmistakable touch of grace*. New York, NY: Free Press-Simon and Schuster.

**87** Senge, P. (1994). *The fifth discipline fieldbook: Strategies and tools for building a learning organization* (p. 377). New York, NY: Crown Business.

**88** Kiblinger. K.B. (2017). *Buddhist inclusivism: Attitudes towards religious others* (p. 91). Abingdon, UK: Routledge.

**89** Forbes, H. (2009). *Dare to love* (p. 78). Boulder, CO: Beyond Consequences Institute.

**90** Siegel, D. & Bryson, T. (2011). *The whole-brain child*. New York, NY: Random House.

**91** Silani, G., Lamm, C., Ruff, C. C., & Singer, T. (2013). Right supramarginal gyrus is crucial to overcome emotional egocentricity bias in social judgments. *Journal of Neuroscience, 33*(39), 15466–15476.doi:10.1523/ JNEUROSCI.1488-13.2013

**92** Klimecki, O. M., Leiberg, S., Lamm, C., & Singer, T. (2013). Functional neural plasticity and associated changes in positive affect after compassion training. *Cerebral Cortex, 23*(7), 1552–1561. doi:10.1093/cercor/ bhs14

**93** Hofmann, S. G., Grossman, P., & Hinton, D. E. (2011). Loving-Kindness and compassion meditation: Potential for psychological interventions. *Clinical Psychology Review, 31*(7), 1126–1132. doi:10.1016/j. cpr.2011.07.003

**94** Hitzmann, S. (2016, August 17). The MELT method: Why vagal tone is so important. Retrieved October 6, 2017, from https://www.meltmethod.com/blog/vagus-nerve

**95** Cohen, L. (2002). *Playful parenting*. New York, NY: Ballantine Books.

**96** Cohen, L. (2017). Personal Communication, November 20, 2017.

**97** Markham, L. (2016). How to use a conversation journal to sweeten and deepen your relationship with your child. *AhaParenting.com*. Retrieved October 1, 2017, from http://www.ahaparenting.com/blog/ how-to-use-a-conversation- journal-to-sweeten-and-deepen-your-relationship-with-your-child

**98** Gottman, J. M., & Levenson, R. W. (1992). Marital processes predictive of later dissolution: Behavior, physiology, and health. *Journal of Personality and Social Psychology, 63*(2), 221–233.

**99** Pinquart, M. (2017). Associations of parenting dimensions and styles with externalizing problems of children and adolescents: An updated meta-analysis. *Developmental Psychology, 53*(5), 873-932. http://dx.doi. org/10.1037/dev0000295

**100** Joussemet, M., Landry, R., & Koestner, R. (2008). A self-determination theory perspective on parenting. *Canadian Psychology, 49*, 194–200. doi:10.1037/a0012754

**101** Rose, M. B. (2003). *The heart of parenting* (p. 1). Encinitas, CA: PuddleDancer Press.

**102** Grolnick, W. S., & Pomerantz, E. M. (2009). Issues and challenges in studying parental control: Toward a new conceptualization. *Child Development Perspectives, 3*(3), 165–170. doi:10.1111/j.1750-8606.2009.00099.x

**103** Stafford, M., Kuh, D. L., Gale, C. R., Mishra, G., & Richards, M. (2016). Parent–child relationships and offspring's positive mental wellbeing from adolescence to early older age. *Journal of Positive Psychology, 11*(3), 326–337. doi:10.1080/17439760.2015.1081971

**104** Laurin, J. C., Joussemet, M., Tremblay, R. E., & Boivin, M. (2015). Early forms of controlling parenting and the development of childhood anxiety. *Journal of Child and Family Studies*, *24*(11), 3279–3292. doi:10.1007/s10826-015-0131-9

**105** Hong, R. Y., Lee, S. S. M., Chng, R. Y., Zhou, Y., Tsai, F.-F., & Tan, S. H. (2017). Developmental trajectories of maladaptive perfectionism in middle childhood. *Journal of Personality*, *85*(3), 409–422. doi:10.1111/jopy.12249

**106** Strayer, J., & Roberts, W. (2004). Empathy and observed anger and aggression in five-year-olds. *Social Development*, *13*(1), 1–13. doi:10.1111/j.1467-9507.2004.00254.x

**107** Wagner, C. R., & Abaied, J. L. (2016). Skin conductance level reactivity moderates the association between parental psychological control and relational aggression in emerging adulthood. *Journal of Youth and Adolescence*, *45*(4), 687–700. doi:10.1007%2Fs10964-016-0422-5

**108** Rosenberg, M. B. (2003). *Teaching children compassionately* (p. 13). Encinitas, CA: PuddleDancer Press.

**109** Kohn, A. (2006). *Unconditional parenting*. New York, NY: Atria Books.

**110** Kakinami, L., Barnett, T. A., Seguin, L., & Paradis, G. (2015, June). Parenting style and obesity risk in children. *Prev Med*, *75*,18-22. doi: 10.1016/j.ypmed.2015.03.005

**111** Gershoff, E. T. (2002). Corporal punishment by parents and associated child behaviors and experiences: A meta-analytic and theoretical review. *Psychological Bulletin*, *128*(4), 539–579. doi:10.1037//0033-2909.128.4.539

**112** University of Texas at Austin. (2016, April 25). Risks of harm from spanking confirmed by analysis of five decades of research [press release]. Retrieved October 6, 2017, https://news.utexas.edu/2016/04/25/risks-of-harm-from-spanking-confirmed-by-researchers

**113** Berlin, L. J., Ipsa, J. M., Fine, M. A., Malone, P. S., Brooks-Gunn, J., Bracy-Smith, C. ... Bai, Y. (2009). Correlates and consequences of spanking and verbal punishment for low-income white, African-American and Mexican American toddlers. *Child Development*, *80*(5), 1403–1420. doi:10.1111/j.1467-8624.2009.01341.x

**114** Straus, M. A., & Paschall, M. J. (2009, July 22). Corporal punishment by mothers and development of children's cognitive ability: A longitudinal study of two nationally representative age cohorts. *Journal of Aggression, Maltreatment & Trauma, 18*(5), 459. doi: 10.1080/10926770903035168

**115** Gershoff, E. T., & Grogan-Kaylor, A. (2016, June). Spanking and child outcomes: Old controversies and new meta-analyses. *Journal of Family Psychology, 30*(4): 453-469. doi: 10.1037/fam0000191

**116** Taylor, C. A., Manganello, J. A., Lee, S. J., & Rice, J. C. (2010). Mothers' spanking of 3-year-old children and subsequent risk of children's aggressive behavior. *Pediatrics*, *125*(5), e1057–e1065. doi:10.1542/peds. 2009-2678

**117** Bender, H. L., Allen, J. P., McElhaney, K. B., Antoinishak, J., Moore, C. M., Kelly, H. O., & Davis, S. M. (2007). Use of harsh physical discipline and developmental outcomes in adolescence. *Development and Psychopathology*, *19*(1), 227–242. doi:10.1017/s0954579407070125

**118** Durant, J., & Ensom, R. (2012). Physical punishment of children: Lessons from 20 years of research. *Canadian Medical Association Journal*, *184*(12), 1373–1377. doi:10.1503/cmaj.101314

**119** McCrory, E. J., DeBrito, S. A, Sebastian, C. L., Mechelli, A., Bird, G., Kelly, P. A., & Viding, E. (2011). Heightened neural reactivity to threat in child victims of family violence. *Current Biology*, *21*(23), 947-948.

**120** Tomoda, A., Suzuki, H., Rabi, K., Sheu, Y.-S., Polcari, A., & Teicher, M. H. (2009). Reduced prefrontal cortical gray matter volume in young adults exposed to harsh corporal punishment. *NeuroImage*, *47*(Suppl. 2), T66–T71. doi:10.1016/j.neuroimage.2009.03.005

**121** Ryan, R. M., Kalil, A., Ziol-Guest, K. M., & Padilla, C. (2016). Socioeconomic gaps in parents' discipline strategies from 1988 to 2011. *Pediatrics*, *138*(6), e2016-0-720. doi:10.1542/peds.2016-0720

**122** Institute for Health Metrics and Evaluation. (2016). The health of young children in America. Retrieved October 6, 2017, http://www.healthdata.org/policy-report/health-young-children-america

**123** Stevens, H. (2016, April 28). New study says spanking doesn't work, makes children's behavior worse. *Chicago Tribune*. Retrieved October 6, 2017, http://www.chicagotribune.com/lifestyles/stevens/ct-spanking-effects-study-balancing-0428-20160428-column.html

**124** Baumrind, D. (1967). Child care practices anteceding three patterns of preschool behavior. *Genetic Psychology Monographs, 75*(1), 43-88.

**125** Maccoby, E., & Martin, J. (1983). Socialization in the context of the family: Parent–child interaction. In P. H. Mussen (Ed.), *Handbook of child psychology* (pp. 1–101). New York, NY: John Wiley & Sons.

**126** Markham, L. (2013). *Peaceful parent, happy kids: How to stop yelling and start connecting.* New York, NY: Perigee Books.

**127** Mandara, J. (2003). The typological approach in child and family psychology: A review of theory, methods, and research. *Clinical Child and Family Psychology Review, 6*(2), 129–146. doi:10.1023/a:1023734627624

**128** Pinker, S. (2011, September 2). The sugary secret of self-control. *The New York Times*. Retrieved October 6, 2017, http://www.nytimes.com/2011/09/04/books/review/willpower-by-roy-f-baumeister-and-john-tierney-book-review.html

**129** Gottman, J. (1998). Raising an emotionally intelligent child: the heart of parenting. New York, NY: Simon & Schuster https://emotioncoaching.gottman.com/about

**130** Calkins, S. D., & Johnson, M. C. (1998). Toddler regulation of distress to frustrating events: Temperamental and maternal correlates. *Infant Behavior and Development, 21*(3), 379–395. doi:10.1016/s0163-6383(98)90015-7

**131** Kennedy, A. E., Rubin, K. H., Hastings, P. D., & Maisel, B. (2004). Longitudinal relations between child vagal-tone and parenting behavior: 2 to 4 years. *Developmental Psychobiology, 45*(1), 10–21. doi:10.1002/dev.20013

**132** Siegel, D., & Bryson, T. (2011). *The whole-brain child.* New York, NY: Random House.

**133** Fabes, R. A., Leonard, S. A., Kupanoff, K., & Martin, C. L. (2001). Parental coping with children's negative emotions: Relations with children's emotional and social responding. *Child Development, 72*(3), 907–920. doi:10.1111/1467-8624.00323

**134** Havighurst, S. S., Wilson, K. R., Harley, A. E., & Prior, M. R. (2009). Tuning in to kids: An emotion-focused parenting program—Initial findings from a community trial. *Journal of Community Psychology, 37*(8), 1008–1023. doi:10.1002/jcop.20345

**135** Denham, S. A. (1993). Maternal emotional responsiveness and toddlers' social-emotional competence. *Journal of Child Psychology and Psychiatry, 34*(5), 715–728. doi:10.1111/j.1469-7610.1993.tb01066.x

**136** Ramsden, S. R., & Hubbard, J. A. (2002). Family expressiveness and parental emotion coaching: Their role in children's emotion regulation and aggression. *Journal of Abnormal Child Psychology, 30*(6), 657–667. doi:10.1023/a:1020819915881

**137** Cassidy, J. (1994). Emotion regulation: Influences of attachment relationships. In N. A. Fox (Ed.), *Emotion regulation: Behavioral and biological considerations* (pp. 228–249). Chicago, IL: University of Chicago Press.

**138** Kohn, A. (2006). *Unconditional parenting.* New York, NY: Atria Books.

**139** Gottman, J. M., Katz, L. F., & Hooven, C. (1997). *Meta-emotion: How families communicate emotionally.* Mahwah, NJ: Lawrence Erlbaum Associates.

**140** Gottman, J. (1997). *Raising an emotionally intelligent child.* New York, NY: Simon & Schuster.

**141** Crowell, J. A., & Feldman, S. S.(1991). Mothers' internal working models of attachment relationships and mother and child behavior during separation and reunion. *Developmental Psychology, 27*, 597-605.

**142** Ginott, H. (2003). *Between parent and child.* New York, NY: Harmony.

**143** Dunn, J., & Kendrick, C. (1982). *Siblings: Love, envy and understanding.* Cambridge, MA: Harvard University Press.

**144** Ornaghi, V., Brazzelli, E., Grazzani, I., & Lucarelli, M. (2016). Does training toddlers in emotion knowledge lead to changes in their prosocial and aggressive behavior toward peers at nursery? *Early Education and Development, 28*(4), 396–414. doi:10.1080/10409289.2016.1238674

**145** Bushman, B. J. (2002). Does venting anger feed or extinguish the flame? Catharsis, rumination, distraction, anger, and aggressive responding. *Personality and Social Psychology Bulletin, 28*(6), 724–731. doi:10.1177/0146167202289002

**146** Davidson, R. J., & Fox, N. A. (1982). Asymmetrical brain activity discriminates between positive and negative affective stimuli in human infants. *Science, 218,* 1235–1237. doi:10.1126/science.7146906

**147** Bailey, B. (2011). *Managing emotional mayhem: The five steps for self-regulation.* Oviedo, FL: Conscious Discipline Press.

**148** Lieberman, M. D., Eisenberger, N.I., Crockett, M.J., Tom, S. M., Pfeifer, J. H., & Way, B. M. . Putting feelings into words: Affect labeling disrupts amygdala activity in response to affective stimuli. *Psychological Science* 2007,18(5), 421-428.

**149** Eanes, R. (2016). *Positive parenting: An essential guide.* New York, NY: TarcherPerigee.

**150** Markham, L. (2013). *Peaceful parent, happy kids: How to stop yelling and start connecting.* New York, NY: Perigee Books.

**151** Siegel, D., & Bryson, T. (2014). *Whole-brain discipline.* New York, NY: Bantam.

**152** Neufeld, G. (c. 2016). A playful approach to discipline. *Neufeldinstitute.org.* Retrieved November 20, 2017, from http://neufeldinstitute.org/a-playful-approach-to-discipline-part-ii/

**153** Rogers, C. (1978). *Carl Rogers on personal power: Inner strength and its revolutionary impact* (pp. 133-134). Philadelphia, PA: Trans-Atlantic Publications.

**154** Wright, L. (n.d.). The ODD child. *The ODD Mom.* Accessed October 19, 2017, http://theoddmom. blogspot.co.uk/p/odd-child.html

**155** Markham, L. (2013). *Peaceful parent, happy kids: How to stop yelling and start connecting.* New York, NY: Perigee Books.

**156** Knost, L. R. (2013). *Whispers through time* (p. 78). Little Hearts Books.

Made in United States
North Haven, CT
14 January 2022

14799526R00137